Balanced Literacy in Action

Two leading Canadian educators share their insights and practical strategies to make balanced literacy work in any elementary classroom.

Anne Brailsford and Jan Coles

SCHOLASTIC

National Library of Canada Cataloguing in Publication

Brailsford, Anne
    Balanced literacy in action / Anne Brailsford and Jan Coles.

ISBN 0-7791-3697-7

1. Reading (Elementary) 2. English language—Composition and exercises—Study and teaching
(Elementary) 3. Literacy programs—Alberta—Edmonton—Case studies. 4. Literacy programs.
I. Coles, Janice, 1942- II. Title.

LB1576.B685 2003   372.6   C2003-905458-6

Editor: Barbara Hehner

Proofreader: Dianne Broad

Production Editor: Lucia Ferrara

Production: Dee Kennedy

Art Director: Noel Upfield

Design and Layout: Julie McNeill/McNeill Design Arts

Specal thanks to Mark Wesner and his class at Keheewin Elementary School
and Adrienne Boon and her class at Steinhauer Elementary School in Edmonton.

Printed and bound in Canada

10 9 8 7 6 5 4 3 2 1   04 05 06 07 08

Table of Contents

Introduction

All teachers have views about "the best way" to teach children to read, and some provide testimonials and research to back up the success of the particular method they use. Reading instruction has a rich history of varied views and pendulum swings in methodology, and over the last century we've seen frequent swings from whole word approaches to intensive phonics and back again. While writing instruction has tended to excite less extremism and argument, there have still been sporadic but intense flurries of "correct spelling, good penmanship, and grammar rules," alternating with "approximated spellings, process writing, and developmental grammar in usage."

Currently we have returned to a period of uncertainty in reading and writing instruction. Whole language advocacy is waning and "back to basics" phonics supporters seem to be in the vocal ascendancy, especially since the publication of Marilyn Jager Adams's (1991) analysis of research that highlighted the importance of early phonics instruction for beginning readers. Language Arts instruction hovers like a craft in midstream. Should we dive into phonics as a primary focus in early reading instruction, or should we cling to the remnants of whole language?

With these extremes on offer, many teachers resort to jumping on the raft of eclecticism. They "do a bit of everything" and hope the strategy will work. Curriculum writers also seem to be sharing this hope, since Language Arts curricula across Canada offer wide-ranging eclecticism as the current choice, presenting seemingly overwhelming expectations and implied methodologies for teaching reading and writing. Sitting on the raft of eclecticism may seem to be a safe, if temporary, position in a time when every citizen has an opinion about the best way to teach reading. However, this raft has not been a safe haven for all school districts. Parents and community members have entered the debate in recent times, and some have demanded particular methodologies.

It is not uncommon to hear parents promoting their views in the local media. Recently, for example, a radio reporter interviewed people in a lineup waiting to register their children at a "traditional" school that promoted systematic phonics, workbook usage, phonetically decodable

texts, spelling rules, and grammatical analysis of sentences. One woman had been queuing cheerfully for three days and nights to try to obtain a placement in the program for her six-year-old grandson. This placement, she enthused, would not only ensure that the child was taught using the correct methods, but would also offer him untold advantages in post-secondary schooling. With such strength of conviction common in many communities, it is unsurprising that school districts have created alternative programs reflecting specific reading and writing methodologies.

With curricula offering eclecticism, and with highly vocal pressure groups demanding particular instructional methodologies in some instances, what do literacy programs in our schools look like at the present time? They tend to span what we call "Pot Pourri," "Surface Unity," and "Single Strand" approaches.

The Pot Pourri approach is the most common one in Canadian schools. In this approach, each teacher plans a program to meet curriculum expectations. The teacher operates the program from a personal philosophy of language learning and teaching. In one class, for example, a teacher may have a strong belief in using a basal reader and teaching the whole class to read from the text. The teacher next door may have an individualized reading program and use trade books. A third teacher may create multilevel reading groups and organize daily guided reading lessons. The Language Arts agenda in Pot Pourri schools may appear disjointed.

In the early days of self-exploration, some schools settle on Surface Unity. They grasp at the concept of unifying school goals in Language Arts, and seek avenues for developing cohesion across their classes. Examples of Surface Unity include adopting school-wide basal reading and spelling series, or engaging in "genre of the month" writing projects in all grades.

The Single Strand approach in Language Arts is a recent one. Groups of parents and educators have promoted the vital importance of one particular aspect of education, and this aspect has become central in specially created alternative programs. Frequently, the "single strand" emphasized in Language Arts is the sequential, systematic teaching of phonics. Whole programs have been structured around this central ideology, with its accompanying features: decodable readers, grammar

rules, and the correct use of spelling and punctuation conventions in early writing.

Pot Pourri, Surface Unity, and Single Strand approaches have arisen in the last decade to fill the literacy vacuum created by disputes about the "right" methodologies and materials for school literacy learning. Schools carry on while debates rage around them, and teachers create literacy learning programs even when the conditions are not ideal and the issues remain unresolved. However, it is our belief that such programs fail to meet the needs of the diverse range of students we find in classrooms.

Pot Pourri schools offer ever-changing expectations in Language Arts and frequently confusing experiences for students. One year, students may feel like successful readers and writers, while another year, they may not be able to engage wholeheartedly in the program. Staff isolation may also be anticipated, because there are so many Language Arts materials, methods, and philosophies operating in these schools.

Surface Unity schools try to achieve staff consensus and continuity for students, but the proposed adoption of one basal and one spelling series across grade levels cannot hope to meet the needs of a wide range of learners. Similarly, while Single Strand programs may offer solid consistency in expectations for students, and a unified staff framework for Language Arts, the methodology and materials used cannot meet every child's literacy learning needs.

The most positive aspect of the last decade of uncertainty is that there is a small, but growing, consensus amongst literacy educators that the time for simple answers and "the one right method" has passed. Educators are emerging from the vacuum and describing alternatives that share "common ground" (Flippo, 2001) and make use of what we already know about children's literacy learning. Embracing complexity and multiplicity in methods and materials is becoming an alternative that should be considered. Cutting through all of the methodological debates is one key question:

> *What kind of literacy learning framework makes the most sense for meeting the needs of every child?*

We believe the answer to that question lies in Balanced Literacy.

Bibliography

Flippo, R. F. "The Study, Findings, and Experts' Points of View" in R. F. Flippo (ed.). *Reading Researchers in Search of Common Ground*. Newark, DE: International Reading Association, 2001, 1-21.

Jager Adams, Marilyn. *Beginning to Read: Thinking and Learning About Print*. Cambridge, MA : MIT Press, 1991.

Part One

Balanced Literacy in Action

1 What Makes Sense in Literacy Education?

What We Mean by a "Balanced" Program

Since there is no one, simple "right way" to teach reading and writing, we believe that a moderate, balanced approach makes sense. A balanced program should not be viewed as yet another special method for teaching reading, spelling, or writing. Instead, it should be understood as an amalgam of several methods, bound together by an underlying framework. Such a framework ensures that, instead of complete eclecticism, in which every teacher follows his or her individual choices, methods and materials can be weighed and evaluated to produce a truly balanced Language Arts program.

"Balance" does not mean that all components of the Language Arts package are given strictly equal amounts of teaching time. Rather, balance that makes sense assigns time according to an area's relative importance in the literacy development of children, thus equalizing their literacy learning opportunities. The framework of a sensible, balanced Language Arts program should:

- cover all areas of Language Arts
- meet the literacy needs of all children
- teach all areas of Language Arts every day
- offer continuity from grade to grade
- use multilevel materials
- provide variety in groupings and communication styles
- allow children to work in their optimal learning "zones."

Covering All Areas of Language Arts

We need to offer a comprehensive Language Arts program that covers the curriculum and does not focus too much on one element. "Single Strand" schools, as noted in the introduction, are not, by their very nature, balanced. They dwell on one aspect of methodology and build programs that feature and enhance that aspect. Balanced programs, by contrast, should ensure that all areas of Language Arts receive attention.

Pendulum swings in Language Arts methodologies favour particular areas. When systematic phonics is in vogue, for example, programs devote significant blocks of time to that instructional area and often fail to pursue a daily writing program or regular use of high quality children's literature. When whole language is pursued, emphasis is placed on literature and writing, but the role of phonics in early reading and the direct teaching of reading and writing strategies receive relatively little attention. A balanced program moves away from pendulum swings, and ensures that no one aspect of Language Arts is emphasized at the expense of another.

When we started the balanced literacy program for grades four to six in Edmonton, we discovered something interesting. Almost all of the teachers had already been providing the children with independent reading on a daily basis. They might have called it different things, such as Drop Everything and Read (D.E.A.R.), Uninterrupted Sustained Silent Reading (U.S.S.R.), or free reading, but the intent was to offer the children some time to read self-selected books. In addition to independent reading, teachers had done one or two novel studies each year and some teachers had dipped into basal anthologies. The activity most consistently pursued by most teachers, however, was independent reading. Although they had never intended to offer Single Strand programs, one aspect of reading programming had been emphasized more than any other.

The Edmonton teachers who now offer balanced literacy programming in their upper elementary classrooms would be startled to look back at their previous practices. Now their programs include shared readings of common texts, class lessons on key reading strategies, reading aloud, guided reading, and literature circles, in addition to independent reading. Their program is far more comprehensive in the reading area, and also expands to include daily word study and writing.

Meeting Children's Needs

When we think about the concept of being comprehensive, we also have to consider whom we intend to reach when we plan Language Arts programs. Every teacher wants to meet the needs of all learners in the classroom but, in reality, this type of comprehensiveness does not always occur. After years of working with students who need active remedial help in reading, Irene Fountas and Gay Su Pinnell (2001) note that our first

job in literacy education is to ensure that we are offering "good first teaching" in our classrooms. Maybe, they suggest, we can reduce the need for remediation if we create classrooms where we meet the needs of more children. In this process we could also meet the needs of the children who have received remediation and are ready to reintegrate into the classroom setting.

Four schools participated in the pilot year of our balanced literacy program in Edmonton Public Schools (1997-1998) and registered their grades one and two classes. During that year, the focus was placed on initiating the word study (word recognition and spelling) and reading components. At the end of the year, all the children in the school district were tested in reading, using the Highest Level of Achievement Test (HLAT), a locally normed version of the Canadian Test of Basic Skills (CTBS). District scores were calculated, and the results from the classrooms in the balanced literacy schools were compared with the district's scores. Although we interpreted the results cautiously, since the numbers were so small, it was encouraging that the balanced literacy program produced solid progress in reading, above the district's scores, for grades one and two. (See Appendix C for a more detailed presentation of the results.) The program also appeared to meet the needs of the children with special needs, and was particularly powerful when partnered with Reading Recovery©.

Reading Recovery© teachers at two of the pilot schools believed that a significant factor in their students' reading growth was that their Reading Recovery© children were reading at instructional level in the classroom as well as in their remedial sessions. The multilevel materials and groupings in the balanced literacy program allowed these readers success not only in their one-to-one Reading Recovery© sessions but also in the classroom. Furthermore, in the second year of balanced literacy at those schools, the Reading Recovery© teachers noted that fewer children needed the intense work of Reading Recovery© than in previous years.

In the second year (1998-1999), 18 schools decided to join the project. The program was enhanced to provide a strong writing component in addition to the word study and reading areas. The Highest Level of Achievement Test (HLAT) was given in reading and writing. Again, comparisons between district scores and balanced literacy results indicated progress for balanced literacy schools that was above the district's overall scores. (See Appendix C.)

In September 2002, Anne Mulgrew, Supervisor of Student Assessment, presented a report to trustees and principals that compared Reading and

Writing test results for schools with and without balanced literacy programs. (See Appendix C for test results and more about this study.) The literacy achievement results from the Edmonton Public Schools that had been implementing a structured, long-term balanced literacy program, with accompanying teacher inservice, indicated that considerable progress had been made. This was especially encouraging in view of the high numbers of disadvantaged youngsters enrolled in those schools.

Teaching All Language Arts Areas Every Day

We need to teach all areas of Language Arts on a daily basis so that children have a regular, predictable program. This may seem obvious, but it is often abused in practice. For example, a grade two class is writing a story and progressing through the draft, revision, editing, and publication stages during their Language Arts time-slot, over a two-and-a-half-week period. The children are absorbed in their task and their products are generally pleasing, but they have been focusing exclusively on writing for more than two weeks, while reading has been placed on the back burner.

The advanced readers will likely continue reading at home and in odd moments at school. Since they tend to finish assigned projects more quickly, they have more spare time to pick up books and read in self-regulated ways; in fact, they create their own balanced programs! However, for the children reading at grade level and below, a program that features "binges" in Language Arts is not helpful. Children need consistent exposure to books and active daily instruction to permit them to progress as readers. They rely on teachers to plot programs that balance components and allow them to experience a full range of Language Arts every day.

There are other distractions that weave their way into classroom life and sometimes prevent a balanced literacy program from operating smoothly. These may be described as "non-literacy intervals." Such gaps in literacy programming can pass unnoticed, accepted as a normal part of daily routines. They include such things as collecting lunch money; announcements on the intercom system; school assemblies; and speakers promoting traffic safety, dental hygiene, and physical fitness programs.

In Edmonton, where balanced literacy programs have been running successfully for several years, we try to minimize these non-literacy

intervals that can cut down precious instructional time each day. We request that there be only brief morning announcements and no repeated intercom messages. At one school where lunch money collection consumed time in the past, an aide or the school secretary now collects the money before the school day starts. We recommend that school assemblies fill afternoon time slots to prevent intrusion into Language Arts time, which is usually featured in morning programming. In short, we suggest that if schools want to have Language Arts as a priority, they should demonstrate that priority by focusing only on literacy learning during the times allocated for it. Let us give you a particular example of how this can work.

In one Edmonton school, parents frequently brought their children to school late. The teacher had tried to change the lateness patterns by sending notes home and talking with parents but, when no changes occurred, had made program accommodations. For the first 20 minutes each morning, the children came in and completed "busy work" in teacher-prepared booklets. Finally, when most of the children had arrived, Language Arts instruction started. However, when initiating the balanced literacy program, the teacher realized that every minute would be vital. She gathered the parents together and told them there would be a change of plan. Every day, the Language Arts program would begin promptly with the word study block, focusing on word recognition, phonics, and spelling. This component would be taught at that time each day, starting on time to enable all components of the new Language Arts program to be fitted in. Interestingly, that was the end of the problems with lateness. The parents, understanding that an important instructional component would be featured first thing each day, now have their children at school on time.

Even when teacher and students are in the classroom and focused on learning, assessment demands can cut into instructional time. In Edmonton, we are required to do standardized provincial or district literacy tests each year. Fortunately these are not very time consuming and eat up only a small portion of potential instructional time. During a recent interprovincial meeting, one teacher described a three-week period of yearly testing that occurs in her province. Almost a month of instructional time devoted to formal testing is excessive, eating away at our ability to provide predictable, daily programming in Language Arts.

In addition to district or provincial evaluations, some schools impose excessive testing of their own. It is quite commonplace, for example, to administer the Gates-MacGinitie reading test two or even three times a

year, in addition to mandated testing. Some schools use criterion-referenced testing in a similar manner. For example, each grade might work on story writing with monthly rubrics to evaluate written products at the conclusion of each project. Such sweeps of testing, although well intentioned, are unnecessary and erode instructional time. By contrast, when assessment to guide instruction is a normal part of the daily program, assessment and instruction become a fused and time-effective cycle within Language Arts time.

Maximizing instructional time has to underpin any successful program, and we have to be vigilant in making sure that happens. Demonstrations are powerful (Cambourne, 1988) and our actions transmit our seriousness about Language Arts to children and parents.

Offering Continuity from Grade to Grade

Having a predictable, daily Language Arts program offers continuity for children within each grade. However, the concept of continuity also needs to be stretched across grades. We divide schooling into grades for convenience, yet learning to listen, speak, read, and write are continuous experiences that the mind does not break into grade levels or years. Children should not be expected to work out the Language Arts agenda for the first two to three months of each school year; rather, their engagement in language learning should be uninterrupted. To offer sense and balance to children, we need to make the transitions from grade to grade as seamless as possible.

In the Edmonton balanced literacy project, we started with primary grades (Brailsford, 2002). Indeed, we had only intended it to be an "early years" project, providing a well-structured Language Arts program over the first three years of schooling. While continuity of learning was one of our stated aims, at first that continuity was limited to grades one through three. Then the teachers themselves requested more continuity.

The kindergarten teachers at the balanced literacy schools noted, quite rightly, that they were an important part of the literacy learning continuum and they asked to be included in the project. We responded by adding kindergarten teacher inservices to the agenda in the second year of the project (1998-99). Then upper elementary teachers at the balanced literacy schools suggested that they should be included, too. It was logical, after all, to build on the continuity of learning established in the primary grades. A new program was crafted for grades four to six teachers

and a professional development program was established (Brailsford, 2003). This was piloted in the 1998-99 school year and progressed to full implementation in the third year of the project. Thus, there was a grassroots movement for continuity in Language Arts programming in the balanced literacy schools.

Now, principals in balanced literacy schools in the Edmonton project can see the development of a school literacy community within their own schools, with teachers of various grades "talking the same language" when they describe their programs and the progress of their students. Principals observe that, at grade transitions, teachers know what the next teacher will be talking about and can pass on materials that are relevant to the continued progress of individual children, such as their book levels and strategy needs.

Teachers talk about feeling that they are part of a literacy team, both in the school and across schools in the district. This sense of teamwork is enhanced by school-wide inservices and by an open invitation for teachers to visit other balanced literacy classrooms. Indeed, with almost 60 percent of Edmonton Public Schools now engaged in the balanced literacy program, it is possible for teachers to speak of continuity for children even when they change schools. Moves are no longer as disruptive to learning, since many children can move from one balanced literacy school to another. Teachers know exactly what information is required by the new teacher to ease the transition.

Using Multilevel Materials

Most basal readers, and all single-book, whole class novel studies, promote the use of one level of material that the entire class is expected to read. (Spelling series and writing texts also direct their content to the at-grade-level student.) None of these "one text for all students" programs provides equal literacy opportunities for all children. A typical basal program might offer anthologies, novel studies, and teachers' guides with related links to writing, grammar, and assessment. Children are expected to read the accounts and stories in the anthologies and novels, and then to complete follow-up work. The texts can be anticipated to be lacking in challenge for the advanced reader, too difficult for the reader who is below grade expectations, and just right for the at-grade-level reader. The result is that the program may be offering reasonable literacy learning experiences for only a third to a half of the class.

Similarly, engaging in a whole class book study, such as reading *Mystery in the Frozen Lands* by Martyn Godfrey in a grade six class, can create unequal literacy learning experiences. Although the book is an excellent historical novel about an Arctic voyage to trace the missing members of the Franklin expedition, reading one text with an entire class raises the same issues as using a basal reader. Teachers have attempted to bypass this problem by taping the novel or reading the book aloud for below-grade-level readers. There is no question that hearing the story is a rewarding experience for children who cannot read the book for themselves, but this read-aloud activity should not replace reading. Used consistently, this well-meaning approach reduces actual reading opportunities for weaker readers! In fact, since it is not unusual to see a "one novel for the class" activity expanded to cover combined grades, *Mystery in the Frozen Lands* may be presented to a grades five-six class. Clearly, as the range of readers increases, the ability of one book to serve all needs decreases.

Reading Recovery© (Clay, 1991, 1993) shows us that young readers progress successfully when they move through gradients of text that offer the right amount of challenge. Appropriate textual support, when combined with students' increasing range of strategies, permits them to develop as readers. We need to offer multilevel materials to create reading growth in our elementary classrooms. Children progress as readers when they are reading at their instructional and independent levels, and we need to match texts to their "growing edge" (Gillet and Temple, 1982; Fountas and Pinnell, 1996, 1999).

Reading Recovery© has taught us that children need to read "just right" books to maximize their reading growth. Our challenge is to translate this powerful message into sensible practice for the classroom, where there may be 25 to 30 readers, rather than the one reader served in the Reading Recovery© session.

We need to group readers with similar needs and provide books with appropriate supports and challenges. In the Edmonton balanced literacy program, we have found that readers in grades one and two need to move through relatively fine textual gradients. We use materials levelled with the Fountas and Pinnell criteria (1996), and we also have a "teacher levelling" committee which meets occasionally to adjust levels. Children are grouped, not quite as rigorously as in Reading Recovery©, but as closely as possible to their instructional levels for guided reading lessons. Materials for classroom use are multilevel, to ensure that all readers can engage in successful reading experiences. Thus, materials such as Bookshop (Scholastic), PM

> **Reading and Comprehension**
>
> Instructional level:
> comprehension = 70-89%
> word recognition = 90-94%
>
> Independent level:
> comprehension = 90% +
> word recognition 95% +

Starters (Nelson), and Alphakids (Scholastic) form the foundations of the program, because they offer whole books that can be levelled.

Recently, Fountas and Pinnell (2001) created levels that stretched to grade six. Although these levels can be used to offer guidelines, we have not found it necessary to create such finely levelled text gradients in upper elementary grades. We use broad levelling criteria that explore areas such as text genre, background knowledge requirements, time perspective, themes, plot development, linguistic complexity, and text structure (Brailsford, 2003). Book levelling decisions are tempered by teacher experience to ensure that we can provide books that offer success for readers. Since factors such as background knowledge and vocabulary match may be quite idiosyncratic, we think of levelling as a local folk art rather than as a prescribed science.

The upper elementary program used by Edmonton Public Schools is designed to ensure that children are exposed to multilevel texts in a way that works for a large classroom. Books at several reading levels are clustered into themes, so that the entire class is reading materials that can be discussed communally and shared on co-operative learning days. In addition, each theme comprises a teacher "read-aloud" book; shared reading materials that are read using supportive reading techniques; and class lessons that teach strategies to be applied during guided reading lessons, literature circles, or independent reading.

Supportive Reading Techniques

Choral Reading:
- reading aloud together (teacher and students)
- can be done with the whole class, in small groups, or with partners

Paired Reading
- two students reading aloud together
- one student needs to be a more proficient reader than the other
- students read in chorus, until the less-proficient reader signals to "go solo"
- the more proficient reader is taught to give positive feedback and to return to choral reading when the partner needs support

(Northern Alberta Reading Specialists' Council, 1991; Topping, 1989)

3-Ring Circus:
The class is divided into three groups
- Group 1: each student reads the text silently and independently
- Group 2: students read in pairs (chorally or using Paired Reading techniques)
- Group 3: as a group, the students read chorally with the teacher

(Cunningham, Hall and Sigmon, 1999)

Mystery in the Frozen Lands by Martyn Godfrey is an example of a book that is part of a grade six collection whose theme is "The North." The books in this theme are selected to meet the needs of readers of varying abilities. With whole class strategy lessons, read alouds, shared reading of common texts, and multilevel books for guided reading and literature circles, all children can participate in exploring the theme and in strategy learning. However, no child will be at frustration level in reading, and all children can be guaranteed feelings of success and actual progress as readers.

When we started the Edmonton project, no publishing companies were levelling texts for upper elementary students, so we needed to start from scratch. We received assistance when Literacy Place (Scholastic) became available after our first year, since that program provided themed and levelled materials. With their three-book selections in each theme, we could meet the needs of readers above grade level, at grade level, and just below grade level. We found, however, that we needed to add extra books to meet the reading needs of children requiring more support than was offered in the easiest books in each themed set. We also decided to add a more challenging book, to be read aloud by the teacher, so that we could tie each theme together.

The Scholastic Literacy Place materials allow us to add more balance to our program. Previously we had focused on levelling novels, but Literacy Place also includes nonfiction. We believe that it is important for readers to have a balance of fiction and nonfiction resources, since they require the reader to use different strategies. Readers also need a balance of genres. Although avid readers can go on binges of reading every book written by, for example, Gordon Korman, instructionally we want to offer more than a diet of humorous adventure tales. We need to expose children to poetry, plays, historical fiction, mystery stories, biographies, news accounts, and historical accounts of significant events.

We are not suggesting that each teacher keep a full range of supplies in his or her individual classroom to meet all the needs of the class. In the Edmonton project we found that the most economical and sensible plan was to create a school bookroom that housed the multilevel materials. The teachers are now aware of all the available resources and can borrow selections as needed for their classrooms.

The North Theme
(grade six)

Read-Aloud Book (Challenging)
Trapped in Ice
by Eric Walters
or
Gentle Ben
by Walt Morey
(Alternatively, the teacher might select one title as the read-aloud book and use the other for students who need more challenges than those offered by the "above grade level" novel.)

Hard
(Above Grade Level)
Black Star, Bright Dawn
by Scott O'Dell

Average
(At Grade Level)
Mystery of the Frozen Lands
by Martyn Godfrey

Easy
(1-2 Grade Levels Below)
Winter Camp
by Kirkpatrick Hill
or
Yuit
by Yvette Edmonds

Easy Plus
(3 Grade Levels Below)
Silver
by Gloria Whelan

Using Variety in Instructional Groupings and Communication Styles

Variety in classroom groupings permits the teacher to balance instructional methods and materials, and also facilitates the use of diverse communication styles by the teacher and students. In the course of a Language Arts session, the teacher can organize both whole class portions and group work to ensure that children's needs are met. Whole class sessions, of course, lend themselves to direct, explicit instruction, with everyone using the same materials. Small groups have the flexibility to permit grouping children with similar needs. They also allow time for some individual teacher-child contact. Although direct instruction can occur in small groups, this setting encourages more informal discussions and conversations, and lends itself to matching communication to the children's personal needs.

Whole Class Teaching

It is possible to meet the needs of a wide range of learners in whole class, explicit teaching when:

- materials are multilevel, or supported reading strategies are built in, to ensure that all readers can participate
- activities, such as hands-on tasks, engage class members
- lessons are brief, focused, and paced
- follow-up activities are multilevel, so that students may practise concepts successfully.

In the balanced literacy program used in Edmonton Public Schools, whole group, explicit teaching occurs in the word study period.

Hands-on activities, even at the upper elementary level, permit the children to engage in an active, tactile way. For example, students are asked to sort word cards to match word patterns, and to manipulate letter strips to form words in word-building activities such as Making Big Words (Cunningham and Hall, 1994.) In addition, basic word study is enhanced by challenge components for students who can learn faster, while review sessions are included for children who need more support.

In the upper elementary program, strategy lessons in reading are taught directly to the whole class. This teaching is meaningful to the students because the content stems from the class read-aloud book or from shared readings of magazines. Transfer of learning occurs when the children apply these strategies during guided reading. For example, the students are taught to analyze character traits during a class strategy lesson using the read-aloud book. Then they use the same analysis strategies to identify character traits as they read instructional-level texts in their guided reading groups.

Similarly, whole class demonstrations of an aspect of the writing process always preface individual writing periods. The children are introduced to concepts through direct instruction and practical demonstrations, and then apply these concepts to personal writing.

Word Study Components in the Balanced Literacy Program

Learning to Read and Spell High-Frequency Words
(Moderate Teacher Support)
Each week the teacher introduces a few high-usage function words and these words are practised regularly, using hands-on activities. For example, the students may tap out and chant the letters of each word (primary grades), or draw word trees to illustrate word building from root words (upper elementary grades). Class word dictionaries are built over the course of the year: Word Walls for primary grades and Tricky Word Corners for upper elementary grades.

Working with Word Patterns for Word Recognition and Spelling
Students engage in action-oriented activities to learn how to use phonic elements, word patterns, and analogies: "If you recognize that word, how will it help you to work out this new word?" The word-building activities from the Making Words (Cunningham and Hall, 1994) and Making Big Words (Cunningham and Hall, 1994) lessons may be used. The word construction activities are followed by transfer lessons that enable the children to use word patterns to recognize and spell new words.

Small Group Teaching

Small groups create clusters of children who share the same instructional needs. They also provide opportunities for individual communication between teacher and child. Guided reading, for example, allows teachers to group children with similar reading needs and to provide appropriate materials and strategies. It also allows both small group and individual contacts. For example, while individuals in the small group read a portion of the text to themselves, the teacher has time to work diagnostically, and individually, with one or two students. Similarly, guided writing permits the teacher to communicate with individual students and to group together students who have similar support needs for mini-conferences. In small group and individual contacts, informal conversations and incidental teaching flourish. The teacher has the opportunity to have literacy conversations with class members and can grasp valuable "teachable moments" as the children apply what they have learned.

Working in the Children's Optimal "Zones"

To engage in successful learning, children need to be working at their "growing edge." Vygotsky describes this area as the "zone of proximal development" (1978) where children can progress with support from others. If work is too easy, growth stagnates. If work is too difficult, no growth is possible because the child is always frustrated. Only if we provide Language Arts programs that permit children to work in their "zones" can progress occur. The skill is to accommodate zones within multilevel groupings, diversity in communication styles, and multilevel methods and materials, to ensure that all children make progress as literacy learners.

In the balanced literacy program (Brailsford, 2002, 2003) used in Edmonton Public Schools, various Language Arts components provide complete support, moderate support, and decreasing assistance, all during the course of the daily Language Arts period. For example, the teacher who reads aloud to the children and demonstrates writing strategies is offering complete support.

Moderate support occurs during shared reading, when the children read using a variety of supportive techniques: for example, choral reading as a class or in groups, buddy reading, and 3-Ring Circus (Cunningham, Hall and Sigmon, 1999; see page 14 for a description of this strategy). In the upper elementary program, shared readings of common texts by teacher and class are often accompanied by a class strategy lesson, in which the children learn a new reading strategy with teacher direction. At all elementary grade levels, moderate support occurs in guided reading groups, where the children read multilevel texts and apply problem solving strategies to reading, with scaffolded assistance from the teacher.

Reading Components in the Balanced Literacy Program

Read Aloud (Total Teacher Support)
The teacher reads aloud to the whole class and models fluent, expressive reading.

Shared Reading (Moderate Teacher Support)
The teacher and students read a text aloud together, to enable all class members to share common content. (Sometimes alternate supported reading techniques are used such as Paired Reading and buddy choral reading.)

Guided Reading (Moderate Teacher Support)
Students are grouped according to their instructional-reading levels. Each group reads a text with support from the teacher.

Class Strategy Lesson: Grades 4–6 (Moderate Teacher Support)
The teacher provides direct instruction on a reading strategy for the whole class. Print content from read-aloud and shared reading sessions is used. Class strategy lessons are used with upper elementary classes.

Independent Reading (Minimal Teacher Support)
Students read personally selected books. In earlier grades, the teacher provides levelled tubs of books. The children gradually progress to free selection of materials.

(Brailsford, 2003)

In writing, moderate support is offered when the teacher provides demonstrations and mini-lessons for the whole class. The students use the demonstrated techniques when they engage in their own writing. Moderate support is maintained for children who struggle with aspects of their own writing, when the teacher gathers together groups of children who require similar assistance. For other children, teacher support can be decreased as their writing confidence increases.

There has been a common perception that children starting kindergarten and grade one need a great deal of support in their literacy learning, but become independent by upper elementary grades. However, observations indicate that, although children do mature as learners, all students need support when they are learning new concepts. Hence, a Language Arts program even at the grade six level should include the provision of support. Grade six students need to work in their "zones" just like their younger buddies in grade one. "He is not an independent worker" is not a fair comment if the work provided is too difficult for a youngster. However, all children can demonstrate independence when they are working on sufficiently easy materials to ensure their success.

Let us take a moment to clarify again what we mean by "support." As noted earlier in this chapter, teachers often provide total support to weaker readers by preparing audiotapes of texts or by arranging to have books read aloud to them. However, since these are listening activities, they should not be the children's major "reading" experiences. We feel strongly that support strategies should enhance children's engagement with print and not serve to avoid it.

In the Edmonton program, children are read to every day in all elementary grades (total teacher support). However, they also engage in

Writing Components in the Balanced Literacy Program

Writing Demonstrations (Total to Moderate Support)
- The teacher models an aspect of writing and talks aloud while the writing is drafted. For example, the teacher verbalizes writing-related thoughts when modelling a journal entry or writing a lead for a story (total support).
- In mini-lessons, a brief lesson is taught on a writing craft: for example, using dialogue or using a writer's checklist for editing (total support).
- Both teacher and class pool ideas, and share the writing process to create a class text (moderate support).

Guided Writing (Moderate Support)
The students work on their own writing (drafting, revising, editing, and publishing) with the teacher providing assistance as needed, for example, through conferences and flexible support groups.

Individual Writing (Minimal Support)
The students initiate and complete their own writing, checking with the teacher occasionally as needed.

(Brailsford, 2003)

shared readings of common texts at all grade levels (moderate teacher support). Shared readings are completed with all children tracking texts, and support is offered through whole-group choral reading, buddy reading, and Paired Reading (Northern Alberta Reading Specialists' Council, 1991; Topping, 1989). Topping's research, and related research completed in Edmonton Public Schools (Northern Alberta Reading Specialists' Council, 1991), shows us that readers can read more complex materials when supported with specific buddy reading techniques.

The students in the Edmonton program, however, also do daily guided reading at their instructional levels, as well as independent reading with slightly easier texts. The variety in program offerings ensures that all children are actually reading every day, not just listening to others read.

In this chapter, we have laid out the framework of a sensible, balanced Language Arts program. If we structure a program with this framework in mind, what will it look like in classroom use? In the next chapter, we will look into the daily life of Bonaventure School, which has taken steps to promote comprehensive and continuous literacy learning for children in the elementary grades.

Bibliography

Professional References

Brailsford, Anne. *Balanced Literacy: Division 1*. Edmonton, AB: Resource Development, Edmonton Public Schools, 2002.

Brailsford, Anne. *Balanced Literacy: Division 2*. Edmonton, AB: Resource Development, Edmonton Public Schools, 2003.

Cambourne, Brian. *The Whole Story*. Auckland. NZ: Ashton Scholastic, 1988.

Clay, Marie M. *Reading Recovery: A Guidebook for Teachers in Training*. Auckland, NZ: Heinemann, 1993

Clay, Marie M. *Becoming Literate: the Construction of Inner Control*. Auckland, NZ: Heinneman, 1991.

Cunningham, Patricia M., Hall, Dorothy P. and Sigmon, Cheryl M. *The Teacher's Guide to the Four Blocks: A Multimethod, Multilevel Framework for Grades 1-3*. Greensboro, NC: Carson-Dellosa, 1999.

Fountas, Irene C. and Pinnell Gay Su. *Guiding Readers and Writers Grades 3-6: Teaching Comprehension, Genre, and Content Literacy.* Portsmouth. NH: Heinemann, 2001.

Fountas, Irene C. and Pinnell, Gay Su. *Matching Books to Readers: Using Levelled Books in Guided Reading, K-3.* Portsmouth, NH: Heinemann, 1999.

Fountas, Irene C. and Pinnell, Gay Su. *Guided Reading: Good First Teaching for All Children.* Portsmouth, NH: Heinemann, 1996.

Gillett, Jean Wallace and Temple, Charles. *Understanding Reading Problems: Assessment and Instruction.* Toronto: Little, Brown and Company, 1982.

Northern Alberta Reading Specialists' Council. *Paired Reading: Positive Reading Practice* . (Manual by Anne Brailsford, with accompanying training videotape) Distributed in Kelowna, British Columbia: Filmwest, 1991.

Topping, Keith. "Peer Tutoring and Paired Reading: Combining two powerful techniques," *The Reading Teacher.* 42 (7), 1989, 488-494.

Vygotsky, Lev. *Mind in Society: The Development of Higher Psychological Processes.* Edited by M. Coles, V. John-Steiner, S. Scribner and E. Souberman. Cambridge, Mass.: Harvard University Press, 1978.

Children's Books

Edmonds. Yvette. *Yuit.* Toronto: Napoleon Publishing, 1993.

Godfrey, Martyn. *Mystery in the Frozen Lands.* Toronto: James Lorimer & Company, 1988.

Hill, Kirkpatrick. *Winter Camp.* New York: Puffin Books, 1993.

Morey, Walt. *Gentle Ben.* New York: Puffin Books, 1965.

O'Dell, Scott. *Black Star, Bright Dawn.* Boston: Ballantine Books, 1988.

Walters, Eric. *Trapped in Ice.* Toronto: Puffin Books, 1997.

Whelan, Gloria. *Silver.* New York: Random House, 1988.

Reading Series

Alphakids: Scholastic

Beanbags: Scholastic

Bookshop: Scholastic

Literacy Place: Scholastic

PM Starters: Nelson

Chapter

2 A Balanced Literacy Program in Action: Primary Class

Bonaventure School

Bonaventure School is located in the suburbs. Surrounded by dense housing estates and the occasional strip mall, it provides an island of green playing fields in its brick and stucco neighbourhood. Children attending the school live in modest frame houses, in the nearby trailer courts, in low-rental apartments and townhouses, or in the small area of larger executive homes. As is true of schools in all large Canadian cities, the student population is ethnically mixed, and new immigrants move into the neighbourhood each year. The school, part of a large urban school district, serves a growing population and has portable classrooms to accommodate the overflow. Over five hundred children attend Bonaventure as their neighbourhood school.

Movement Towards Balanced Literacy Programming

Three years ago, the staff and principal decided to join the school district's balanced literacy project in an attempt to meet the diverse needs of their school population. In the first year of their enrolment in the project, teachers of grades one to three attended a two-and-a-half-day initial training session and then once-a-month inservices. As they learned new techniques, materials, methods, and organizational groupings, they were supported by a balanced literacy consultant who came to the school each month. The consultant taught demonstration lessons in the classrooms, coached teachers, and ran lunchtime meetings to focus on areas that the teachers had identified as needing more explanation.

During that first year, the school janitor helped the primary teachers to clear out a dusty stockroom that had contained old textbooks and assorted bundles and boxes of materials whose educational significance

had been lost over the years. Once the room was cleaned, the teachers placed levelled books on the shelves, with the materials in each level arranged in brightly coloured plastic crates. The levelled books were borrowed by teachers for their multilevel guided reading groups. At the same time, a professional library was started in the staff room. Books on the balanced literacy project's professional reading list were housed in a bookcase near the coffee area, and teachers were encouraged to borrow them.

In the first year of the project, the two kindergarten teachers attended their own inservices organized by the district's balanced literacy consultants. Here they learned about shared reading groups, word activities, and incorporating literacy into centres. They became more aware of developmentally appropriate practices that would further young children's knowledge about print. The kindergarten teachers added suitable books to the professional library, for example, *Month-by-Month Reading and Writing for Kindergarten* (Hall and Cunningham, 1997).

In the second year of the project, while the primary teachers continued their inservices and coaching, the upper elementary teachers enrolled in the balanced literacy program. They attended similar initial training sessions and monthly inservices, received demonstration lessons and coaching from a balanced literacy consultant, and attended monthly lunchtime meetings with the consultant. The school's centralized book room was also expanded to include levelled guided reading materials for students in grades four to six. The upper elementary teachers added new books to the staff's professional development library. The principal included a balanced literacy section in each staff meeting to enable the staff to exchange news and ideas.

As we prepare to enter a classroom to get a closer view of balanced literacy in action, it is now the third year of Bonaventure School's inclusion in the project. Most of the kindergarten and primary classroom teachers have completed two years of balanced literacy inservices and coaching. Now they simply attend two "updater" inservices a year, although they are welcome to seek consultant advice or review their practices by attending years one and two inservices for kindergarten and primary teachers new to the project, if they feel the need. The primary teachers in Bonaventure School continue to meet for one or two lunchtimes a month to share ideas and readings and to review materials that could be added to their supplies.

The Teacher

Darlene Hunka has been teaching children in the primary grades for 20 years, at various schools in the area. She transferred to Bonaventure Elementary School at the beginning of this school year, and is participating in intensive professional development sessions. All of the other primary teachers completed their two years of balanced literacy training last June. Darlene Hunka is the only staff member currently immersed in the first year of training and this is her first year of teaching a balanced literacy program. It's a Monday morning in March, and by now program routines and teacher expectations are well established in her grade one class.

Materials and Classroom Organization

In Mrs. Hunka's class, children sit around tables to give everyone an unobstructed view of chalkboards and pocket charts on one wall, as well as the Word Wall dictionary, challenge words chart, and text structure organizers (Brailsford, 2002) on the opposite wall. The other two walls are covered with posters of poems and chants; some commercially produced, some penned by the teacher with the children's help, and some composed by individual children. Beneath the Word Wall dictionary, wall-length bookshelves house tubs of levelled books, metal cookie trays with magnetic letters, selections of large writing-organizer sheets, crayons, felt pens, paints, and piles of plain and coloured paper. A horseshoe-shaped table and wipe-off magnetic easel, used for guided reading sessions and other activities, stand in one corner of the room. A big book easel, with a selection of big books currently in use, is placed on a rug in another corner of the room. Nearby is the audio-visual station, with a tape recorder and a computer.

The School Day Starts: Word Wall

There's a general buzz of chatter and laughter as the children arrive and head to their desks. Mrs. Hunka greets them all, takes attendance, and gets ready to introduce the week's five "high usage" Word Wall words.

Each day, Mrs. Hunka spends ten minutes practising high-frequency word patterns with the children. She emphasizes word recognition and spelling of the words, using hands-on practice activities. The intent is to build automatic recall of words that are needed constantly in reading and writing. Five new core words are introduced each week, plus three optional challenge words for the advanced spellers. At the conclusion of each week, the core words are filed on a wall dictionary that is visible to each child, providing a handy reference.

The week's new words, printed on thin card, will be presented to the children in alphabetical order to ease transfer into their individual Word Wall dictionaries. The words are: friend, into, make, play, and where.

Mrs. Hunka: (holding up the card so that everyone can see it) Our first word today is **friend**. "My best *friend* is coming for a sleep-over." Let's chant the letters in **friend**, clapping our hands once as we say each letter, and we'll say the word when we've finished spelling it. Ready ...

Children and Mrs. Hunka: (teacher finger tracking under each letter as it's verbalized) **f ... r ... i ... e ... n ... d ... friend**.

Mrs. Hunka: Nice going. Now I want you to spell **friend** again, and this time, instead of clapping for each letter that you name, I'd like you to write those letters in the air with your finger as you say them. Let's do (deepening her voice) **our enormous giant letters**. Get ready...

Children and Mrs. Hunka: (drawing huge letters in the air as they chant) **... f ... r ... i ... e ... n ... d ... friend**.

Mrs. Hunka places **friend** in the top slot of a nearby pocket chart.

This Week's Word Wall Words

⌞friend⌝

Mrs. Hunka: Super job! Our next word is (holding up the card) **into**: "The bear went back *into* its cave." Get ready to clap the letters as you spell them out loud.

Children and Mrs. Hunka: (teacher finger tracking) **i ... n ... t ... o ... into**.

Mrs. Hunka: All right! We're going to chant the letters again and write them in the air, but this time we're going to use (lightening her voice) our tiny elf letters. Ready ...

Children and Mrs. Hunka: (drawing tiny letters in the air) **i ... n ... t ... o ... into**.

Mrs. Hunka puts **into** below **friend** in the pocket chart.

This Week's Word Wall Words

⌞friend⌝

⌞into⌝

Mrs. Hunka: Way to go! Now we'll clap for **make**: "I'm going to *make* some delicious blueberry muffins." Ready ...

The word spelling sequence is repeated for the remaining words, with the children using various "tactile reinforcer" movements such as clapping, making giant or elf letters, and so on. As this initial work on each word unfolds, Mrs. Hunka continues to place the word cards in the pocket chart.

This Week's Word Wall Words

friend

into

make

play

where

When all the words have been practised, Mrs. Hunka and the class reread them before moving on to the challenge words.

Mrs. Hunka: Let's look at this week's challenge words, for those of you who decide to do them. The words I've chosen link to our Science project: **chicken**, **hatch**, and **shell**. (As she says each word, she places it in the pocket chart.)

Challenge Words

chicken

hatch

shell

Note: At this time of year, Mrs. Hunka has the school's incubator in the room and the children observe, discuss, and record the embryo-to-birth progress of baby chicks.

Who can tell me a sentence with the word **chicken** in it? Go ahead, Petra.

Petra: The chicken lived at the farm.

Mrs. Hunka: Good sentence. How about a sentence for the word hatch?

Appropriate sentences are provided for **hatch** and **shell**; then Mrs. Hunka asks the children to take out their Word Wall dictionaries and pencils. Mrs. Hunka uses this time to allow the children to transfer the words into their personal Word Wall dictionaries, and to engage the children in printing practice.

Mrs. Hunka: Steve, remind us which letter is at the beginning of the word (points) **friend**. (Steve says **f**. She asks the children to locate the **Ff** page, and verbalizes the alphabet through to **f** as she moves around the room helping the few children who still have difficulties with alphabetical order.) Everybody's on the right page for printing **friend**. Put your pencil point at the beginning of the next empty line on your **f** page, just below the word **family** (moving around as she speaks, checking that everybody has the right spot) ... that's where you're going to print **friend**.

Grade one child finds the place in his dictionary.

Mrs. Hunka: Watch how I print each letter to make **friend** ... very carefully ... all of them sitting on the line (printing the word on the board as she talks). Now I'd like you to print **friend** on the line where your pencil point is sitting. Very best printing, please!

Ff
from
family
friend

Grade one child prints the word.

The same procedure unfolds as all five words are printed into Word Wall dictionaries. At the end of the day, each child will take a sheet of this week's five words home for reading and spelling practice with family members. The "challenge" words will be included as optional words for those children who wish to work on them. In class, tomorrow, there will be a clap-and-chant review of today's words, followed by additional practice using a different activity, such as *Ruler Tap, Wordo, Cloze with Sentences and Paragraphs*, or *Be a Mind Reader* (Brailsford, 2002; Cunningham, 1995).

Mrs. Hunka: (seeing that every child has finished Word Wall dictionary work) Clear your desks, please. We're going to read a favourite story together.

Transition into Making Words

A Making Words lesson will follow the brief, shared rereading of a book that was initially introduced at Halloween, then placed in the browsing box for independent reading times. Mrs. Hunka quickly checks the "jobs" chart. She asks Lorraine and Mike to put a Making Words stick on each desk, and directs Greg, Stephanie, Jodi, Emma, Nick, and Rob to place specific letters by each stick. (She has already put the pertinent letter containers on the back table.)

When the six letters are rearranged at the end of the Making Words lesson, they will form the word "nights" (Lesson in Cunningham and Hall, 1994, p.93).

Teachers use a utility box (usually used for nails and screws) from the local hardware store. Letters are stored in the drawers.

Mrs. Hunka calls the children over to the carpeted big book corner, and places on the easel *It Didn't Frighten Me* by Janet Goss and Jerome Harste. Many of the children notice the selected book, and grins of anticipation light up their faces. They enjoy a shared reading of a familiar book, and the children completing jobs return to the group quickly.

Mrs. Hunka: Super reading, everybody! That's a great story, isn't it? (She puts the book back into the browsing box — a large cardboard box containing familiar big books — as the children return to their desks.)

Making Words

Today, Mrs. Hunka is working on a Making Words lesson. The children will progress from building two-letter words to making a six-letter word.

Mrs. Hunka always does a letter check at the beginning of the Making Words lesson. She asks the children to hold up each letter in turn.

Mrs. Hunka: Show me your **i** (holding up a larger version **i**) ... show me your **g** (holds up the large version **g**) ... show me your **h** ...

As the letters are named, children who are missing a specific letter help themselves from the letter containers at the back table, and Mrs. Hunka places the large letter cards in the bottom pocket of the pocket chart.

Mrs. Hunka: (scanning the room to ensure that everyone has a stick and letters) Remember our rule: letters flat on your desk, lower-case side up. Leave your stick empty until you're ready to build a word.

Being, of necessity, a proficient right-to-left as well as upside-down reader, from her position by the pocket chart Mrs. Hunka can see the words being built, because every letter card has the lower-case letter on one side and its upper-case equivalent on the flip side. Mrs. Hunka holds "class sized" versions of the words she'll be asking the children to make, ensuring that the children can't see what's printed on the cards until they have made the words.

Making Words Lessons

Making Words lessons focus the children's attention on phonetic and visual-sound patterns while they build words. The children built two-letter and three-letter words and advance to more complex words within each lesson. The activities are multilevel, in that all children can make the simpler words and receive support from a model to build the more difficult word patterns. Making Words lessons, in this balanced literacy program, are always followed by Sort and Transfer sessions on the next day. These sessions emphasize recognition of visual sound patterns and transferring that knowledge to build new words. Teachers plan for one 25-minute lesson each day. As the children progress through grades two and three, Making Words lessons often give way to other hands-on word recognition and spelling activities.

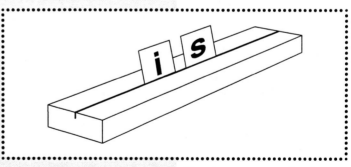

There's a groove running down one side of the sticks. When the children are asked to make a particular word, they'll place their letter cards upright in the groove.

Mrs. Hunka: Two-letter words first. (Mrs. Hunka places the numeral **2** at the left side of the top pocket.) Show me two fingers. Our word is ... (smiling) **is**. "Today *is* Monday." Say the word **is** very slowly and make the word in your stick.

As the children verbalize **is**, they place **i** and **s** in their sticks with a great deal of confidence. Seeing that all attempts are accurate, Mrs. Hunka asks Jenny to use the large letters to make the word in the pocket chart.

Mrs. Hunka: Nice going, Jenny. Everybody, check that your word is exactly like Jenny's ... yes, you all made **is** beautifully. (She places her **is** word card under the numeral **2** in the pocket chart.) Now take out the last letter of your word. (Mrs. Hunka models moving the **s** out of the pocket chart, and the children move their last letters from their sticks.) Let's make another two-letter word by finding a new last letter. We'll make **it**: "That's a plane. Did you see *it* fly through the cloud?" ... Say the word **i...t** very slowly, and make the word in your stick. (pauses) I see everybody's finished. Jason, come and make the word **it** in the pocket chart, please ... Well done, Jason, and well done, all of you! (She places her **it** word card below **is** in the pocket chart.)

Mrs. Hunka: (placing the numeral **3** at the top of the pocket chart, and to the right of the two-letter words column) Let's move on to three-letter words. Show me three fingers ... Okay. The first word is **hit**: "I *hit* a baseball." Say the word **hit** slowly: **h...i...t**, and make the word in your stick.

When the children have made **hit** successfully, Mrs. Hunka asks them to change the first letter to make the word **sit**. Then the students are asked to "clear their sticks," start again, and make the word **his**.

The activity continues at a brisk pace, with the children making four-letter and five-letter words.

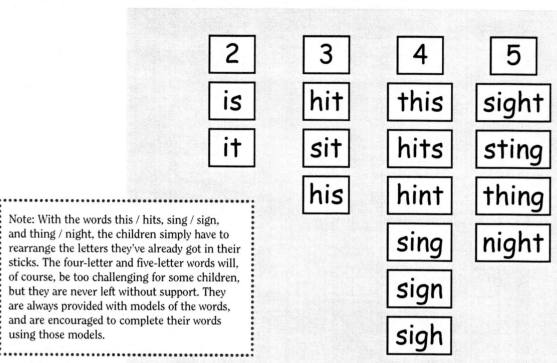

Note: With the words this / hits, sing / sign, and thing / night, the children simply have to rearrange the letters they've already got in their sticks. The four-letter and five-letter words will, of course, be too challenging for some children, but they are never left without support. They are always provided with models of the words, and are encouraged to complete their words using those models.

Mrs. Hunka: You did a super job making these words! Let's read the words in each column, together, starting with the two-letter words. (She points to each word as it's read.) Now comes the really tough part: I want you to use all six letters to make the mystery word. Go for it!

Some of the children have already realized that the mystery word is **nights**, so they make the word quickly. Other children take more time, attempting to use all of their letters to make a meaningful word. Mrs. Hunka moves around the room offering help where needed, and sees that most children have completed the activity. She decides to give the remaining two children a clue.

Mrs. Hunka: One minute to go. I've got a clue for those of you who haven't yet figured out the mystery word: If you add an **s** to one of our five-letter words (points to them in the pocket chart), you'll make the mystery word. (The last two children figure out the word quickly.) Mercedes, make the word for us in the pocket chart ... thank you. (Mrs. Hunka places her **nights** word card in the pocket chart.) On a count of three, say the mystery word, please: one, two, three ... (every child verbalizes **nights**). Who can give us a sentence with *nights* in it?

Sadie: Nights are cold in winter.

Mrs. Hunka: Good sentence, Sadie.

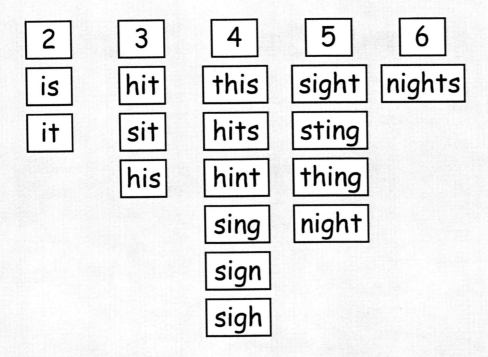

Note: The mystery word could also be **things**.

Mrs. Hunka comments on the good word-building strategies she's noticed on her travels around the room, and says they'll use those words to recognize and build new words on Tuesday.

The children are reminded to place their letter cards on their desks; then the children who handed out the letters collect them and put them away. Lorraine and Mike collect the sticks.

Shared Reading

Each day Mrs. Hunka spends approximately 15 minutes reading first a familiar book, poem, or chant, and then a new one, with the class. Shared reading is a time for supported reading practice, when all children can

experience engagement with print. It is also a time when reading strategies are taught. Today, Mrs. Hunka is going to emphasize:

- increasing comprehension by linking experiential knowledge with story information
- word recognition strategies:
  - using rhyming patterns
  - using prompts to help work out words
  - using picture cues and integrating them with other sources, for example, syntax, meaning, and graphic cues.

Teaching Tip

Eliciting experiential, background knowledge, whether via illustrations or text, "primes" the children's thinking about what might occur, before the story unfolds.

Mrs. Hunka: One group at a time, we're going to move back into the shared reading corner: Rob's group, Sean's, Tracy's (and so on, until all children are on the rug). Let's take a look at the story I've chosen for us today. We've read *It Didn't Frighten Me* before, but this book (placing a big book on the easel) is a new one for us. Let's look at the front cover. Marcia, what do you think this story's going to be about?

Marcia: It's about clowns.

Mrs. Hunka: (getting ready to finger track along the title) Right on! This clown is called Smarty Pants.

Nick: (chuckling) That's what my Dad calls me when I tell him something he doesn't know!

Mrs. Hunka: He does? Well this Smarty Pants is a clown. Who can tell me anything about clowns? (seeing one girl's hand shoot up first) Lorraine?

Lorraine: Well, they do funny things ... and tricks that make you laugh ... and they're on TV.

Alex: I saw some clowns when I went to the rodeo, doing back flips and stuff ... and one of 'em flipped right over a bull when it ran at him ... and that old bull got a big surprise! My Dad says they're really brave, them clowns 'cause they help cowboys that fall off get away from the bull.

Mrs. Hunka: The clowns get the bull's attention away from the cowboy (lots of children nodding enthusiastically) and give that cowboy time to get out of the way to safety, and they make us laugh when they are doing it!

Jason: Yeah! You should just see the cowboys run! And the clowns, sometimes they make real neat balloons and stuff, and give'em to you!

Sadie: Yeah! I got a balloon dog last summer when me and my mom went to the big parade!

Mrs. Hunka: So, we know quite a lot about clowns. We know they make us laugh by being funny and doing tricks. We see them on TV, maybe in a circus show. We see them helping to keep cowboys out of danger at the rodeo, and they might make balloon animals for us at parades. Let's look at the pictures, and see what Smarty Pants the clown gets up to in this story. I wonder if he's funny and makes us laugh?

An animated, fast-paced discussion ensues about Smarty Pants driving a racing car, flying an "aeroplane" (as this New Zealand-authored book spells it), playing a trumpet, swimming, and so on. His pet dog tags along and, as Esther notes, always looks scared.

Many storybooks that children read are written by authors who live in English-speaking countries other than Canada. Some spellings are slightly different, such as aeroplane/airplane, Mum/Mom, centre/center. With teacher mediation the children get used to differences, initially pointing them out as they occur, then completely accepting them, as reading fluency and confidence increase.

Mrs. Hunka: (turning back to the beginning of the story, pointer on the first word, ready to track the print) I'm going to read the first two pages, and I'd like you to join in when you can.

I am a smarty pants, (p. 1)
Rum-tum-toe.
Here is a racing car.
See me go. (p. 2)

Mrs. Hunka's left-to-right tracking, her sweep back to the left for the next line, and her progression from top to bottom on each page of this narrative format, will reinforce the children's understanding of directionality. (By this stage of the year, directionality is generally established, but the teacher's tracking keeps the children focused on the print itself.) In addition, Mrs. Hunka varies the way she tracks, running her hand under the lines of print on the repeated refrain, and using word-by-word pointing on the new word addition to each pattern, for example, "See me go" and "See me fly."

The language used across the first two pages establishes language and rhyming patterns that will be carried through most of the story. Mrs. Hunka knows that a brisk read-through, followed by discussion, will provide the children with more "advance organizer" expectations about what is to follow.

Embedded in this particular language pattern, there's a jingle that alters slightly for each event in order to produce rhyming patterns, for example: Rum-tum-toe / See me go; Rum-tum-tie / See me fly. Rhyming patterns often prove useful for predicting new words, for example: Rum-tum-tee / See me ski.

Various children are able to read the first line chorally with Mrs. Hunka. Some drop out hesitantly at "Rum," and some after "Rum-tum," with many having difficulty reading "toe." Since jingles don't have to make sense, this one doesn't provide any context clues for word recognition support. Its rhyming partner, "go" — which most, if not all of the children can read — comes on the next page, and the rhyming pattern hasn't yet been established.

The majority of the children resume confident choral reading of the last two lines.

Mrs. Hunka (smiling): Nice going, everybody. That second line was a little tricky, wasn't it? Where he's kind of singing to himself: "Rum-tum-toe." Can you find, in what we've read so far, a word that rhymes with "toe"?

Mike: Yeah, it's "go," at the end there. "Rum-tum-toe, see me go."

Mrs. Hunka: Good for you, Mike. Now, everybody, a clue for you: the clown always sings "Rum-tum," but the word after "Rum-tum" changes each time. Thinking about what we've read on these two pages, where might we look if we need help figuring out that word? Tracy?

Tracy: Well, if it's the same as this one — we could check the last word, 'cause it should sound the same. It should rhyme."

Mrs. Hunka: Hmm ... we can check that out, can't we? Let's do it now. (She turns the page and points to both "tie" and "fly.")

**I am a smarty pants,
Rum-tum-tie.
Here is an aeroplane.
See me fly.**

Tracy: Yeah, see? "Rum-tum-tie, see me fly."

Earl: But, Mrs. Hunka, the words aren't spelled the same at the end there — that can't be right.

Mrs. Hunka: Rhyming words often have the same spelling pattern, the same letters, at the end of the words, but not always, Earl. Good point, though. In this particular story, some of the rhyming words just sound the same at the end, and don't have the same spelling patterns. Okay, everybody, let's start at the beginning again. Now we know what to expect, and we'll read about Smarty Pants' adventures. (She flips back to the beginning.) One, two, three ...

The children read the first four adventures briskly, with a good deal of confidence, then Mrs. Hunka calls a halt as she turns the page to reveal the fifth adventure.

Mrs. Hunka: Let's stop here, for a moment. Ah ... you've already noticed that I've covered a word.

> **I am a smarty pants,**
> **Rum-tum-tee.**
> **Here is a**
> **See me ski.**

Let's read to that part.

All: "I am a smarty pants, rum-tum-tee. Here is a ..."

Gurnam: (laughing at the picture) It could be "slope" ... he could be going down the ski slope!

Mrs. Hunka: "Here is a slope." Hmm ... does that sound right? (Assents come from everyone.) Yes, we could say that. Does it make sense? (All agree it makes sense.) Uh huh, "Here is a slope" makes sense. So "slope" sounds right, and it makes sense. Let's see if "slope" checks out. (She lifts up the flap covering the first letter, exposing the **m**.) What do you think?

> **I am a smarty pants,**
> **Rum-tum-tee.**
> **Here is a m**
> **See me ski.**

Mercedes: No, it's not "slope." "Slope" doesn't start with (letter name) **m.** And it can't be "hill," then. I thought it was "hill," but that starts with (letter name) **h.**

Mrs. Hunka: You're right. It's not "slope" or "hill." Neither of them check out as starting with an **m.** You're getting warmer, though. Let's read ahead.

All: "See me ski." (Though there are some hesitations at "ski," the clear picture of Smarty Pants skiing assists the students.)

Mrs. Hunka: So we know he's skiing. Where do you ski that starts with an **m**?

Val: (waving her hand excitedly) I know, I know — it's "mountain"! We went skiing in the mountains at Christmas.

Mrs. Hunka: Let's check that out. "Mountain" begins with (sound) **m** (lifts the entire flap) and ...?

All the children: Mountain!

Mrs. Hunka: "Here is a mountain." Well done, Val!

The class and Mrs. Hunka finish choral reading the book. Every child has been totally involved with Smarty Pants' adventures, rhythms, and rhymes for 15 well-focused minutes.

Guided Reading and Independent Reading Stations

Mrs. Hunka works with two guided reading groups each day. As she spends time with one group, the other students are working at reading stations.

Guided Reading

Guided Reading provides opportunities for children to read instructional level materials and for the teacher to work on reading strategies with small groups and individual children. The independent reading stations offer reading practice time for the students. The types of reading stations that Mrs. Hunka uses are shown below.

Reading Stations

Browsing Box: Tubs of familiar big and small books from shared reading sessions. The children can read these with a buddy, independently, or as a group with a leader who tracks print. Sometimes, sentence strips are left with a book and the children remake the story on the rug or in a pocket chart.

Levelled Books: Tubs of carefully levelled books for "Independent Level" reading. These need to be books that can be read with a minimum of 95 percent contextual word recognition, and 90 percent comprehension by each child. A tub is recommended to each child, though he/she is welcome to read books from tubs that are below that level. For example, Steve is reading Level D books in his guided reading group, but is selecting from the A, B, and C books for levelled tubs.

Listening/Technology: Audiotapes and books for a listening centre. Mrs. Hunka has one computer in the room and she combines this with the listening materials. Good quality "literacy boosting" software such as Wiggleworks (Scholastic) Story Webs and Multimedia Literature (MacMillan McGraw Hill) are used for the computer.

ABC/Word Study: Activities that boost letter and word recognition abilities. The children build Word Wall words with tactile materials; practise making small words from longer words with letter tiles; do word sorts into patterns; and play word games such as Snap and Concentration Pairs with word wall words.

Read Around the Room: Reading all the stories, charts, chants, and poems on display in the room (Fountas and Pinnell, 1996). The children use pointers and read the print on the walls with a buddy. Mrs. Hunka ensures that poem charts and samples of class writing are left up, to give rich print sources for her Read Around the Room group.

> **Poetry:** Overheads of poems and an overhead projector, which the children can use for group shared readings.
>
> **Drama:** Props and copies of simple plays are provided. The children can dramatize their own oral retellings of stories, use scripts, or write and perform their own scripts.

On this day in March, Mrs. Hunka is moving the children towards the goal of all the reading stations, independent reading itself. The groups can now concentrate on reading from levelled tubs and Mrs. Hunka has included these as an activity for most groups. Mrs. Hunka and the children check the Reading Stations pocket chart together. Collecting the material they need, the children move to their specified stations.

The children are placed in groups according to their current Instructional Reading Levels. Fountas and Pinnell (1996) describe nine reading levels in grade one. Children develop as readers at different rates. For example, Moon group members are reading Level H materials at the present time (anticipated "average" level around May of first grade). Sun group members are reading Level D materials (anticipated "average" level at December of first grade). The composition of group members changes as reading needs change. Four, or a maximum of five, groups will be underway at any given time, depending on the reading level needs of the class. Some teachers formulate their groups homogeneously so that they draw out an established group for guided reading: for example, the Sun group or Rainbow group. Other teachers organize heterogeneous reading station groups and call together children from several station groups for their guided reading lessons. Both methods work well.

The children work for 20 minutes at one station, and then move to their next designated station for the following 20 minutes. For example, the Sun group begins with guided reading and then moves to levelled book tubs; the Moon group starts at levelled book tubs and then moves to the listening and reading station. Mrs. Hunka makes sure that the children who work at independent reading stations know what they're doing; then she joins the group at the guided reading table.

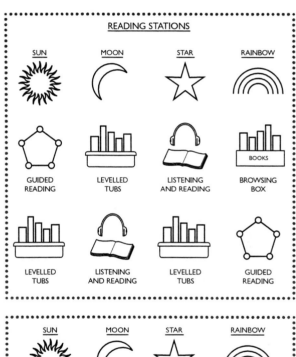

Rereading Familiar Books

Mrs. Hunka has trained the children to reread books at the beginning of a lesson. She has left copies of *Run! Run!* (Level C) and *Will You Play With Us?* (Level D) on the table. The children of the Sun group are busy rereading the two familiar books, on their own or with a partner. Mrs. Hunka monitors and prompts where necessary.

Six copies of *Tails* sit face up on the table, one for each of the children and one for the teacher. Mrs. Hunka has prepared a lesson plan for the Sun group, and she keeps it handy to ensure that she covers all of the planned items.

<table>
<tr><td colspan="2">DIVISION ONE
GUIDED READING PLAN FOR NARRATIVE OR EXPOSITORY TEXT
Date: March 11, 2002   Grade: 1   Group: Sun
Text: Tails   Level: D   Earl, Stephanie, Jodi, Steve & Emma</td></tr>
<tr><td colspan="2">Supports: Repeat pattern: Whose Tail is _____? Rhyme patterns on pp. 3/5 (word ending letter), 7/9 and 11/13. Experiential knowledge of animals. Picture clues.
Challenges: Word recognition and vocabulary concepts, e.g., curly, feathered, stumpy, scaly. Concept of "looking up the answers" (last page).</td></tr>
<tr><td></td><td>Teacher Does</td></tr>
<tr><td valign="top">Introduction
• Predictions and building background knowledge
• Link to children's experience
• Point out supports and some challenges</td><td valign="top">Children reread "Will You Play With Us?" (Level D) and "Run! Run!" (Level C)
New Book
• Look at front and back covers. Choral read plot summary.
• Predictions: What kind of animals might you find in this book? What might their tails be like? Note on clip chart, e.g.,
    Crocodile: green, long
    Tiger: striped, furry
• Choral read to p. 5. Purpose: Let's be detectives. Can you find out what the animals are from pictures of their tails? Discuss after reading together.
• Point out word ending pattern (pp. 3/5). Look at 5/7.</td></tr>
</table>

Children Reading	Children read the rest of the book.
• Set comprehension purpose • Set activity for early finishers • Teacher listens to children read, and checks on strategies used and needs of readers • Use prompts	Purpose: Who has no tail? Early finishers reread the book with a partner. Listen to Steve and Emma read. Monitor for: Does it make sense, sound right, check out/look right? (Clay's strategies) Prompt for: If you know _____, how does it help you work out _____?
Conclusion	Purpose question: Who has no tail? Discuss.
• Check purpose question • Check on comprehension • Discuss successes • Mention a "Good Reading" strategy • Discuss challenges	a) Review animals and their tails. Teach group how to use the answer key. Review predictions on introductory list. b) pp. 8/9 Discuss the "story in pictures" depicting the crocodile and the lizard. Good reader strategy from Steve and Emma. (Point out) Discuss challenges observed.
Follow-up Activities	**Students Do**
Reread next time. Make own book using the pattern.	Draw partial picture of another animal with a tail. Use in next guided reading group to make up a text for rereading.

Lesson Planner, *Balanced Literacy: Division 1*, Brailsford, 2002.

Introduction to the New Book

Mrs. Hunka: We're going to read a new book today. (Mrs. Hunka opens the book so that the children can see the front and back cover spread. She then distributes the books and the children look at their front and back covers.) The book's title is ...

Earl: (pointing) Tails! That's a tiger's tail there. See, there's stripes on it. And that one at the top's a crocodile ... or ... alligator!

Predictions and Linking the New Book with Prior Experiences

Mrs. Hunka: I think you're right about the tiger, Earl. And we'll find out, when we read, whether we're looking at a crocodile or alligator tail. Let's check the back cover. (She turns the book over, and reads/finger tracks.) "Can you tell an animal by its tail? Find out if you can in this book about different kinds of tails."

Emma: You can tell it by its tail, Mrs. Hunka. That one there (pointing to a flat tail with a rounded end)—that's a beaver. I've seen one in the lake at my Grandpa's farm. It's got a tail just like that one.

Mrs. Hunka: So we think there's a beaver in the book. What kind of tail does it have?

Emma: Round ... and flat.

Mrs. Hunka: (writing on the whiteboard on the easel next to her) Let's have two columns:

Animals	What their tails are like
beaver	round and flat

Mrs. Hunka: What other animals do you think we'll find in this book?

Mrs. Hunka makes a chart of the predicted animals and their tail characteristics. These characteristics feature prominently in the book and will be a "challenge" when the children read on their own.

Earl: A tiger!

Mrs. Hunka: Yes, you noticed a tiger's tail before. And what's his tail like?

Steve: Striped.

Earl: And furry.

Mrs. Hunka: So we'll write down tiger on our chart and what its tail is like.

Animals	What their tails are like
beaver	round and flat
tiger	striped and furry

Mrs. Hunka collects predictions from each child and maps them on the chart. The vocabulary to describe the tails is quite challenging in this book, and Mrs. Hunka is exploring some of the possible concepts before reading. She is creating anticipation in the children so that they can problem solve more effectively when they read.

Mrs. Hunka: So we've thought about the animals we might find in the book and what their tails may be like. Now you need to be detectives when we read some of the book together. In this book the author doesn't tell you the names of the animals right away. Let's read to page 5 and see if we can match the animals to their tails.

Choral Reading

Mrs. Hunka and the children choral read a small portion of the book. This provides opportunities for discussing supports and challenges.

All: (reading chorally with the teacher) "Whose tail is long?"

Emma: It's a horse! (Nods and smiles from everyone; Emma's love of horses is well known.)

Mrs. Hunka: Good detective work! The picture gave you the clue.

All: (continuing to read with the teacher) "Whose tail is ... (various verbalizations, including "curled," "a curl"; nothing from Steve).

Earl: That's a pig, so it's gotta be a curled tail.

Mrs. Hunka: Let's take a closer look at the word. Some of you think it's "curled" or "a curl." Does "Whose tail is *curled*?" sound right? (All say yes.) Yes it does. Does it make sense? (Nods come from all.) Yes, it sounds right and makes sense. What about: "Whose tail is a *curl*?" (It's agreed that "a curl" could sound right and make sense.) Let me jot your "a curl" and "curled" predictions on the whiteboard here. And I'm going to print this word from the book (points to the text's "curly") right below:

a curl
curled
curly

Jodi: Hey — "a curl" — that's *two* words. It can't be "a curl."

Stephanie: And *they're* not the same (pointing to "curled" and "curly"). They're different at the end there.

Mrs. Hunka: Good checking, Jodi and Stephanie. If I wipe off "a"—the word "a"——we're left with the word ...?

Jodi: Curl! And "curl" is at the beginning of the other words!

Mrs. Hunka: Uh-huh ... Do these two words (pointing to "curl" and "curly" without verbalizing them) look the same?

Emma: A bit. But that (pointing to "curly") has a **y** at the end.

Steve: So it's "curly"!

Mrs. Hunka: Yes, Steve! "Whose tail is *curly*?" That sounds right, makes sense, *and* checks out. You know, people, I really liked the way you predicted words that sounded right and made sense, and I liked the way you checked out word endings to choose the right word. Nice going, everyone. Let's read on together.

The supportive choral reading concludes at the end of page 5, with the teacher continuing to model word recognition strategies (for "short" and "furry" tails) and the children volunteering predictions about the animals attached to those tails. The children then reread the story to that point, since they can now do so with a fair degree of fluency. Mrs. Hunka next asks them to check pages 3 ("Whose tail is curly?") and 5 ("Whose tail is furry?"), and elicits the information that (in addition to the language pattern of "Whose tail is ...?") there might also be word-ending patterns that could be useful if word recognition problems occur. She gets them to check the word-ending pattern on pages 7 and 9: "stumpy" and "bumpy".

Purpose Question for Independent Reading

Mrs. Hunka sets a purpose question to focus the children on an important story idea. They then read the rest of the book on their own.

Mrs. Hunka: Now, I want you to read to the end of the story to find out who, in this story, *doesn't* have a tail. When you've finished reading, read the book again with a buddy.

The children begin reading to the end of the story, all of them reading aloud in quiet voices, since no one in this particular group has yet reached the developmental stage of reading silently. Mrs. Hunka sits next to Steve.

One-on-One Help

Teachers employ various methods for recording the strategies they observe individual children using, and the strategies the children still need to learn. As long as the "assess-on-the-go" records inform subsequent instruction (Brailsford, 2002), the selected method should be whatever the teacher finds most useful. Mrs. Hunka uses a file folder of a different colour for each guided reading group, with a record sheet for each child paper-clipped to the folder. The records are, therefore, available for instant perusal and action during guided reading sessions, and readily transferable to the children's individual records folders to become part of their literacy progress "history."

Mrs. Hunka gets Steve's current record sheet from the file folder and notes that Steve is usually successful in using picture cues, but he needs continued help, like the rest of this group, in monitoring textual cues.

Name: Steve

Date: Feb. 13th

Title: My Circus Family, Level C

Checking for:
- Use of picture cues
- Self-correction behaviours

Strategies used:
- Read this text quite fluently, like rest of group. Consider Level D soon.
- Self-initiated check of picture clues-twice on "bikes" and "plates"

Strategies needed:
Okay on this text

Date: Feb. 21st

Title: Run! Run!, Level C

Checking for:
- Self-initiated corrections (rereading and reading ahead)
- Use of graphic details

Strategies used:
- Finger tracking still
- Picture cues
- Self-initiated check on word on previous page ("away")

N.B. One self-correction

Strategies needed:
More work on self-correction, but fairly fluent on book. Move to Level D.

Date: Mar. 1st
Title: Friends, Level D
Checking for:
- Self-corrections
- Use of graphic cues (1st/last letters and analogies, e.g., "It looks like ..."

Strategies used:
- Picture cues
- Sound sequencing: p-ull (graphic detail)

Strategies needed:
Work on self-correcting: omitted "cuddle" on back page and read on with no self-correction

Date: Mar. 11th
Title: Tails, Level D
Checking for:
- Self-corrections
- Use of graphic cues

Strategies used:

Strategies needed:

As Steve reads to her, Mrs. Hunka jots down his ability to use picture clues and his awareness of some word endings to further aid word recognition.

Steve: Whose tail is (pausing and glancing at picture) feathery?

Mrs. Hunka: Feathery makes sense and sounds right. Now check it out and look at the ending very carefully.

Steve: It's a **d**. (He rereads.) Whose tail is feathered?

Mrs. Hunka: Good checking, Steve. I like the way you looked carefully at that word ending.

Mrs. Hunka reinforces the positive strategies that Steve uses, but notes that he still needs support to check out textual details. She will need to continue to emphasize prompts that focus Steve on discrimination of word endings, and watch for his self-initiated correction in that area. As Steve moves away to reread the book with a partner, she takes a few seconds to complete his record sheet notations:

Date: Mar. 11th
Title: Tails, Level D
Checking for:
- Self-corrections
- Use of graphic cues

Strategies used:
- Pictures (studied them for "scaly" and "prickly": couldn't work out "scaly"
- Corrected word ending ("feathery"/"feathered") WITH a prompt from me
- Reread the sentence independently
- Worked out "curly" with support

Strategies needed:
- Prompts to get him to self-correct and attend to print details
- Work on praising self-corrections

Mrs. Hunka listens to Emma read, while the other students reread the book with their buddies.

Mrs. Hunka sets a simple activity for the early finishers: reread the book with a buddy. As the children progress through the levels, they may be asked to answer the purpose questions on sticky notes or in a response journal.

Group Discussion

Mrs. Hunka: You've read the book again with a partner, so let's talk about what you found out. Who has no tail in the book?

Jodi: It's a boy at the end

Emma: It could be a girl.

Mrs. Hunka: These pictures don't often show us the whole animal or person, do they?

Jodi: We could say a person doesn't have a tail.

Earl: Or a kid.

Mrs. Hunka: So, what animals did we find in the book?

Mrs. Hunka leads the group through a comparison of the animals and types of tails they had suggested initially, and the animals they actually found in the book.

Stephanie: It tells you at the back.

Mrs. Hunka does not go through all of the challenges before the reading but leaves the children with some personal problem solving. In this case, Stephanie has found the answer key to the animals and Mrs. Hunka seizes the opportunity to discuss this new text format.

Mrs. Hunka: Let's look at the back of the book. Stephanie's right. We can check our detective work because the answers are at the back (pointing to the word "Answers").

The group checks one or two of the answers on pages where the animals were uncertain: "Was it a crocodile or an alligator?" (page 9)

Mrs. Hunka: Let's look at the crocodile picture. This is unusual because it shows us the whole scene and two whole animals. I wonder what's happening here?

Emma: The crocodile's looking for lunch!

Steve: And it's going to be the lizard!

Stephanie: Or the lizard gets away to feed her babies.

Mrs. Hunka: Those are good ideas. The book's author doesn't tell us what really happened. On this page (points to page 9) I saw Emma do something that good readers do: she fixed a mistake. She read, "Whose tail is lumpy?" And then she stopped and thought, and read it again, "Whose tail is bumpy?" I liked the way you read it again and fixed it, Emma. (She reviews a good reader strategy.) Do you remember why you changed "lumpy" to "bumpy"?

Emma: It started with a **b**, not **l**.

Mrs. Hunka: Yes… you looked carefully at the letters in the word. Now let's turn to page 7 and read that page together.

All: "Whose tail is stumpy?"

Mrs. Hunka: You all worked out that tricky word "stumpy." Do you know what a stumpy tail looks like?

Jodi: It's brown.

Mrs. Hunka: That bear's tail is brown, you're right, but you could see a stumpy black tail, too. (She pauses. The children are clearly puzzled by the word, and Mrs. Hunka needs to explain.) It means it's short and cut-off, not long like the horses' tail. Next time I'll leave this book out so that you can read it again. When we move stations, remember you'll go to the levelled tubs. Which tubs will you choose books from?

Earl: From the green triangle, the red triangle, and the yellow triangle.

Mrs. Hunka initiates a change of stations and the Rainbow group joins her for their guided reading lesson on Level F books. By the time the recess bell sounds, Mrs. Hunka has worked with two guided reading groups and heard (diagnostically) four children read. Just before clear-up time, she asks the listening station group to share their favourite part of the story they were reading. Mrs. Hunka always asks one or two groups to share an aspect of their reading with the class at the conclusion of reading station time, and she keeps the sharing sessions brief and focused.

The entire guided reading and independent reading stations session has lasted 40 minutes, and each child has been engaged in reading activities at two stations. The children head out for recess, as does their teacher, who has playground supervision duty this morning.

Read-Aloud Links Into Writing

After recess, it's time for the read-aloud and writing components of the balanced literacy Language Arts program. Read alouds give Mrs. Hunka wonderful opportunities to expose the children to high quality literature, to show her enjoyment of books, to model good reading strategies and fluency, and to "spin off" into writing.

Last week during a read-aloud session, the class loved hearing the story *That Magnetic Dog* by Bruce Whatley. After reading the story of Skitty, the magnetic dog of the title, to the class, Mrs. Hunka facilitated the group discussion about the dog who was so magnetic that food seemed to stick to him everywhere he went! She used a text structure organizer for a descriptive paragraph to write down the children's thoughts, thus giving them more exposure to descriptive paragraph writing.

Throughout the year, Mrs. Hunka has used the organizers after some read-aloud sessions to model how to organize thoughts on text structure forms. What follows is the descriptive paragraph organizer that was completed on Skitty.

Descriptive Paragraph Organizer A

Title: Skitty the Magnetic Dog

Introduction: Opening Sentence [general statement about the topic]

Skitty is like a magnet. She ~~gets~~ attracts food to her just by looking with her special look.

Idea 1

She looks at Mom and gets a biscuit.

Idea 2

She goes near the table at supper time and food seems to come to her.

Idea 3

She looks at a baby and gets his ice cream.

Idea 4

Skitty looks at a ^peanut butter and honey sandwich and gets some.

Conclusion: Closing Sentence [summary statement about the topic]

Skitty looks with her magnetic eyes and everyone feeds her.

Text Structure Organizer, *Balanced Literacy: Division 1* (Brailsford, 2002)

Today, Mrs. Hunka is going to build on the knowledge of descriptive paragraph writing that the children gained when writing the Skitty account. She will move them beyond a class account and into individual writing.

Mrs. Hunka: Let's read our paragraph that we wrote about Skitty the magnetic dog last week. (Mrs. Hunka tracks the print and she and the class choral read their Skitty paragraph.) Now, I'm going to read you a story about a different dog who's just as much fun as Skitty.

For today's story, Mrs. Hunka has selected *Sit, Truman!* by Dan Harper, another delightful dog story. She tells the class the title and author, and they discuss the front and back cover illustrations.

Val: Oh, it's probably about dog training, 'cause it's "Sit, Truman!" My Mom took Blackie to that class, to 'beedyence class, and Blackie did real good!

Mrs. Hunka: So Blackie went to obedience classes, Val, and you think maybe that's what Truman will do? (Val nods enthusiastically.) Maybe that will happen in this story. What do you think, Mike?

Mike: That Truman… he might get into lots of adventures, running all over the place, chasing things… and getting into trouble.

Mrs. Hunka elicits a few more predictions about story content, and tells the class that Truman is a special kind of big dog called a mastiff. She shows some of the pictures and they talk a little about mastiff characteristics. "Slobber" and "drooling" vocabulary items cause some glee, as does Truman's habit of slaking his thirst by using the toilet bowl.

As Mrs. Hunka reads *Sit, Truman!* to the class, and shows the children Cara and Barry Moser's hilarious illustrations, she's mindful that she's going to use today's read-aloud session as a bridge into individual descriptive paragraph writing. She has hung on the wall a large poster-

sized laminated version of a simple text structure organizer for a descriptive paragraph. Nearby, she has placed a washable marker.

When the story has been read and enjoyed, Mrs. Hunka reminds the children about the paragraph they wrote about Skitty.

Mrs. Hunka: Truman isn't magnetic like Skitty, is he?

Lorraine: No, but he gets into trouble.

Mrs. Hunka: Just like Skitty! If we write about Truman, what could our title be?

Val: Truman the Trouble!

Mrs. Hunka: That would be a great title. It catches your attention because both words start with **tr**: Truman and Trouble! (She writes the title on the organizer and invites the class to reread it with her.) Now we need an introduction, a beginning. How shall we start?

Mercedes: We could put: Truman is a big dog.

Gurnam: And he gets into lots of trouble. We could put that, too!

Mrs. Hunka: (repeating) "Truman is a big dog and he gets into lots of trouble" Thumbs up if you think this sentence will make a good introduction. (There are thumbs up from everyone.) Okay, we know how to spell Truman from the title. Read the spelling of Truman for me, Sean.
Sean: (slowly, eye-voice matching from the title) Big **T** — 'cause it's his name — **T... r... u... m... a... n** (verbalizing letter names).

Mrs. Hunka (printing): Well done, with that capital **T**, Sean. **T... r... u... m... a... n. Truman... is...** Emma, can you come and write **is** for us?

(Emma comes to the front and prints **is** on the chart.)

Emma: It's a Word Wall word.

Mrs. Hunka: Good for you. It is on our Word Wall and that's a good place to look when you need words for writing. Now we were saying: "Truman is a b... i... g dog." Jodi, can you come and write **dog** for us? Let's say the word very slowly. That will help Jodi to listen to the sounds when she writes the word. (Jodi prints **dog** on the chart.) Let's add Gurnam's idea: "and he gets into lots of trouble." Gurnam come and write the first part: and he gets... (Gurnam prints the words and then Mrs. Hunka prints the rest of the sentence.) What do we need at the end of the sentence? Thanks Jenny — yes, we need a period right there at the end. Let's read our introduction together. (The class choral read the introduction.) Now, let's write our ideas about Truman here. (She indicates Ideas 1 through 4 on the chart.) What's our first idea about Truman going to be, Greg?

Greg: (thinking) Truman ... (grinning) drops spit over everything. He gets things very wet.

Mrs. Hunka prints exactly what Greg has said, beside Idea 1 on the chart. She asks various children to generate details for the remaining ideas, asking children to spell some words along the way, and inviting some children to print a few words on their own. Mrs. Hunka reminds the children of spelling resources: "You could check the Word Wall," "Say the word slowly and write the sounds you hear," and "You know 'sit.' Could that help you work out 'spit'?" The children are asked to think of a concluding sentence to tie in everything that's been written so far.

Petra: Truman is hard to train... but everybody loves him.

Mrs. Hunka: (printing) A super conclusion, Petra! **Tru... man... is hard... to...** Can you print train, Petra?

Petra prints **tran**.

Mrs. Hunka: Truman is hard to train (printing) **but... everybody... loves him.** All right, let's read what we've written. (The children and teacher choral read the ideas on the organizer.)

Descriptive Paragraph Organizer A

Title:	Truman the Trouble
Introduction:	Opening Sentence [general statement about the topic] Truman is a big dog and he gets into lots of trouble.
Idea 1	Truman drops spit over everything. He gets things very wet.
Idea 2	He drincs from the toilet.
Idea 3	He bugs the little dog Oscar.
Idea 4	Truman puts his head in the mailbox.
Conclusion:	Closing Sentence [summary statement about the topic] Truman is hard to tran but everybody loves him.

Text-Structure Organizer, *Balanced Literacy: Division 1* (Brailsford, 2002)

Mrs. Hunka: Good reading, everybody. Now I want you to write about a favourite pet or an animal you know. Let's think about some ideas. (Mrs. Hunka jots down brainstormed ideas on the board.)

- a favourite pet
- a special animal

Joanne: Could it be a toy… a stuffed animal?

Mrs. Hunka: Good idea. Are you thinking of writing about one of your stuffed animals, Joanne?

Joanne: Yes, my Granny got me a lion for Christmas.

Mrs. Hunka: Let's add a stuffed animal on the list. (Prints the idea.)

- a favourite pet
- a special animal
- a stuffed toy animal

Mrs. Hunka: If you were writing about a favourite pet, which would you write about?

Tracy: My hamster. He's got a new cage.

Mrs. Hunka: So let's add those ideas. (The children add ideas and Mrs. Hunka compiles the list.)

- a favourite pet
  - a hamster
  - a puppy
  - a snake
  - a cat

- a special animal
  - Grandpa's dog
  - our neighbour's turtle
  - Becky the baby elephant at the zoo

- a stuffed toy animal
  - a lion
  - my penguin
  - Curious George monkey

Mrs. Hunka: Close your eyes. I want all of you to think of the animal you're going to write about. (She gives them time to think.) Now, whisper to the person next to you and tell them what you're going to write about.

The children whisper their ideas while the teacher distributes the 11 x 17 inch organizers.

Mrs. Hunka takes the group story about Truman down from the wall, because she wants the children to generate their own ideas. The read aloud has taken 15 minutes, and the writing demonstration a further 10 minutes. The children now have around 25 minutes in which to produce their own animal paragraphs, with as much or as little support as needed.

Most of the children can put their thoughts on the organizers. Mrs. Hunka draws together Earl, Jodi, Emma, and Greg, who sometimes have difficulties starting their writing. She convenes a support group for five

Teaching Tip

Large 11 x 17 inch writing organizers are used for grade one students to allow them plenty of space.

minutes and helps them to talk through their introductions. She then circulates among the other children and provides prompts to stimulate ideas. She encourages the children to reread as they write, to help them formulate cohesive sentences.

Mrs. Hunka will start the afternoon with a sharing session when she will encourage children to read their paragraphs to a partner, and then ask two or three children to read aloud their ideas. Tomorrow, Mrs. Hunka plans to work on revising ideas in writing. She'll use the class writing about Truman and invite the children to add elaborations and modify ideas. Then the children will work on revising their own paragraphs.

Language Arts finishes for the morning, but Mrs. Hunka has clear ideas about the strategies and materials she'll use this afternoon and tomorrow to ensure continuous growth in Language Arts.

Bibliography

Professional References

Brailsford, Anne. *Balanced Literacy: Division 1.* Edmonton, Alberta: Resource Development, Edmonton Public Schools, 2002.

Cunningham, Patricia M. *Phonics They Use: Words for Reading and Writing.* New York: HarperCollins, 1995.

Cunningham, Patricia M. and Hall, Dorothy P. *Making Words.* Parsippany, NJ: Good Apple, 1994.

Fountas, Irene C. and Pinnell, Gay Su. *Guided Reading: Good First Teaching For All Children.* Portsmouth, NH: Heinemann, 1996.

Hall, Dorothy P. and Cunningham, Patricia M. *Month-by-Month Reading and Writing for Kindergarten.* Greensboro, NC: Carson-Dellosa, 1997.

McCarrier, A., Pinnell, Gay Su, and Fountas, Irene C. *Interactive Writing.* Portsmouth, NH: Heinemann, 2000.

Children's Books

Cowley, Joy. *Smarty Pants.* Auckland, New Zealand: Shortland Publications/Ginn, 1980.

Harper, Dan. *Sit, Truman!* New York: Harcourt, 2001.

Whatley, Bruce. *That Magnetic Dog.* Sydney, Australia: HarperCollins, 1994.

Bookshop Texts

Goss, Janet L. & Harste, Jerome C. *It Didn't Frighten Me.* New York: Mondo, 1995.

Hong, M. *Friends.* New York: Mondo, 1995.

Lake, Mary Dixon. *My Circus Family.* New York: Mondo, 1995.

Vandine, JoAnn. *Run! Run!* New York: Mondo, 1995.

Vaughan, M. *Tails.* New York: Mondo, 1986.

Yatsevitch Phinney, Margaret. *Will You Play With Us?* New York: Mondo, 1995.

Software Series

Story Webs and Multimedia Literature (MacMillan McGraw Hill)

Wiggleworks (Scholastic)

A Balanced Literacy Program in Action: Upper Elementary Class

The Teacher

During Bonaventure School's third year in the project, upper elementary teachers are enrolled in their second year of coaching and inservice in balanced literacy. Martin Schmidt is one of those teachers. Always curious to find new ways of helping his class to become better readers and writers, Mr. Schmidt has immersed himself in the balanced literacy inservices and professional readings. He has taught upper elementary students for three years and presently teaches a grade four class. His classroom is in a portable unit built in the play area near the main building. He has 28 students in his class this year and we join him on a cold, snowy March morning, when the portable's overworked heating system is noisily keeping the group warm.

Materials and Classroom Organization

Looking around the room, we can see balanced literacy materials amongst the displays of students' art work and writing samples. On the walls are text structure

Persuasive Writing Organizer
Title:
State arguments: (What is your viewpoint?)

Reason 1	Reason 2	Reason 3	Reason 4	Reason 5

Summary of argument:

STRONG WORDS

because	beg
persuade	plead
request	ask

(Text Structure Organizers: Brailsford [b], 2002)

organizers, accompanied by brightly coloured word cards. Each word card contains a cue word for a particular organizer. For example, the text structure organizer for persuasive writing is accompanied by the word cards **because**, **plead**, **persuade**, **beg**, **request**, and **ask**. On the long shelf under the window, smaller text structure organizers are arranged in baskets for students to use as they plan a writing project.

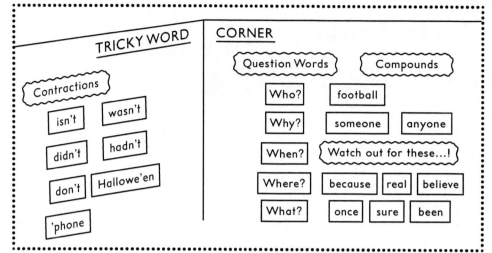

In one corner of the room, a Tricky Word Corner is arranged. Coloured paper delineates the areas where the word cards are arranged. These are key words that have recently given students some difficulties during their writing.

A class-sized book leans against the blackboard ledge. The front cover proclaims: "The True Story of…" Inside are the students' illustrated versions of fairy tales, modelled on the text structure of *The True Story of the Three Little Pigs* by Jon Scieszka. The school library is well stocked for independent reading time, but on the window shelf are five book tubs containing samples of levelled books for students who have difficulty making independent book selections and still need some support from the teacher.

A round table placed near the coat racks is used for guided reading groups. To one side, there is a flip chart on which the teacher can illustrate instructional points during lessons. In cubby holes at the side are four tubs of levelled reading materials, ready for guided reading sessions.

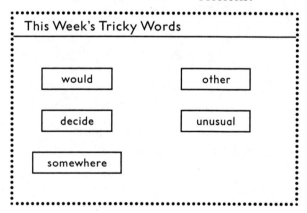

Beside the board there is a chart listing the week's tricky words and a pocket chart for the Making Big Words lesson. A reading corner, with an old battered couch and floor cushions, is squeezed into an area by the emergency exit. There is a wall chart in the corner listing students' book recommendations.

The School Day Starts

As the students move into the room, they greet Mr. Schmidt and read at their desks, on the floor cushions, or on the couch in the book corner. Some of them get sticky notes from a basket and write comments about a book they have read. They post their comments on the book recommendation chart on the wall in the corner, and read new notes that other students are placing on the chart. A few students go to the levelled tubs and exchange their books for new ones.

The intercom crackles into life and a child makes a brief announcement about a floor hockey game in the gym at lunchtime and a cookie sale at recess.

AWESOME BOOKS

Firewing by Kenneth Oppel is the third book in his fantasy bat series. The other books are Silverwing and Sunwing. You have to read these books to get into the story and the wonderful world of bats. Terrific book! Put your name up here if you'd like to talk about the books with me in sharing time.

Josh

Word Study

Mr. Schmidt announces word study time, and the students move to their desks. Mr. Schmidt plans ahead for a month of word study periods, mapping out a balance of activities to meet class needs. For example, this week Mr. Schmidt has worked on:

- reviews of high-frequency words
- word building with a Making Big Words activity (Cunningham and Hall, 1994)
- use of visual-sound patterns in spelling and word recognition by doing sorts of the word patterns in the Making Big Words activity
- transfer of word patterns into word recognition and spelling by building new words stemming from the word sorts
- using context clues by engaging the class in a Guess The Covered Word activity (Cunningham and Hall, 1998), using a paragraph.

Today, Mr. Schmidt leads the class in a snappy review of tricky words by getting them involved in a chant.

Word Study

Word study is a daily period in the upper elementary, balanced literacy classroom. From 20 to 25 minutes are spent on word recognition and spelling. Reviewing high-frequency words, analyzing multisyllabic words, using prefixes and suffixes, working with visual-sound patterns, and utilizing context clues are the types of concepts featured in the word study period. Activities are usually hands-on and quickly paced. Supports and challenges are built into lessons.

Mr. Schmidt: Let's focus on the words that have been giving us some difficulties. When you really give attention to the details in words, and practise spelling them, it helps you to remember them. Find **would** in this week's list of tricky words. Can somebody give me **would** in a sentence?

Abdul: He would be late to school as he missed his alarm clock.

Mr. Schmidt: Great sentence. Lead the cheer Abdul!

Abdul: Give me a **W.**

Class: W!

Abdul: Give me an **O.** (The class cheers animatedly through the word's letters.)

Abdul: And what have you got?

Class: WOULD!

Mr. Schmidt then leads a practice of **because** (a review word from the Tricky Word Corner) in the same fast-paced way, before moving to a review of other tricky words by playing The Wheel (Cunningham and Hall, 1998).

Mr. Schmidt: Maya, start us with our review. Choose a tricky word and draw the letter lines on the board.

Maya looks at the Tricky Word Corner and selects a word. She comes forward and draws four letter lines on the chalkboard.

```
 ___  ___  ___  ___
```

Maya elicits letter predictions from various members of the class.

Raoul: Is there a **p**?

Maya: There is no **p** in the word. (She writes **p** under the word and crosses it out to remind other students which letter has been predicted.)

```
      ___  ___  ___  ___
  p̶
```

Grace: Is there an **e**?

Maya: There is an **e**. (She writes it on the appropriate letter line.)

```
           e
      ___  ___  ___  ___
  p̶
```

Grace: Is there an **s**?

Maya: There isn't an **s**. (She puts **s** on the board and crosses it out.)

```
           e
      ___  ___  ___  ___
  p̶ s̶
```

Josh: I have a word prediction. It's **been**.

Maya: Sorry, it isn't **been**.

Zoltan: Is there an **r**?

Maya: There's an **r**. (She writes the new letter prediction). You may have another turn.

r e _ _
p s

Zoltan: I have a word prediction for my second turn. It's **real**!

Maya: That's right! Can you spell it? (Zoltan spells the word and Maya completes the word puzzle on the blackboard.) What is your sentence?

r e a l
p s

Zoltan: The animal was real and not just a photograph.

Zoltan comes up for his turn and other words are reviewed using this game for 15 minutes. Mr. Schmidt knows that the students enjoy the game and love to take control of word practice. He also knows that, to play, they need to check the Tricky Word Corner constantly, and are thus focusing attention on the words they have struggled with in writing time. Mr. Schmidt often uses quick, active word games in word study time.

The Reading Hour

After 20 minutes of word study, Mr. Schmidt moves the class on to the reading hour. The class is working on the "Join In" theme from Literacy Place (Scholastic). This theme focuses on people working together to help each other in the community or to solve a problem together.

"Join In" is a fiction theme in the book study component, although it has fiction and nonfiction articles in the magazine. Mr. Schmidt has used the Literacy Place magazine to introduce the theme for the unit. He has also started the class on book study, using the three levelled novels (above average, at grade level, and below grade level) from the Literacy Place unit for guided reading. He has added *The Trouble with Tuck* by Theodore Taylor as a book to read aloud to the class, and also *True Blue* by Joan Elste for two readers who need more support in guided reading than the easiest Literacy Place text can offer.

Mr. Schmidt uses multilevel books for all of his book study units. The number of levels required in the unit depends on the composition of the class each year. In occasional years only Hard (above grade level), Average (at grade level), and Easy (just below grade level) sets of themed books are

Reading Hour Components

The reading hour occurs daily in the upper elementary balanced literacy program. There are five flexible components planned for the reading hour:

Read Aloud: The teacher reads aloud to the class. The selected book often links to the theme. Content from the class read-aloud book is frequently used for a class strategy lesson.

Shared Reading: Materials that are written at "one level"— for example, the textbooks or a story the class reads together — are always shared with the class through co-operative reading techniques such as buddy reading, choral reading in rows or groups, Paired Reading (Northern Alberta Reading Specialists' Council, 1991; Topping, 1989) or 3-Ring Circus (Cunningham, Hall and Sigmon, 1999). The magazines from Literacy Place (Scholastic), often used to introduce a themed unit, are always read with shared reading techniques. Similarly, if a class play is read, small groups of students take each part to ensure that all readers are supported when reading "one level" of materials.

Class Strategy Lesson: The teacher, using content from the read-aloud book or a shared reading session, introduces a new reading strategy or reviews one previously taught. Such strategies could include: summarizing information, predicting from prior knowledge, character analysis, relating events to experiences, inferring from actions of characters, or using a glossary. Strategies are taught to the whole group and then applied to instructional level texts in guided reading lessons.

Book Study: Students are grouped according to their needs, and read books well within their zones of comfort. One or two groups meet with the teacher for a guided reading group each day. Meanwhile, the other groups read assigned chapters of their books and then work on literature response activities or activities related to the class strategy lesson. All the books used in guided reading are multilevel and all relate to a central theme: for example, survival, journeys, or making a difference in the community. Co-operative days are planned, on which each group shares its book with the other groups. Book studies are also completed using the literature circles techniques (Daniels, 2002) or with book clubs and prompts (Day, Spiegel, McLellan, and Brown, 2002). During those book studies, the teacher can work with each group in turn, or integrate guided reading lessons into the Literature Circles and book clubs.

Independent Reading: Students read self-selected books. The teacher guides students who still need support in the book selection process.

Teachers plan the reading hour by selecting a balance of components. For example, on one day the class may engage in a class strategy lesson, shared reading, and independent reading. The next day, the students engage in a read aloud and guided reading.

needed. In most recent years, Mr. Schmidt has needed to add an Easy Plus book (two to three grades below grade level) and, sometimes, he may need to add an Extra Challenging text (two to three grades above grade level). Levelled book recommendations to supplement the Literacy Place core texts can be found in the revised *Teacher's Tool Kit for Literacy Place* (2002).

The Read Aloud

Today Mr. Schmidt plans to read a chapter of *The Trouble with Tuck* to the class. He will then use the content to teach a class strategy lesson on how to reflect on the story by using a double entry journal. The strategy lesson will be followed by a guided reading lesson.

The plan for today's Reading Hour is:

Components	Times (approximate)
Read aloud	15 minutes
Class strategy lesson	15 minutes
Guided reading/group work	30 minutes

Mr. Schmidt begins by reading the first sentence of Chapter 5 (page 27) to the class: "If there was ever any doubt whatsoever about the special status of Friar Tuck Golden Boy at 911 West Cheltenham, no matter what he did or didn't do, the doubt was removed the following summer when Tuck was nearly two years old."

Mr. Schmidt: I wonder why the author said that right at the beginning of the chapter?

Mr. Schmidt has decided to discuss the opening of the chapter because he plans to use this portion of the text in the class strategy lesson. He wants to get the students thinking about the introduction so that they will be able to relate to the content of the demonstration he will provide in the strategy lesson.

Matt: Because the dog's going to do something brave again.

Mr. Schmidt: Why are you thinking that, Matt?

Matt: Well…Tuck just rushed that man who was attacking Helen in the park. He could do something else.

Mr. Schmidt: To give him special status? What's it like to have "special status," do you think?

Zoltan: It means everyone respects the dog — really likes him.

Maria: Like they think he's special.

Matt: So maybe he *does* do something else that makes him special.

Mr. Schmidt: Let's read on and see.

Mr. Schmidt reads the chapter aloud and it is revealed that Tuck, the family's young dog who is especially close to Helen, rescues the girl when she hits her head on a diving board and sinks to the bottom of a swimming pool. Mr. Schmidt now uses the opening sentence from the chapter, the one he has previously utilized for chapter predictions, to model reflective journal writing. He has pinned a large piece of chart paper on the board and has ruled a column down the middle of the page.

> ## The "Join In" Unit
>
> Read-Aloud Book
> The Trouble with Tuck
> by Theodore Taylor
>
> **Hard**
> (Above Grade Level)
> The Green Angels
> by Nicky Millard
> (Literacy Place)
>
> **Average**
> (At Grade Level)
> Smoky and the Gorilla
> by Sylvia McNicoll
> (Literacy Place)
>
> **Easy**
> (1-2 Grade Levels Below)
> The Lunchbox Mystery
> by Alison Lohans
> (Literacy Place)
>
> **Easy Plus**
> (3 Grade Levels Below)
> True Blue
> by Joan Elste

Class Strategy Lesson

Mr. Schmidt: When we read a story, it helps us to understand what it's about if we think about an event or a character, or something somebody says. I'm going to show you a new way of thinking about the story, using your literature response journals. We have been working on journal entries that retell part of the story, and that relate or link ideas to other stories or to your experiences. Today, we are going to reflect. I have put the prompts that help you to reflect on a chart. Let's look at them.

Mr. Schmidt reviews the list of interpretive prompts that he has selected from *Retelling, Relating and Reflecting: Beyond the 3Rs* (Schwartz and Bone, 1995).

The class is familiar with using the Schwartz and Bone prompts for retelling and relating, and Mr. Schmidt is now going to expand their knowledge to include reflective thinking in their literature response journals. Although the techniques will be taught in a whole class lesson, the students will apply them to reflect on the instructional level books they are reading in guided reading time.

Reflecting about what you read:
- I wonder ....
- I wonder why he/she did that ....
  he/she said that ....
- I wonder if ....
- I understand ....
- I'm not sure about ....
- I believe that ....
- I think that ....
- The part of the chapter that is interesting is ....
- I don't like ....
- I wish that ....
- I guess that ....
- I imagine that ....

Mr. Schmidt: When we reflect on the story, we predict, wonder, or interpret part of the story. Now we can't wonder about everything in the story, so we need to think about something particular in the story. Do you remember, this morning, that I read you the first sentence of the chapter and asked you to predict and wonder about what might happen here? (*He reads again the sentence from* The Trouble with Tuck.) That's an important sentence because it sets up your thinking for the rest of the chapter — you know something important's going to happen. I'm going to use it for my response to the chapter. When you're doing this kind of response, you write one quote from the book, an important idea that is right from the pages of the book, on the left side of your page. (Mr. Schmidt prints the key sentence in the left column of his board chart.)

Quote	Reflections
If there was ever any doubt whatsoever about the special status of Friar Tuck Golden Boy at 911 West Cheltenham, no matter what he did and didn't do, the doubt was removed the following summer when Tuck was nearly two years old.	

(Chapter 5: *The Trouble with Tuck* by T. Taylor)

Mr. Schmidt: Now I'm going to look at the reflecting prompts, and I'll select "I wonder if...." My thoughts go in the right-hand column. (Mr. Schmidt verbalizes his thoughts and writes in the column.)

Quote	Reflections
If there was ever any doubt whatsoever about the special status of Friar Tuck Golden Boy at 911 West Cheltenham, no matter what he did and didn't do, the doubt was removed the following summer when Tuck was nearly two years old.	I wonder if Tuck is going to do something really special to make him very important in the house.

(Chapter 5: *The Trouble with Tuck* by T. Taylor)

Mr. Schmidt: When I first read that sentence I wondered if Tuck was going to do something else that gave him special status in the house. He was already very special because…. Now I could put lots of things here: he was good to play with or slept on Helen's bed when she was scared, but I think I'll focus on one really important thing…

Anna: That attack on Helen, in the park. He saved her!

Mr. Schmidt: Yes, that certainly would have given him special status. I'll put that down. (He adds the sentence to the chart.) "He was already very special because he had saved Helen from a man who was trying to attack her in the park." I'm thinking that Tuck is going to do something very important again. At the beginning of the chapter I thought he'd likely attack a robber who had broken into the house. Now I'm wondering if he might stop a mean dog from knocking down a child.

Quote	Reflections
If there was ever any doubt whatsoever about the special status of Friar Tuck Golden Boy at 911 West Cheltenham, no matter what he did and didn't do, the doubt was removed the following summer when Tuck was nearly two years old.	I wonder if Tuck is going to do something really special to make him very important in the house. He was already very special because he had saved Helen from a man who was trying to attack her in the park. I think he is now going to do something that will make sure the family never forgets him. Maybe he will show courage and attack a thief who is breaking into their house. I also wonder if a ~~mean~~ vicious dog might knock down a toddler and Tuck might rush in to save the baby.

(Chapter 5: *The Trouble with Tuck* by T. Taylor)

Mr. Schmidt continues to alternate between talking through his thought processes and writing his journal entry on the chart. The students add ideas and he incorporates some into the journal entry. This class strategy lesson on how to reflect when reading, and how to write reflections in a double-entry journal, lasts about 15 minutes. Then Mr. Schmidt makes the transition into guided reading.

Guided Reading

Mr. Schmidt has elected to teach this module using guided reading groups, his preferred method for using multilevel materials. However, for variety during the school year, he uses literature circles (Daniels, 2002) for one module, and book clubs with prompts (Day, Spiegel, McLellan, and Brown, 2002) for another module.

Mr. Schmidt: When you're reading your own novels today I want you to reflect about an important idea, and then try your own reflection journal entry once you've finished reading. To help you, I'm giving each group an important idea from each book, and I want you to reflect on it. Use the prompts — they'll help you. (Mr. Schmidt points to the wall chart, "Reflecting about what you read.")

Mr. Schmidt provides the first page of a double-entry journal, with each group's quotation in the left-hand column, for each novel study group. He then assigns each group their day's reading.

Mr. Schmidt: Green Angels, you read Chapter 7, "Invasion" and the quote for your reflection journal entry is here. (He hands them the sample set-up page with the quotation already in the left-hand column).

The Green Angels group are reading the Literacy Place "above grade level" selection for this module.

Quote	Reflections
"What do you think he'll do?" she asked.	
"I dunno. Maybe nothing. Depends on what the rest of the gang think." (page 38)	

Once all of the groups' chapters are assigned, Mr. Schmidt tells the class that he will be working with the Lunchbox Mystery group today. That group moves to the guided reading table while the other groups pursue their reading and journal entries.

Planning the Guided Reading Lesson

Before the lesson, Mr. Schmidt reread the chapter to help him to decide
what supports the text offered and what challenges it would present to
this group of readers. He entered his comments on a guided reading
lesson plan. As supports, he noted that the chapter continued with the
same viewpoint and time sequence as the previous part of the novel, and
that the problem was unchanged. As challenges, he noted that a new
minor character was introduced and one or two word recognition/
vocabulary items might cause some difficulties, such as "swatted at
mosquitoes" and "glint of water." In the introduction to the lesson, Mr.
Schmidt decided to link the old chapter to the new one to reaffirm the
continuity of the problem and the main plot, to encourage the students
to predict events for the new chapter, and to link with the class strategy
lesson about reflecting on content. He thought the challenges were
relatively minor and wanted to leave the students with some problem
solving during their reading, so he did not mention the new vocabulary
or the new minor character.

DIVISION TWO
GUIDED READING PLAN FOR NARRATIVE OR EXPOSITORY TEXT
Date: March 13, 2002   **Grade:** 4
Text: The Lunchbox Mystery   **Chapter:** 4

Supports:	Same viewpoint and time sequence as last chapter: Same problem (lunch box contents being stolen/who is the thief?): same major characters
Challenges:	New minor character (Tanya's sister Amy): vocabulary concepts, e.g., "glint of water" (p. 32), "swatted at mosquitoes" (p. 33), "glared" (p. 29)

	Teacher Does

Introduction
• Link to previous chapter(s)
• Build background knowledge
• Link to strategy lesson
• Point out supports and challenges
	Look at p. 27; choral read last sentence.
	    Discuss: "What problems do J.J. and Derek have now?"
	New chapter: Look at title, "Another Detective."
	    Link to reflecting prompt and use starters, e.g., "What are you wondering about when you read the title?"
	Choral read first paragraph. Purpose: to think about their journal quote as they read.
	[Challenges minor: Leave as "problems to solve."]

Children Reading
• Set purpose
• Set activity for early finishers
• Teacher listens to children read, and checks on strategies used and needs of readers
	Children read chapter.
	Purposes: Does Derek quit as a detective?
	          Who is the other detective?
	Activity for early finishers: jot down the answers.
	Read diagnostically with Micha.
	          Check on comprehension.
	          Check on self-correcting behaviours.
	          Fill in Oral Reading Observation Checklist.

Conclusion
• Check purpose question
• Check on comprehension
• Select from:
  - Review link to strategy lesson
  - Discuss challenges
  - Mention a "Good Reading" strategy
  - Predict for next chapter
	Review: Does Derek quit?
	          Who is the other detective?
	Orally review reflections on the quote to be used in the double entry journal.
	Challenges: "glint of water," etc., and new character
	Good reader strategy (from observations of Micha)
	What will happen next? Set up purpose questions for tomorrow. What do they do with the tin cans? Will the plan catch the thief?

Follow-up Activities Double Entry Journal	**Children Do** Journal response and read Chapter 5 tomorrow.

Lesson Planner, *Balanced Literacy: Division 2*, Brailsford, 2002.

Mr. Schmidt moves to the guided reading table where The Lunchbox Mystery group is gathered. This group is reading the "below grade level" text from the Literacy Place module.

Mr. Schmidt: Let's remind ourselves about how the previous chapter ended. Turn to page 27 and let's read the last sentence together. (The group chorally reads "Somehow they'd have to catch that criminal and prove it wasn't them!") So, what problems do J.J. and Derek have now?

Anna: Mr. Muller thinks they could be the lunchbox robbers.

Josh: Because he saw Derek in the classroom.

Mr. Schmidt: Wasn't it okay for Derek to be in the classroom?

Josh: It was recess and he'd seen somebody fiddling with his lunchbox, so J.J. went to Mr. Muller, the teacher.

Laurie: And he went to check it out.

Josh: And he found Derek there, so he thinks… could it be Derek robbing the boxes?

Mr. Schmidt: So Mr. Muller is suspicious of the boys …

Micha: He'll keep an eye on them, I think.

Mr. Schmidt: Mmm, so let's look what happens next. The next chapter is called, "Another Detective." What are you wondering about when you see that title?

Mr. Schmidt deliberately uses an "I wonder…" question here to link with the class strategy lesson on reflecting when reading.

Laurie: Maybe the kid they saw with the lunchboxes was another detective on the case.

Micha: Or they get a real detective… like a policeman to check it out.

Anna: Mr. Muller could be a detective too.

Mr. Schmidt: That title sure makes you wonder. We've got a lot to find out when we read this chapter. Let's read the first paragraph together. Your quote for your response journal comes from this paragraph.

Teaching Tip

Oral discussion based on an "I wonder…" prompt will be helpful to assist the students with their thoughts before reading and making their journal responses. Links to the class strategy lesson are part of a guided reading lesson to help the students to transfer learning from one context to another.

The group chorally reads the first paragraph: " 'I think we should forget about being detectives. If I get in trouble at school, I'll probably be grounded for a week,' Derek said after school that day. The two boys were riding their skateboards down Cameron Street towards the river."

Mr. Schmidt: The quote for your journal is the first two sentences. What was Derek thinking here? Do you wonder if they should give up being detectives?

Mr. Schmidt provides support to give confidence to this group, who are reading below grade level. Choral reading of a small section of text is often used to help the readers move into a new chapter. In this case, Mr. Schmidt takes the opportunity to do shared reading of the portion of the text that the children will be using for their new double-entry journals.

Josh: That's why they'll hand over the case to a real policeman, I think.

Micha: It's not worth getting into all that trouble.

Anna: Mr. Muller will take over the case.

Laurie: I don't think J.J. will give up.

Mr. Schmidt: Let's use a prompt, Laurie: "I wonder if…"

Mr. Schmidt takes the opportunity to weave a reflective prompt into the discussion. Again, transfer of learning is a conscious plan that Mr. Schmidt puts into operation. He grabs the teachable moment in this case.

Laurie: I wonder if another kid will become a detective with them — maybe Shaun.

Micha: Not Shaun. He's such a bully.

Mr. Schmidt: You'll have some interesting thoughts for your journals and you may discover whether Derek does give up being a detective when you read the next part of the book. When you read the chapter see if you learn whether Derek quits being a detective. I also want you to read to find out who the other detective is. The chapter title said, "Another Detective," so who is it?

Mr. Schmidt turns the page on the flip chart and reveals the two purpose questions:

> Do the boys stop being detectives?
>
> Who will be the other detective?

Mr. Schmidt: I am going to read with Micha today. While you are reading the chapter, think about the questions. If you finish reading early, jot down your answers in your journals. Use a yellow sticky note to mark difficult ideas or words on a page, and we'll look at them afterwards.

Micha: (reading aloud to Mr. Schmidt) " 'Man, that was cool what you did to Shaun!' J.J. said."

Mr. Schmidt: What's J.J. thinking about there?

Micha: Tanya and Shaun.

Mr. Schmidt: What happened?

Purpose Questions

Mr. Schmidt always sets purpose questions before the students begin to read. This focuses the children on key ideas. (As they move up the grades, it would be a good idea for students to set their own purpose questions before reading.) The purpose questions then become an activity for "early finishers." When students finish reading, they respond to the purpose questions in their journals. However, lessons should not be delayed if some readers have not finished responding to the purpose questions in writing. The written response is intended primarily for students who complete their reading, since the purpose questions are always discussed orally.

Micha: Like, Tanya went at Shaun with her karate stuff when he was bullying Derek and J.J. (Micha carries on reading.) "I'm going to get my Mom to let me take karate too. I'm already… sinied… signied… up…"

Mr. Schmidt: Can you read that sentence again and think about what would make sense there: What do you do when you want to start a class?

Micha: You sign up for a class. "I'm already signed up."

Mr. Schmidt: That makes sense.

Micha: (reading on) " 'Nooooooo,' winned Amy… whined Amy."

Mr. Schmidt: I like the way you went back and checked that word. Why did you change your mind?

Mr. Schmidt notes a time when Micha self-corrects a miscue and reinforces the boy's good use of a strategy. Noticing positive use of strategies is a key feature of Mr. Schmidt's guided reading lessons.

Name: Micha   Date: March 13th

Book: The Lunchbox Mystery   Page Number: p29-32

Word or Phrase from Passage	Miscue (Word or Phrase)	Self-corrects miscue	Miscue is meaningful	Miscue is gramatically correct	Miscue is phonetically similiar to text
I'm already signed up	sinied __ signied	corrected with prompt			
____ whined Amy	winned ___ sc	✓	(-)	(✓) ed ending	(✓)
Away to catch the criminal	crim ____ sc	✓	(-)	(✓)	(✓) beginning

- ☐ reads slowly
- ☑ reads at a appropriate rate
- ☐ reads too quickly
- ☐ is easily distracted from reading
- ☐ is somewhat distracted
- ☑ attends to reading
- ☐ reads in a staggered, choppy manner
- ☑ reads with inconsistent fluency
- ☐ reads fluently
- ☐ reads with little or no expression
- ☑ reads with some expression
- ☐ reads with strong expression
- ☐ does not attend to punctuation cues
- ☑ attends to punctuation cues inconsistently
- ☐ attend to punctuation cues

Comments:
- Self corrected 2/3 miscues: corrected one when prompt provided. Improvement here
- Comprehension was good. Micha understands events and Vocabulary eg. signed & whined

Which reading behaviour did I discuss with the student?

Self-corrected: going back and checking- ensuring it made sense/rereading

Observation Records: Brailford 2003

Micha: Well she... like she wasn't winning anything. She was pouting.

Mr. Schmidt: So "whined" made more sense.

Micha nods. Mr. Schmidt makes notes about Micha's reading on the boy's Oral Reading Observations chart.

As the children finish reading their chapter, they write responses to the purpose questions in their journals.

Mr. Schmidt: Put your pencils down. You've all finished reading, so let's talk about what you are thinking at this stage.

Reviewing the Purpose Questions

When the class has finished reading, Mr. Schmidt concludes the guided reading lesson by reviewing the purpose questions, discussing some of the challenges, linking to the class strategy lesson, mentioning a good reader strategy, and linking to the new chapter.

Mr. Schmidt: Will the boys stop being detectives?

Anna: No.

Mr. Schmidt: Can you show me something you read that made you decide that, Anna?

Anna: Well it says here at the end, they make a plan to catch the lunchbox criminal, so they can't be giving up.

Mr. Schmidt: So it doesn't actually say, right there in the book, "They won't stop being detectives," but you can still gather some clues that suggest they are going to carry on. One of those clues — which Anna found — is that they are still making plans to catch the thief.

Teaching Tip

During guided reading lessons, there is always time for individual diagnostic work with one or two students. This provides opportunities to focus on the strategies each student needs to progress as a reader. Mr. Schmidt knows that Micha needs help with comprehending ideas and with using self-correction strategies for word recognition. Both areas receive attention.

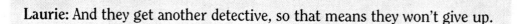

Laurie: And they get another detective, so that means they won't give up.

Josh: The other detective is Tanya… who beat up Shaun!

Mr. Schmidt: So you found out who the other detective was. And you got another clue to say they wouldn't give up being detectives. When you are writing in your journals and thinking about that quote from the beginning of the chapter, what might you be thinking about?

Mr. Schmidt encourages the students to reflect on their discussion at the beginning of the chapter. The students are asked to revise their ideas on the basis of their reading. This discussion will help them with their follow-up reflective journal entry.

Micha: Well, I think Derek was scared of carrying on being a detective at the beginning, and then he changed his mind —

Anna: — because J.J. wouldn't let him give up.

Josh: I think it's because Tanya had a good plan. They couldn't give up if there was a new plan.

Laurie: Derek stopped being scared when Tanya became a detective.

Mr. Schmidt: So you've got lots to think about when you write your journals. And then you can share your thinking before you start reading your new chapters tomorrow. Were there any words or ideas in the chapter that you found tricky?

Laurie: I've got a sticky on page 32. It says they could see the "glint of water." I wasn't sure what "glint" meant.

Mr. Schmidt had expected this vocabulary item would be tricky for the group when he read the chapter before the lesson. He did not mention

Teaching Tip

Mr. Schmidt often asks students to use text to prove a point. This does not mean that all questions can be answered by quoting from the text. However, he encourages the class to reflect about their reading, to move easily from personal thoughts to text and back again.

the word in the introduction to the lesson but was pleased when a reader realized that the word concept was a problem for her. Self-initiated questioning is more valuable than solving all of the students' problems before reading. Had they not raised this issue, then Mr. Schmidt might have reviewed the word in context as part of the conclusion to the lesson.

Mr. Schmidt: He could see bits of water through the branches…

Anna: Like a glow of water…

Mr. Schmidt: Maybe a sparkle, or he could see the water shining in a little glimpse. I was wondering about page 33. (Mr. Schmidt points out the line that includes "swatted at mosquitoes" and the meaning is discussed.)

Mr. Schmidt raises a phrase that he thinks will be challenging to the class since nobody in the group self-initiated clarification of this expression. However, he finds that the students are experiencing no difficulty with the phrase and so he can quickly move on.

The students say they have no further questions. Mr. Schmidt mentions the new character, Amy. Everyone understands that she is Tanya's little sister, so no extra clarifications are needed.

In the conclusion of the lesson, Mr. Schmidt often summarizes a good reading strategy that he has observed during the individualized diagnostic reading time with a student. These strategy summaries will be repeated during the year, so that the group members will have multiple opportunities to learn good reading strategies.

Mr. Schmidt: I want to mention a good reading strategy that Micha used this morning. Let's find page 30 and look at that line where Amy is saying "Noooooo." When Micha first read the line he said, " 'Noooooo,' winned Amy," and then said to himself, "That didn't make sense. She isn't winning anything!" He reminded himself that Amy was being pouty so he fixed it up and corrected: "'Noooooo,' whined Amy." Micha used a great

strategy. He corrected when his reading didn't make sense. Before we finish, let's think about what will happen next.

Micha: They have to do the plan.

Mr. Schmidt: It doesn't say what that plan is. What are you thinking?

Anna: It's got tin cans in it. It says so.

Mr. Schmidt: I wonder what they will do with the tins.

Josh: Put them in the lunchboxes so that the thief will only find empty cans.

Mr. Schmidt: When you are reading tomorrow, you can read to find out what they do with the tin cans — and whether the plan will catch the thief.

Mr. Schmidt sets the group up with a purpose question for tomorrow and prepares the ground for independent reading of the next chapter. Tomorrow this group will be working on their own as Mr. Schmidt moves to guide another reading group. Mr. Schmidt remains flexible about how much time he will spend with the various reading groups. It is likely he will work with the groups who need extra support more frequently than with those who are comprehending their texts with ease.

Mr. Schmidt does a quick check around the other groups who have been reading and working on their reflection journal entries. Then it is time for recess.

Writing

After the recess break, Mr. Schmidt introduces the writing session. The class has already completed a text structure organizer on forest fires, a major concern each summer in the area. (See class organizer below.) Then the students created their own plans.

Next, Mr. Schmidt took the class plan and demonstrated how to change an outline into sentences and paragraphs. The students then converted their own outlines into text.

Today, Mr. Schmidt wants the group to focus on revising their accounts. He focuses on writing more interesting leads to catch a reader's attention. His mini-lesson is short and focused to permit plenty of time for the students to continue with their own writing.

> ### The Writing Session
>
> The writing session takes approximately 35 minutes daily. The teacher provides a 10-minute demonstration or mini-lesson, and then the students write, accessing support from the teacher when needed. In the writing session discussed here, Mr. Schmidt combines Language Arts with Social Studies, since the class is writing about forest fires in Alberta, part of a study of natural resources in the province.
>
> The text structure organizers used for planning writing topics are used in all writing projects, in both Language Arts and in content areas. Over the grades, as students become more familiar with the text structures, they can plan their writing without formal use of an organizer. In this lesson, the organizational planner is necessary because the class is just being introduced to problem-solution writing.

Mini-Lesson/ Demonstration

Mr. Schmidt: Today, I want us to look at the beginnings of our accounts — the first paragraph and especially the lead sentence, the first sentence. We need to grab the readers' attention with our lead sentences. When we say there's a problem, we want readers to wake up and be

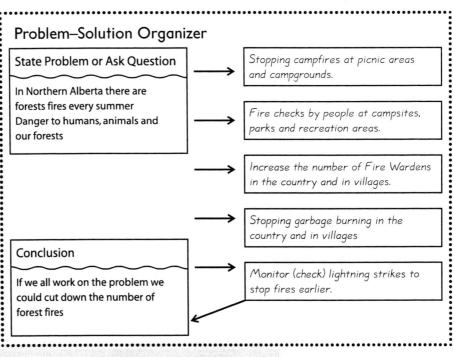

aware there really IS a problem! Let's look at the problem-solution account we wrote as a class. Let's look at our lead and second sentence in the introduction and ask ourselves, "Does this grab your attention? Does this problem sound serious?"

> A problem in our area is that every summer we get forest fires. Some are started by lightning strikes that we can't stop, but others are caused by things we could prevent.

Let's read the first sentence, our lead sentence, together. (Class reads it chorally.) Does that grab your attention?

Jenny: It's a bit boring.

Riku: It says what the problem is okay.

Jenny: But it could get your attention more.

Mr. Schmidt: Riku's on target when he says that the problem is clear in our writing, but we've got to be sure a reader doesn't fall asleep before reaching the second sentence. I'm going to suggest we paint a bit of a picture with words to make sure that our readers can really see the problem. What about saying, "Every summer, flames leap high in the trees, and black smoke covers areas of forest"?

> ~~A problem in our area is that every summer we get forest fires.~~
> ~~Some are started by lightning strikes that we can't stop, but~~
> ~~others are caused by things we could prevent.~~
>
> Every summer, flames leap high in the trees and black smoke covers areas of forest.

Mr. Schmidt demonstrates how revisions can occur in writing.

Mr. Schmidt: Does that give us more of a picture?

Anna: What about "thick black smoke" 'cause it's really choky stuff?

Mr. Schmidt: (adding to the chart) We could add "and thick, black smoke" and then add your other good idea "chokes areas of forest."

> Every summer, flames leap high in the trees and ^thick black smoke chokes
> ~~covers~~ areas of forest.

Mr. Schmidt models using carats to insert ideas.

Mike: Let's say "pine trees" too. Then they'll know how high the flames are. Pine trees are tall.

Mr. Schmidt: So if we put, "Every summer, flames leap high in the tall pine trees and thick black smoke chokes areas of forest," would that be a more attention-grabbing picture?

> Every summer, flames leap high in the ^tall pine trees and ^thick black smoke chokes
> ~~covers~~ areas of forest.

Jess: Could we add a bit more, like "Animals rush away from the smoke and fire"?

Mr. Schmidt: We could add to our introductory ideas: "Animals rush away from the smoke and fire."

Ben: We could say, "Animals race for their lives."

Mr. Schmidt: … and even "to escape from the disaster." "Disaster" tells people it is a serious problem. So now we have a lead and a backup sentence. Let's reread them.

> Every summer, flames leap high in the ‸tall pine‸ trees and ‸thick‸ black smoke chokes ~~covers~~ areas of forest. Animals race for their lives to escape from the disaster.

We've painted a picture with words now, but is the problem clear?

Riku: I think we have to say it's a forest fire somewhere, to make it clear. Some people haven't seen forest fires, so they won't know.

Mr. Schmidt: "The forest fire season has started again in Northern Alberta."

Riku: That says it.

Mr. Schmidt adds to the chart.

> Every summer, flames leap high in the ‸tall pine‸ trees and ‸thick‸ black smoke chokes ~~covers~~ areas of forest. Animals race for their lives to escape from the disaster. The forest fire season has started again in Northern Alberta.

Mr. Schmidt: Let's read it together. As we read, ask yourselves: Does it grab my attention? Is the problem clear?

The class rereads the sentences and agrees with the changes.

Later that day, Mr. Schmidt will add to the Writer's Checklist for Problem-Solution writing on the wall. The children refer to the wall chart when they do individual and partner revisions and editing.

Introduction:
I have a lead sentence.
My introduction grabs your attention.
My introduction makes the problem clear.

Transition to Student Writing

Mr. Schmidt: Now, when you do your writing today I want you to look especially at your introduction. Check your lead sentence and for the first few sentences that make the introduction. I'm going to write two questions on the board. (He writes: Does it grab my attention? Is the problem clear?) You can ask yourself these questions when you reread your problem-solution writing. If you finish early, partner with someone else and read each other's introductions. Make suggestions to each other.

Mr. Schmidt writes the questions and the students turn to their own writing. He removes the class writing sample, so that the children will generate their own ideas. Then he circulates around the room, and conferences briefly with two or three students. He gathers four students together for five minutes, forming a mini-support group to help them work on their lead sentences.

Flexible Support Groups

Flexible support groups are formed daily in writing, as Mr. Schmidt finds students who share a common need. They meet for a few minutes, receive some direct instruction, and then go back to their own writing.

Summing Up

At the conclusion of the lesson, Mr. Schmidt asks Riku and Maggie to read their introductions to the group. Then, to conclude the lesson, he sums up: "Their introductions caught our attention and made the problem clear."

And with that, Language Arts concludes for the day. As he does each day, Mr. Schmidt has provided the word study, reading, and writing components. Over the course of the school year, he varies the content and organization within the basic components to provide a balanced Language Arts program.

Achieving Success in Literacy Programming

Darlene Hunka and Martin Schmidt offer balanced Language Arts programs in their classrooms. They represent two classrooms within a school that offers balanced literacy education. The children move through the grades within a literacy continuum, building on previous knowledge and progressing in their learning. No child needs to work out the Language Arts agenda for the first months of each grade, because the agenda is school wide, the philosophies and goals consistent, and the expectations clear. All children can benefit from whole group lessons because opportunities are provided to apply strategies on materials that are within their "literacy comfort zones." The children benefit from continual demonstrations of good literacy practices and gain incremental confidence as they experience success at each grade level.

Does this sound like a dream school with dream teachers: a literacy paradise that can bear no comparison with reality? It isn't! Programs like the one at Bonaventure School have been running in Edmonton for the past five years. There are many people like Darlene Hunka teaching grade one, and many like Martin Schmidt teaching grade four. These teachers provide comprehensive programs that both meet children's needs and cover a wide range of curricula outcomes each day. Such teachers form the core of successful balanced literacy education, creating the right environment for children to experience success in literacy learning.

Bibliography

Professional References

Brailsford, Anne. *Balanced Literacy: Division 2*. Edmonton, Alberta: Resource Development, Edmonton Public Schools, 2003.

Cunningham, Patricia M., Hall, Dorothy P. and Sigmon, S. *The Teacher's Guide to the Four Blocks*. Greensboro, NC: Carson-Dellosa, 1999.

Cunningham, Patricia M. and Hall, Dorothy P. *Month-by-Month Phonics for Upper Grades*. Greensboro, NC: Carson-Dellosa, 1998.

Cunningham, Patricia M. and Hall, Dorothy P. *Making Big Words*. Torrance, CA: Good Apple, 1994.

Daniels, Harvey. *Literature Circles: Voice and Choice in Book Clubs and Reading Groups*. Markham, ON: Pembroke, 2002.

Day, Jeni Pollack, Spiegel, Dixie Lee, McLellan, Janet and Brown, Valerie B. *Moving Forward with Literature Circles*. New York: Scholastic, 2002.

Northern Alberta Reading Specialists' Council. *Paired Reading: Positive Reading Practice* (Manual by A. Brailsford, with accompanying training videotape). Distributed in Kelowna, BC: Filmwest, 1991.

Topping, Ken. "Peer Tutoring and Paired Reading: Combining two powerful techniques," *The Reading Teacher*. 42 (7), 1989, 488-494.

Schwartz, Susan and Bone, Maxine. *Retelling, Relating and Reflecting: Beyond the 3Rs*. Toronto: Irwin, 1995.

Children's Books

Elste, Joan. *True Blue*. New York: Grosset and Dunlap, 1996.

Oppel, Kenneth. *Firewing*. Toronto: HarperCollins, 2002.

Oppel, Kenneth. *Sunwing*. Toronto: HarperCollins, 1999.

Oppel, Kenneth. *Silverwing*. Toronto: HarperCollins, 1997.

Scieszka, Jon. *The True Story of the Three Little Pigs!* New York: Viking Penguin, 1989.

Taylor, Theodore. *The Trouble with Tuck*. New York: Avon Camelot, 1981.

Literacy Place Texts

Lohans, Alison. *The Lunchbox Mystery*. Markham, ON: Scholastic Canada, 1990.

McNicoll, Sylvia. *Smoky and the Gorilla.* Markham, ON: Scholastic Canada, 1999.

Millard, Nicky. *The Green Angels.* Markham, ON: Scholastic Canada, 1985.

Teachers' Tool Kit for Literacy Place. Markham, ON: Scholastic Canada, 2002.

At the Core of a Balanced Literacy Program: Skilled Teachers

4

At the core of a balanced literacy program are skilled teachers who are balancing the components, strategies, grouping arrangements, and materials to meet students' needs. These teachers need to be highly trained professionals, because daily literacy programming depends on their expertise.

Darlene Hunka: A Veteran Teacher Encounters New Experiences

As we saw in Chapter 2, veteran teacher Darlene Hunka is teaching in a balanced literacy school for the first time. At her previous school, each teacher followed a "potpourri" approach with little connection across classes and grades. In her former classroom, Mrs. Hunka used a basal reading series that she augmented with worksheets. She also did sessions of shared reading and read to the children every day. She followed a writing conference approach and encouraged the children to write on self-selected topics. Invented spellings were emphasized, but towards the middle of the year she made up spelling lists of high-frequency words that the children needed to learn.

When Darlene Hunka transferred to Bonaventure School, she was excited by the prospect of change but felt some trepidation about engaging in a balanced literacy project. She knew that moving to Bonaventure meant that she would need to make some changes in her Language Arts program, but she was unsure what these would be. Indeed, Darlene Hunka wondered if she had made the right move when she realized that she would no longer have a basal reader to use, and that worksheets were a rarity in the two other grade one classrooms at her new school.

The First Months of Balanced Literacy Training

In the June before she was to start at Bonaventure, Darlene attended a day of workshops about the balanced literacy program she would be using at her new school. She was exposed to the theories underlying the program and given an overview of the word study component. Darlene also met the reading specialist who would serve as her balanced literacy consultant and coach. This consultant would be responsible for all monthly inservices and would work with Darlene in the classroom as she mastered the new materials and strategies. Although she was an experienced teacher, Darlene felt a little overwhelmed by all she had learned and would need to learn.

Darlene was given titles of books and articles to dip into over the summer, and she borrowed these from the balanced literacy professional library in her new school. She also talked to the other primary teachers at Bonaventure. These teachers had already completed their two years of intensive professional development, and had become confident in teaching the program. They invited Darlene to come into their classrooms in the fall to observe their literacy program. Darlene made arrangements with her new principal to spend two mornings in the other grade one classes in September and October.

In August, Darlene visited her new school and classroom. She felt initial panic when she viewed the school's bookroom of levelled reading materials and recognized, once more, the reality that she could no longer rely on a reading series and have her own set of books to use in the classroom. Darlene visited the other teachers as they were setting up their classrooms and looked at their guided reading areas and reading station charts. "Am I ever going to get the hang of this?" she wondered.

That same month, Darlene attended a further one-and-a-half days of inservice. At that time she was introduced to the balanced literacy reading approaches and the writing component. By now, Darlene was getting to know her fellow participants in the workshops. These people would be her professional companions over the next two years, and it reassured her to know that they were all sharing new experiences in the professional development sessions. Darlene felt relief when she learned that new teachers in the balanced literacy program would start introducing the elements slowly and would receive demonstration lessons from the balanced literacy consultants.

In September, Darlene's coach came to the school and demonstrated a Word Wall lesson, and a Special Child activity in which children's names were constructed with large letter cards. Darlene also participated in

small group reviews of Making Words lessons during September's balanced literacy workshop. She made her planned morning visit to Mrs. Reva's grade one class and observed the word study component in action there. Darlene then started the word block in her own classroom, continuing with the "special child" activity and later in September branching out into the simple Making Words lessons from the Cunningham and Hall program (1994).

In October, the coach visited Darlene's classroom and demonstrated the sort-and-transfer part of the Making Words lesson and a shared reading activity where word recognition strategies were taught. Darlene taught a Word Wall activity and a Making Words lesson, and then received constructive feedback from the coach. At this stage, Darlene realized that although she had lots of new techniques to learn, her 20 years of teaching experience could now come into play as well. Darlene was comfortable with the shared reading approach, which she had integrated into her previous classroom. Now she could add new dimensions. For example, Darlene learned that she needed to expose the students to a wide variety of genres, so she began to include informational big books, overheads of early reading plays and overheads of excerpts from children's magazines in her shared reading sessions. She also learned that these sessions were vehicles for strategy teaching, and began to incorporate word recognition and comprehension strategies into each lesson. Blending her "old teaching knowledge" with her new experiences, she felt the quiet confidence of growth.

In other areas, however, Darlene still felt overwhelmed. In guided reading, there were so many things to learn. "Still," she told herself, "my coach said to take it slowly. I'll get several demonstrations… as many as I need over the next two years." She comforted herself with this thought. The challenge was to run a good program while she was learning all the new approaches and strategies. She voiced her worries in a sharing session with other teachers new to the program at her monthly inservice.

"It's not so bad for us, because we are all learning together," noted Rita, whose primary staff was newly enrolled in the balanced literacy professional development program this year.

"That's true, but in some ways it's worse for us," responded Brian, a colleague at Rita's school. "We're having to set up a bookroom from scratch and build all of our professional library. At least yours have already been set up by teachers who've taken the balanced literacy training."

"Yes, but we don't have to be the only people starting out on the new program. Are you feeling panicky because the other teachers at your school are now experienced balanced literacy teachers, and you're the only one new to the program?" Rita queried.

"That's a real part of it," replied Darlene. "But I also feel anxious about all the new things that I personally need to implement in Language Arts."

As the months passed by, Darlene Hunka continued to receive inservice information with her professional development group and classroom visits from her balanced literacy consultant. During these visits, Darlene observed demonstrations of techniques and received feedback on her own teaching of program components. Her anxieties re-emerged when she tried new approaches, but her coach was sensitive to her worries and provided extra demonstrations and coaching sessions. On the days that the balanced literacy consultant visited, Darlene attended lunchtime meetings with the other primary teachers. It was reassuring for her to realize that even the experienced balanced literacy teachers had questions and issues to discuss.

Over the course of the year, Darlene came to feel more at ease. She recognized that the process of change in her Language Arts program would take time and she had that time. The professional development program would last for two years and after that she could join inservice groups in progress for refreshers, or request more time from the balanced literacy consultant for additional demonstrations and coaching.

Reaching a Comfort Level with the Program

When we join Darlene Hunka in March of her first year in the balanced literacy program, she is feeling far more relaxed and confident about her ability to operate a balanced literacy classroom. She has begun to integrate previous expertise with new strategies and materials. Darlene has taken advantage of opportunities to visit other balanced literacy classrooms and has immersed herself in the inservices and teacher sharing sessions. Her principal has been supportive, by allowing Darlene to focus on balanced literacy professional development and refraining from adding other commitments such as introducing a new math program. Her period of anxiety is behind her. The balanced literacy consultant has seen Darlene's initial tentativeness diminish, as she begins to take ownership of her literacy program. Now she discusses the program strategies and materials freely with her colleagues on staff.

A Demonstration Lesson
from the Balanced Literacy Consultant

In March, Marie Blanchard, the balanced literacy consultant, is focusing on refining teaching strategies for guided reading. Now that Darlene has organized her groups and is more familiar with the components of the guided reading lesson and the materials, she is open to learning these refinements. Darlene has already learned to use word-recognition prompts to assist readers to problem-solve, but now she and the students need more exposure to comprehension prompts. Marie comes into Darlene's classroom to run a guided reading group and has the 5Ws and HI prompt cards on the table (that is, cards with **Who? What? Where? When? Why? How?** and **If**... printed on them). During the guided reading group, Marie has used the cards as self-prompts to remind her to ask a variety of questions as the children read *Marvella and the Moon* by Linda Massola. At the conclusion of the lesson, Marie selects the **Why?** cue card.

Ms. Blanchard: I am going to ask you a Why question about the story. Why did Marvella get a surprise when she went to the moon?

Ethan: 'Cause there were no trees or anything there.

Marcia: No flowers and no people.

Ethan: So she felt lonely.

Ms. Blanchard: Where did it tell you that in the story?

Greg: Here. It says, "There were NO trees, NO flowers, NO people."

Mohinder: "And worst of all, NO ROBOTS!"

Ms. Blanchard: Why did that bother Marvella?

Greg: She's a robot, and so she's lonely.

Ms. Blanchard: Sometimes when we ask a Why question, it doesn't tell us the answer in the book right away. We have to look at more than one place, and really think about it, before we can answer a Why question. Can you think of a Why question to ask, Greg?

Greg: Why do you think Marvella was happy when she got back to earth?

Marcia: I think she wasn't lonely.

Ms. Blanchard: Can you tell us a bit more, Marcia? I think she wasn't lonely because …

Marcia: … because there must have been robots on earth, and flowers.

Ms. Blanchard: Can you think of a Why question to ask, Marcia?

Marcia: Why did Marvella want to go to the moon?

Ms. Blanchard: Where should we look to get help with that question?

Petra: At the beginning of the book. (The children flip through to the beginning of the book.)

Ethan: It doesn't say. It just says she looked at the moon and the moon looked back.

Ms. Blanchard: Sometimes with Why questions, the answer isn't right in the book. You have to think about what Marvella is like.

Petra: She's like Curious George.

Mohinder: She wants to know everything — what everything's like.

Ms. Blanchard: Does that give us a clue about why she might have gone to the moon?

Mohinder: She went because she wanted to know what it was like there.

Marcia: She thought the moon was looking at her and she wanted to ask, "Why are you looking at me every night?"

Ms. Blanchard: So she could have planned to ask the moon a Why question?

Marcia: Yep.

Ms. Blanchard: There might be lots of reasons why Marvella wanted to go to the moon. The book doesn't tell us the exact reason, so we have to think in our heads and come up with some good ideas that make sense.

After Marie Blanchard's demonstration lesson, Darlene and Marie spend recess time talking about it and applying comprehension prompts and questions to future lessons. Darlene has learned about these techniques in the large-group inservice that occurred the previous week, but this individualized session with her consultant allows her some time to ask questions and clarify her thinking. We join them in their discussion:

Darlene: Would you ever give them some Why questions to answer as follow-up to the guided reading group, in a reading station afterwards?

Marie: I don't think so. At this stage, we want the children to understand not only the question forms but the sources for finding out information. The Why questions this morning made them look at several parts of the text or required them to use inferential reasoning because the answer wasn't "right there" for them. The search and inference strategies need exploring orally, so that you can remind them that they may need to look at more than one part of the text, or they may need to link ideas to their background knowledge.

Darlene: So they need more guided practice before they answer written questions?

Marie: Most of the time, students should be making up the questions for themselves and for each other, rather than answering teacher-designed written questions. If they can make up a Why question, it shows us they've internalized the question form. Then they can answer each other's questions, which gives them more involvement in the questioning process.

Darlene: So they can make up oral questions, as they did this morning? Can they write some questions for each other?

Marie: Well, we need to ensure that they've experienced enough support, orally, to understand the question forms first. Then they could write a question for the group, moving towards more independence over time.

A Lunchtime Meeting

Following Darlene's visit with her balanced literacy consultant, a lunchtime meeting is held at the school. The primary staff, including Darlene, meet with Marie. While the staff formulate the agenda, Marie serves as a resource.

Meg: We're starting to think about ordering some extra book resources for next year.

Jon: The first year we got the core sets of books: *Bookshop, Beanbags and the PM Starters*. The second year we had a bit of money and we ordered supplementary levelled books to boost up the levels that were sparse. Now we want to try to get some books for our independent reading tubs.

Meg: And we need a few novel sets for our advanced grade three readers.

Darlene: We've got catalogues, but we need some help there.

Marie: It's great that you're planning for next year, and that you can see where your gaps are. For your advanced reader novels, I'd look over some of the novels that the upper elementary staff hasn't put into themed sets. You have quite a selection of those in your bookroom and it's a good starting point before you purchase anything. It may be a good idea for you to start reading some novels to see which ones would be interesting for the children you have in mind. You could check the higher level booklists in Fountas and Pinnell's book, *Guiding Readers and Writers: Grades 3-6*, or look at the United Library Services levelled booklists.

When you look over catalogues to find books for your independent levelled tubs, keep in mind the list of the levels you need. Before you buy too much, consider actually looking over the books. Your book reps will have samples, but if you want to see the full range of options, so that you can compare them, wait until our yearly Book Fair in April. We have all of the major companies coming with their collections of levelled books. If you have a good idea of the levels you need, then the Fair should let you explore many possibilities.

Joan: Maybe we should meet in grade level groups first and see what we need.

Jon: Let's set a date for when we should have co-ordinated all our needs before the Book Fair.

Today's lunch meeting has focused on the practicalities of book selection and ordering. Last month, the meeting discussed using a rubric to evaluate writers' needs, while in January the group wanted to discuss accountability in reading stations. Darlene has been a participant in all of the meetings, both absorbing and expressing ideas.

Applying Inservice Ideas in the Classroom

Darlene has prepared some question form cards (5Ws and HI) since the last inservice and plans to use them in her guided reading groups. At the March inservice, she also learned how to use the text structure organizer for persuasive writing. Ideas were provided for literature links that would stimulate persuasive writing. For the next inservice, Darlene and the other teachers have been asked to share their ideas after using the question prompts and persuasive organizer in their classrooms.

Darlene feels confident about trying the question form prompts after receiving both inservice information and theory, as well as the demonstration lesson in her classroom. She will use a book suggested at the inservice, *The Lighthouse Dog* by Betty Waterton, to engage her children in persuasive writing. Darlene has found a copy in the library and she has decided to read part of the book to the class, up to the point where the lighthouse keeper thought that the Newfie dog was too big and mischievous to keep at the lighthouse. Then the class will do an interactive account with the teacher to persuade the lighthouse keeper to keep the dog (or to let the dog be adopted, whichever the class chooses as a viewpoint). Darlene will take her class's persuasive writing, plus samples of the children's individual writing, to the next inservice. There, the teachers will share their persuasive writing experiences with their colleagues.

The Skilled Primary Teacher

Over the course of the year, Darlene has become used to the rhythm of the inservices, the demonstration lessons and coaching in the classroom, and the independent trials of the new techniques. She had many skills garnered over 20 years of teaching before engaging in the balanced literacy program and professional development sessions. However, after almost a year within the program, she realizes how many more skills she has acquired. "I'll never go back to using one level of material — a basal — in reading," she says now. "This way I can reach all of the kids. I know what to do when they're at different reading levels in

the classroom, and I'm learning new strategies to help them to problem-solve when they read."

**The core of a good balanced literacy program
is the expertise of the teacher.**

Martin Schmidt:
A New Teacher Tries Balanced Literacy

Martin came to Bonaventure School as a newly trained teacher three years ago. In his first months of teaching, Martin used the resources available. He used the class novel sets from the storeroom, and borrowed the chapter comprehension questions designed by a fellow grade four teacher. Martin provided spelling lessons using the grade level spelling text, and gave students the chance to do independent reading each day. He read aloud to his class and engaged them in writing, using the five-stage process approach he had learned in his university classes and teaching practicums: brainstorming/planning, drafting, revising, editing, and publishing/final copy.

During his first year of teaching, two things occurred that started to influence Martin's thinking about Language Arts. First, he observed that not all students could engage effectively in classroom novel studies. Some of his students couldn't read the novel he'd chosen. Martin explored this with his grade four teaching colleague, who told him, "Ask somebody to read the book to them at home, borrow an aide to read it to them, or tape the story. They need to feel part of the group when you do the novel study." Martin started to tape each chapter of the story, but this didn't seem to be totally successful because, when he watched his group of weaker readers, they were certainly listening but rarely following the print in the text. Martin realized that the students who needed reading practice the most were not receiving any!

The second influential experience occurred at a staff meeting. The primary teachers had been asked to report back to the rest of the staff

about their new balanced literacy professional development sessions. The primary teachers ran a 30-minute information session about how they were setting up a bookroom for multilevel reading texts that would meet the needs of the varying levels of readers in the class. Martin asked questions about their guided reading lessons and later requested time to visit the primary classes as the teachers introduced balanced literacy techniques and materials into their rooms.

After Martin had observed guided reading lessons and word level activities, he decided to try some multilevel approaches in his own classroom. He begged a bit of time from the balanced literacy consultant to discuss how he could manage multilevel novel studies, and she suggested theming some books at different levels. He raided the storeroom and sorted through the piles of novels. Linda, who taught a grade four-five class at his school, joined Martin because she had recognized that novel studies in a combined grade presented difficulties. Both teachers read books and clustered them into themes. They found books for a "Settlers" theme, for part of a "Children in War" theme, and for a "Humorous/Adventure" theme. The principal then provided some funding to buy small sets of books to fill in the themes. For example, the teachers found that they needed easier books for the "Settlers" theme and a challenging book for the "Humorous/Adventure" theme.

Martin launched his first multilevel novel study in April of his first year of teaching. He ran his version of themed book clubs and rotated around his groups each day. The students were provided with response journals and completed activities that related to the novels: for example, a poster depicting a main character, or a paragraph describing an alternate book ending.

At the same time, Martin became dissatisfied with a "one-level" spelling series text that was jam-packed with rather tedious exercises. He watched the primary teachers, gained advice from them, and tried some Making Big Words lessons (Cunningham and Hall, 1994) with his class.

In these ways, Martin was on the road to change in meeting children's literacy needs even before he was enrolled in balanced literacy training. His forays into multilevel methods and materials arose from personal observations of his class's needs. The potential for addressing those needs emerged when he connected with the balanced literacy program in operation in the primary grades.

Balanced Literacy Training Begins

Bonaventure School staff decided to expand balanced literacy from the primary to upper elementary grades for the next school year, and Martin was delighted with this decision. Although he was already taking the first steps to create a multilevel Language Arts program with a colleague, he was keen to learn new approaches that he could add to his budding program.

When he attended the June inservice day, Martin felt at ease with the ideas he heard and engaged enthusiastically with the discussions and trials of new techniques. In some ways, the information couldn't come fast enough for him: he wanted to learn guided reading techniques when most of his colleagues were struggling with the idea that multilevel reading materials were necessary to meet the needs of upper elementary students.

In August, following the next inservice sessions, Martin decided to start his class on the themed and levelled books that he'd put together the previous year for the "Settlers" theme. He would run this unit with a book club approach until he found out more about guided reading from his professional development sessions. When he knew more details about how to run upper elementary guided reading lessons, he planned to start a Literacy Place module. Martin thought that he'd use the nonfiction "Fact Finders" module once he had completed the "Settlers" theme. In addition, he would start the word study block instead of using the spelling series. In writing he could maintain his process writing approach, but he realized that he needed to add daily writing demonstrations and mini-lessons, and needed to broaden the students' experiences by introducing them to different text structures rather than always featuring self-selected topics.

Working With the Balanced Literacy Consultant

Since Marie Blanchard, the balanced literacy reading specialist and coach for the primary grades, already had a full schedule, Ken Cotton, another balanced literacy consultant, worked with her at Bonaventure School to provide support to the upper elementary teachers.

In September, Ken provided a demonstration on techniques for the word study block. Martin felt quite confident with these approaches and taught a Making Big Words lesson in October so that Ken could observe

and provide him with feedback on his teaching strategies. After school they discussed the lesson.

Ken: The kids were really involved, Martin. Even when you reached the more complex words, the weaker spellers were still trying the words and modelling the correct spellings when the word was built in the pocket chart.

Martin: The hands-on word building is perfect for them.

Ken: One thing I noticed is that you didn't ask the students to say the word slowly as they built each word.

Martin: I wondered if that would sound a bit babyish for a grade four class.

Ken: Well, we're doing it so that the students can hear the sound sequences in words. It's an important step, especially if they don't go through that stage intuitively as they spell more complex words. I wonder if you could explain to the class that "saying a word slowly" is the same as "stretching" a word so that you can hear all the sounds as you spell it. Then you could just say "stretch the word" when you teach the lesson.

Martin: I like that, but you're right — I would need to practise linking the idea of "saying the word slowly" with the term "stretch" for a while.

Before Christmas of Martin's first year in the project, Ken taught his class a strategy/shared reading lesson and two guided reading lessons. He started off the module "Fact Finders" from Literacy Place with a shared reading lesson featuring the magazine, and combined this session with a class strategy lesson on visual scanning of reports and articles to maximize comprehension.

Ken gave a brief introduction to the theme and the class looked at the list of contents in the "Fact Finders" magazine. He then moved on to reading an article with the class ("Weather Dogs on Patrol," page 14):

Mr. Cotton: When we're reading a magazine article, it's always a good idea to read the title first. Let's read it together.

Class: (in chorus with Ken) "Weather Dogs on Patrol."

Mr. Cotton: Strange title. Do you have any idea what this account is going to be about?

Zoltan: Maybe some dogs trained to spot storms — like seeing eye dogs, only weather dogs.

Mr. Cotton: That's a possibility. Let's read the heading underneath the title and see if it gives us some clues.

Class: (reading chorally) "If there's a storm brewing anywhere on the Canadian prairies, that's where you'll find the Fighting Prairie Weather Dog."

Ryan: They're fighting dogs!

Mr. Cotton: It doesn't give us much more information does it? Except...

Maya: It's on the Prairies.

Mr. Cotton: Yes, it tells us an area in Canada. Sometimes it really helps to scan over an article to see if it can give us some clues on the topic. We can see the main account (pointing to the printed main body of the text of the article) but the article provides supports in other places, places where we can look for information. Let your eyes scan over the article and tell me where you can find extra details. (The students scan the article.)

Mr. Cotton: What did you find?

Abdul: Photographs of a storm, and a weather balloon… and a tornado.

Mr. Cotton: Did they give you any clues about the article?

Abdul: It's definitely about bad weather.

Alexa: There's a bit in a box that tells you about the name "Weather Dogs."

Mr. Cotton: Can you show us that part?

Alexa points to the box highlighted in purple on page 15.

Mr. Cotton: So photographs and boxes at the side can often tell us more about the magazine article. Let's look at this box that Alexa found and read it together.

The class, in tandem with Ken, reads the information chorally and discovers that weather dogs are really people who track storm systems and warn people of the dangers of approaching bad weather. They were named after the prairie dogs who sit near their burrows and watch for danger.

Zoltan: So they aren't real dogs at all!

Mr. Cotton: That box at the side of the account gave us some information that we really needed. It told us about who the weather dogs were. Can anybody tell us in their own words?

Continuing with the lesson, Ken shows the class how graphics, sidebars, and highlighted boxes can be found in nonfiction accounts. He teaches them to scan the article and the extensions before reading the main body of the account; this is a useful skill they will eventually transfer to other subject areas in school and magazines in their daily lives.

After the demonstration, Martin and Ken talk through some points.

Martin: I noticed you always read with the class when they were reading chorally.

Ken: Yes, I did that consciously, to provide a model of fluent, expressive reading. I don't want to say, "Look, there's an exclamation mark. Read that with expression." It's more powerful to provide a model and I'm the model.

Martin: So how do you manage that when we read in rows, or several students read one part in a play?

Ken: I choral read with each row, or each part. I carry on modelling and supporting.

Martin: I get it. Can we talk about how to incorporate this type of scanning into my guided reading lessons?

Ken: I'd practise it a little more — with another article or two, and then transfer to your read-aloud book and guided reading.

Martin: I'm reading Wayne Lynch's book, *Penguins!*, for the read aloud.

Ken: Let's look at it. So here you've got lots you can introduce to the class as things to be scanned. There's the table of contents, the index at the back, the coloured photographs with explanations below, the world map of penguins, and the pictorial layout of the types of penguins. You could start a classroom chart on the visual scanning of nonfiction books and list and illustrate the things you might look for. (Ken sketches ideas on scrap paper.)

Scanning can help you find out information in nonfiction books. Look out for:

Contents: Provide an illustration for each new area you discover.
Photographs
Highlighted boxes
Graphics
Checklists
Index
Glossary

Ken: When you start the guided reading books, you could add other examples. In *Swimming with Sea Lions* there are footnotes illustrated by sun symbols. In *Big Ben*, the coloured photographs are clustered in the middle of the book, and there's a timeline at the end of the book. *Animals at Risk* has an interesting fact box for each animal, and a map of endangered species at the end.

Martin: *Wild, Wild Wolves* (Milton, 1992), that I'm going to use as an Easy Plus book, has magnification circles on some of the illustrations... a bit like a magnifying glass.

Ken: So you could add circles as illustrations of magnified images that give additional information you can obtain from scanning.

Martin: And we can add to this chart all year... when we find some new items.

Ken: Yes. It'll increase student awareness of the need to read nonfiction materials a little differently from tackling narratives. It will also increase students' comprehension about what they are reading.

Becoming Confident

By the time we join Martin in March of the second year, teaching the lessons described in Chapter 3, he is feeling confident about implementing all aspects of the Balanced Literacy program and even adding some refinements. He recently talked to Ken, his balanced literacy consultant, about continuing with guided reading for most modules but adding literature circles (Daniels, 2002) and a book club unit each year.

Martin: I was doing book discussion groups on themed books just before I started balanced literacy training. I liked them, although I felt the groups maybe didn't have enough structure. They seemed a bit aimless in their discussions at times.

Ken: Were you doing modelling and demonstration lessons at that stage?

Martin: No, not at all. I guess I just expected them to discuss — that was a bit optimistic, I think!

Ken: Well, now you could add class strategy lessons, demos with tips on group discussions. I'd still plan a core comprehension strategy. It could be prompts using the 3Rs comprehension approach from Schwartz and Bone. Then I'd do some demos on each set of prompts. Start with the prompts for retelling and demo how they can be used in a discussion group. Then you can move on to relating and reflecting over time.

Martin: The prompts would give the groups a bit more focus.

Ken: They would. And when you do literature circles, the various roles each group member takes provide some structure and focus. Do you want me to demo a prompts strategy lesson when I come?

Martin: No, let me try it, and I'd appreciate you giving me some feedback on things I could change or add.

The months that Martin Schmidt spent attending the monthly inservices, reading the professional resources, observing the demonstration lessons, and receiving coaching on his own teaching of balanced literacy techniques have, by March of his second year, paid off. He has developed a comprehensive Language Arts program that meets the needs of his students and is a confident and competent user of a wide range of grouping arrangements, materials and strategies to support each child's learning. Next year Martin will serve as a mentor for a new teacher coming on staff, who will begin attending balanced literacy professional development sessions.

A Journey Just Beginning

Darlene and Martin have not arrived at a professional development "destination" when they have completed the two years of training offered in their balanced literacy program. Rather, they have reached the departure gate for a professional literacy journey that will continue throughout their careers. In the process of encountering change, they have also learned how to filter change through a theoretical literacy framework. This may immunize them against all the "quick fix" programs that surge through the literacy learning field every few years. The greater their understanding of how children become readers and writers, the more careful consumers of methods and materials they will become.

Bibliography

Professional References

Cunningham, Patricia M. and Hall, D. *Making Words*. Torrance, CA: Good Apple, 1994.

Cunningham, Patricia M. and Hall, D. *Making Big Words*. Torrance, CA: Good Apple, 1994.

Daniels, Harvey. *Literature Circles: Voice and Choice in Book Clubs and Reading Groups*. Markham, ON: Pembroke, 2002.

Fountas, Irene C., and Pinnell, Gay Su. *Guiding Readers and Writers: Grades 3-6*. Portsmouth, NH: Heinemann, 2001.

Fountas, Irene C. and Pinnell, Gay Su. *Matching Books to Readers: Using Levelled Books in Guided Reading, K-3*. Portsmouth, NH: Heinemann, 1999.

Schwartz, Susan and Bone, Maxine. *Retelling, Relating and Reflecting: Beyond the 3Rs*. Toronto: Irwin, 1995.

Children's Books

Lynch, Wayne. *Penguins!* Willowdale, ON: Firefly, 1999.

Milton, Joyce. *Wild, Wild Wolves*. New York: Random House, 1992.

Waterton, Betty. *The Lighthouse Dog*. Victoria, BC: Orca, 1997.

Bookshop Texts

Massola, Linda. *Marvella and the Moon*. New York: Mondo, 1995.

Literacy Place Texts (Scholastic)

Bailey, Lydia. *Animals at Risk*. Markham, ON: Scholastic Canada, 1993.

Fact Finders Magazine. Markham, ON: Scholastic Canada, 1999.

McGovern, Ann. *Swimming with Sea Lions*. Sydney, Australia: Scholastic, 1992.

Scanlan, Lawrence. *Big Ben*. Richmond Hill, ON: Scholastic Canada, 1994.

Part Two

Sensible Steps for Implementing a School-Wide
Balanced Literacy Program

The Professional Journey

The professional journey towards school-wide implementation of a balanced literacy program involves the school district, the school, and each teacher.

At the district level, consideration needs to be given to the kinds of support that can be offered to schools and teachers to enable them to move towards a comprehensive and unified Language Arts program. Such support could include: providing forums for discussions in the early stages of implementation, organizing and putting into operation the professional development model; and providing resources such as educational videotapes, books, and articles for loan to schools.

Within each school that is planning a movement into balanced literacy programming, an environment that supports change is necessary. Even in the early stages, administrators need to be participants in staff discussions about balanced literacy and involved in the change process. For example, in the program in Edmonton, some administrators attended all of the inservices along with their teachers, demonstrating by their actions that they were part of the team initiating the program. Administrators must be willing to make changes in the school setting, such as creating professional development time at staff meetings, encouraging the initiation and expansion of a staff professional library, minimizing intercom messages to avoid teaching-learning interruptions, setting up assemblies and events so that they avoid timetable conflicts with Language Arts, and communicating with parents about the new program.

Finally, each teacher has to make a significant commitment of time and professional energies during the movement into balanced literacy programming. In the initial stages, it is entirely normal for teachers to experience the full range of human emotions that accompany change, from extreme doubt through passive acceptance to enthusiasm and commitment.

Kathryn Au, Jacquelin Carroll, and Judith Scheu talk about the process of educational change in their book, *Balanced Literacy Instruction: A Teacher's Resource Book* (1997). They suggest that the "majority of resources (for) professional development should be dedicated to the *goers*, the teachers most willing and able to take new ideas to heart and to make immediate changes in their practices" (page 342). Their view was that these teachers can then serve as models for other teachers. While that route is likely the easiest to take when implementing a balanced literacy program, it is not the one we travelled in the Edmonton and area Balanced Literacy Program. A major premise underlying the program is that children need to experience continuity in Language Arts. Accordingly, we asked interested schools to register first grade teachers, with the expressed intention of moving the program through the grades over time, eventually including all of the teachers in those schools. As the reading specialists-consultants offering the professional development, we needed to work harder to welcome *all* teachers into the project, recognizing that they enter new programs with varying levels of comfort and interest.

Although we did not take the easiest route to promoting professional change, we found the outcomes to be interesting. As we worked with large numbers of teachers over a five-year period, it was fascinating to observe how some teachers' initial misgivings moved into commitment to the program and appreciation of the techniques and approaches they were learning. We suspect these changes were brought about, in part, by the long-term inservice component. Teachers felt supported as they watched their balanced literacy consultant teach demonstration lessons in their classrooms, and they developed increasing comfort with the coaching model as they moved from support to independence in implementing the program. Most of all, teachers warmed to the program as they saw the approaches, strategies, and materials providing success for their young literacy learners. Hence, we recommend not restricting professional development to the "goers" (Au, Carroll and Scheu, 1997) but instead including all teachers within a school. This recommendation, however, comes with an accompanying note of caution. *Professional development plans have to include a strong teacher support system in which teachers can build a relationship with a coach-mentor.* In addition, extra time has to be taken in the early stages of initiating a school-wide balanced literacy program, to build awareness and knowledge of the program itself.

Bibliography

Au, Kathryn H., Carroll, Jacquelin H., and Scheu, Judith. *Balanced Literacy Instruction: A Teacher's Resource Book*. Norwood, MA: Christopher-Gordon, 1997.

1 Raising Awareness

Change in literacy practices usually follows an evolutionary rather than revolutionary process. In the Edmonton Balanced Literacy Program, change occurred in an evolutionary, grassroots manner. From a roughed-out plan of a program, with four schools expressing an interest in piloting it, the program spread from school to school over five years until 92 elementary schools had asked to join the project by the 2002-2003 school year and five districts around Edmonton had requested training for some of their staff. Clearly a transformation like this gains greater impetus when teachers and schools are requesting balanced literacy programming rather than when change is mandated from above.

Often the seeds of change are planted when a small group of teachers or administrators read articles or a book on the topic, or attend a conference and hear a speaker outlining the benefits that will accrue from balanced literacy programming. The ideas are then taken back to a district or school and explored by staff. At that point they either wither on the vine from lack of nutrients, or are nourished through discussion and accessing further information. In the following pages, we will present six methods for raising staff awareness.

1. Inviting a Speaker On Balanced Literacy Programming

The literacy educator can address the theoretical underpinnings of balanced literacy, cite research, and provide practical examples of balanced literacy in action in the classroom. This is also an opportunity for staff to ask questions and discuss the presentation.

The selected speaker should be knowledgeable about balanced literacy theories and models, as well as the developmental process of literacy learning. In addition, choose a speaker who has been actively involved in balanced literacy professional development, and who has taught demonstration lessons in the classroom and coached teachers.

At the District Level

The speaker can be invited to present to the district, with an open invitation to staff. It is helpful, also, if the speaker can meet with selected focus groups such as administrators, reading specialists, and key Language Arts teachers to discuss their particular concerns. For larger groups, it is helpful to break into small discussion groups following the initial presentation.

Discussion Questions at the District Level

The types of prompts that may be helpful in promoting discussion include:

- Is this a sound approach to literacy learning?
    — How powerful is the evidence?
    — Will balanced literacy programming raise literacy achievement for all children?
    — What are the strongest aspects of balanced literacy?
    — What more do we need to know?

- How can the district support the movement into balanced literacy?
    — What is best done by the district?
    — What is best done at the school level?

- What are we doing now that could be modified to support the implementation of balanced literacy?

- What types of consultative support do teachers need in order to implement the program?
    — Who would be available in the district?
    — Do we need to go farther afield?

- How can we work out costs?
    — Do we need a committee or team to get us started by defining our needs?

- How do we introduce this idea to all staff?
    — Do we pilot a program first?

- Can we establish a small network of schools whose staff may be interested in attending balanced literacy awareness inservices?

At the School Level

The speaker addresses the staff on balanced literacy programming and invites discussion and questions. Following the presentation, discussion groups can focus on what they have heard in the presentation, and on new directions they would like to explore.

Discussion Questions at the School Level

The following discussion starters may be useful:

- What do we like best about this approach?

- What do we still need further information about?

- Do any of us use multilevel approaches in word recognition, spelling, reading, and writing?
  — What would we need to modify?

- What kind of support would we need, to help us move into balanced literacy programming?

- Are we prepared for demonstration lessons and coaching in our classrooms?

- Are we ready to commit to a two- to three-year professional development plan?

- How much preparation will we need to do in the first year?

- How can administration help us to focus our energies on balanced literacy professional development, and minimize other commitments for that time period?

- What multilevel materials do we have in the school?
  — What items do we need to prioritize in our purchasing?
  — Where will we put school-wide multilevel materials?

- How can we share balanced literacy programming with our parent group?

2. Viewing Balanced Literacy Videotapes

Videotapes of balanced literacy practices are invariably helpful, painting a vivid, immediate picture of classroom life and providing images that are powerful for teachers. Visual highlights provide useful "starters" before more in-depth professional development occurs.

At the District Level

At the district level, the videotapes can be used to support initial inservices. It may also be possible to run a videotape highlight series, accompanied by informal discussion groups on balanced literacy programming.

At the School Level

Videotapes can be used to accompany a speaker or to stimulate staff discussion at school professional development meetings. They can provide both starting points for discussion and an introduction to balanced literacy techniques that can be applied in the classroom.

Videotape Overviews of Balanced Literacy Programs

- **A Balanced Literacy Program (Pearson Education Canada)**
- **Success in Early Literacy Instruction (Pearson Education Canada)**
- **Successful Classrooms: Effective Teaching Strategies for Raising Achievement in Reading and Writing (Educational Resource Specialists)**

The first two videotapes are from *The Literacy Backbone: Connecting Teaching-Learning Approaches* series. They are part of a staff development program that offers supportive overheads and a plan for teacher sharing, discussion, and reflection.

These two videos feature Andrea Butler, and offer an overview of her conception of a balanced literacy program in primary grades. They introduce modelled, shared, guided, independent, and collaborative reading and writing components and highlight them with refreshingly spontaneous classroom examples.

The third videotape, from California, provides an overview of Language Arts components and the strategies and materials used for teaching a balanced literacy program. Realistic classroom footage of both primary and upper elementary settings allows the viewer to see continuity in programming across the grades and components. Note that California appears to have the requirement that children read grade-level materials in Language Arts in some portion of the day; that is not the case in most Canadian schools. Therefore, the segment of the video entitled "Core Content Curriculum" should be viewed with caution; the strategies for co-operative reading it contains, however, would be most helpful for content area reading where only one level of textbook may be available for students.

Including Phonics in a Balanced Literacy Program

- **Phonics in a Balanced Literacy Classroom (Pearson Education Canada)**

Introduced by Andrea Butler, Pat Cunningham makes a strong case for including hands-on phonics activities in primary and upper elementary classrooms. Pat Cunningham cites brain research that emphasizes how humans learn by analogy and by comparing new patterns with stored information. Although it adheres to a lecture-based format, this videotape offers clear and practical demonstrations of classroom phonics lessons.

Classroom Management

- **Classroom Management (Pearson Education Canada)**
- **Classroom Management: Managing the Day (Heinemann)**
- **Classroom Management: Planning for Effective Teaching (Heinemann)**

All three videotapes feature a primary classroom and provide good overviews of classroom organization and planning. Classroom Management from Pearson's *Literacy Backbone* series presents a large, multi-ethnic grade one class in the early stages of the school year. The teacher is working on developing predictable routines in Language Arts, which is a challenge with her big group and a high number of children with special needs (for example, one-third of the class is learning English as a second language). The Classroom Management tapes by Fountas and Pinnell, from Heinemann's *The Primary Literacy Video Collection*, present a highly organized grade one setting and highlight the daily schedule, establishing group routines, the Language Arts components, and spatial planning. The accompanying teacher-support materials for each of the three videotapes provide discussion points and suggestions for further study and personal reflection.

Book Study Groups

- **Matching Children and Books (Pearson Education Canada)**
- **Guided Literacy: Emergent-Early (Pearson Education Canada)**
- **Using Strategies to Enhance Book Club Discussions (Stenhouse)**

The first two videotapes, from Pearson's *Literacy Backbone* series, feature the book selection process, the use of multilevel texts, and guided reading groups in action in the primary grades. In the third tape, from Stenhouse's *Strategy Instruction in Action* series, footage of a book club session in an intermediate grade includes the book selection process, starting a book club, the teacher's role in facilitating and providing prompts, and actual book club discussions. Although our recommendation would be to provide pre-selected, instructional level books for each group engaged in this type of book study, the video is helpful in illustrating the role of the teacher and the use of comprehension strategies in the groups. It could also provide a model for the type of self-selected, informal book group that children may choose to form in our independent reading period.

Class Strategy Lessons

- **Creating a Culture of Thinking (Primary and intermediate grades)**
- **Modelling Questioning in a Reading Workshop (Primary grade)**
- **Reading and Understanding Nonfiction (Intermediate grade)**
  (All the above from Stenhouse Publishers)

These videotapes from Stenhouse's *Strategy Instruction in Action* series illustrate a strategic approach to reading comprehension. The techniques are excellent, although we prefer the use of instructional level materials in book study groups, and the provision of co-operative reading techniques such as choral reading when one level of text is shared with the whole class. The strategies illustrated can be used with shared-reading and guided-reading materials, and especially in class strategy lessons for grades four through six.

Discussion Questions: Follow-Up to Videotapes

Discussion points emerging from videos may include:

- What did we observe about_____? (the topic featured in the video, such as running a guided reading lesson, teaching strategies during shared readings of nonfiction materials, or doing demonstration lessons in writing)

- What questions emerged from our observations?

- What did we like/not like in the videotaped highlights of an aspect of balanced literacy programming?

- Did we see evidence that this approach was meeting the needs of a diverse group of literacy learners?
  — What supports were offered to the students?
  — What role did the teacher play?
  — Were problem-solving prompts and strategies taught in the lesson we observed?
  — Were multilevel materials and/or methods being used?

- Thinking about what we observed, could we see ourselves implementing these approaches in our classrooms?
  — What help would we need?
  — What do we need to know more about?

3. Reading Articles and Books About Balanced Literacy

Articles and books can provide a more detailed follow-up to the videotaped encapsulations of balanced literacy in action.

At the District Level

A curriculum or Language Arts circular or newsletter can provide information on suitable articles and books for school use. Accompanied by summaries, highlights, and discussion questions, this type of central information about available resources is a useful contribution to schools. A central library of balanced literacy professional resources can be an additional asset at the district level, enabling school staff to peruse materials with a view to purchasing them for school use.

At the School Level

Starting a professional development library in the school would be a good idea. However, library resources may languish on shelves if actions are not taken to engage potential readers.

Starting a Professional Development Library

Here is a selection of articles and chapters that are useful as an introduction to balanced literacy.

Articles

Duffy, Gerald G. and Hoffman, James V. "In pursuit of an illusion: The flawed search for a perfect method," *The Reading Teacher.* (September, 1999), 53 (1), 10-16.

Fitzgerald, Jill. "What is this thing called 'balance' ?" *The Reading Teacher.* (October, 1999), 53 (2), 100-107.

Hoffman, James V. "When bad things happen to good ideas in literacy education: Professional dilemmas, personal decisions, and political traps," *The Reading Teacher.* (October, 1998), 52 (2), 102-112.

Spiegel, Dixie Lee. "Silver bullets, babies, and bath water: Literature response groups in a balanced literacy program," *The Reading Teacher.* (October, 1998), 52 (2), 114-124.

Wilkinson, Ian A.G. and Townsend, Michael A.R. "From Rata to Rimu: Grouping for instruction in best practice New Zealand classrooms," *The Reading Teacher.* (March, 2000), 53 (6), 460-471.

Chapters

Cunningham, Patricia M. "What Should We Do About Phonics ?" in L.B. Gambrell, L.M. Morrow, S.B. Neuman and M. Pressley (eds.), *Best Practices in Literacy Instruction.* New York, NY: The Guilford Press, 1999, 68-89.

Fountas, Irene C. and Pinnell, Gay Su. "Becoming Lifelong Readers and Writers: The Goal of the Intermediate Literacy Program," in *Guiding Readers and Writers, Grades 3-6*. Portsmouth, NH : Heinemann, 2001, 2-13.

Pearson, P. David. "Life in the Radical Middle: A Personal Apology for a Balanced View of Reading," in R.F. Flippo (ed.), *Reading Researchers in Search of Common Ground*. Newark, DE: International Reading Association, 1999, 78-83.

Pearson, P. David and Raphael, Taffy E. "Toward An Ecologically Balanced Literacy Curriculum," in L.B. Gambrell, L.M. Morrow, S.B. Neuman and M. Pressley (eds.), *Best Practices in Literacy Instruction*. New York: The Guilford Press, 1999, 22-33.

Pinnell, Gay Su and Fountas, Irene C. "Selecting and Using Books in the Literacy Program," in *Leveled Books for Readers, Grades 3-6*. Portsmouth, NH : Heinemann, 2002, 1-11.

Spiegel, Dixie Lee. "The Perspective of the Balanced Approach," in S.M. Blair-Larsen and K.A. Williams (eds.), *The Balanced Reading Program: Helping All Students Achieve Success*. Newark, DE: International Reading Association, 1999, 8-23.

Connecting Teachers with Print Resources

Teachers can be connected with print resources for balanced literacy in several ways. For example, to stimulate discussion at a professional development session, an article could be distributed a few days beforehand for all staff to read. Staff could be asked to bring their questions to the meeting. In addition, the district's balanced literacy consultant or a small group of interested teachers could prepare a small core of discussion questions to get the discussion started.

Balanced literacy "bookmark time" is a second possibility: reserving a section of a regular staff meeting for article and book recommendations. Staff, including the administration, could provide brief summaries and two to three key points for readers to note when they peruse the same materials. The titles of the recommended resources could be posted on a "This got me thinking !" bulletin board with room provided for further comments and questions as more people read the resources.

Recommended resources should be placed in an accessible professional development library area.

As a third approach, each teacher could take a turn to introduce a new article or chapter from a professional resource to the staff. For this approach, it is more realistic to select short pieces of text for commentaries, rather than the entire book. The teacher could comment on the material at a regularly scheduled staff meeting.

Discussion Questions After Reading

Prompts to guide the teacher's comments may be helpful:

- What I really found helpful was_____.

- The key ideas for me in this article/chapter were_____.

- What puzzled me was_____.

- I'd like to know more about_____.

- The classroom application here would be_____.

4. Attending Balanced Literacy Conference Sessions

At the District Level

Conference attendance is beneficial to individual staff members, but it is important to disseminate their learning. For example, attendees might share their findings with colleagues through brief contributions to district newsletters or e-mailed curriculum highlights. A "Top Three Points of Interest" e-mail may provide a helpful summary of a session, especially if a phone number or e-mail address is added to allow colleagues to contact the writer for more details. Similarly, the member of staff who attended the conference could be asked to bring back a key article or handout. These could be advertised and sent out to staff who request them.

To: All staff on the balance literacy mailing list
From: Mary Sims, Pine Street School
Subject: Conference: Canadian IRA Regional Literacy Conference
Exemplary Practice in Literacy, Oct 24-26, 2002

Speaker: James V. Hoffman
Sessions: (a) Assessing the Literacy Environment of the Classroom
(b) Levelled Texts in Beginning Reading Instruction:
Moving Beyond the Decodability Debate.

Cc:
Bcc:
X-Attachments:

Top 3 points:
1. Literacy is learned in social settings. Having a rich classroom literacy environment is vital.
2. In recent research that explored classroom literacy environments, excellent classrooms had rich book resources (1000-5000 books), levelled books and local texts (print charts, books, pamphlets, and diagrams created by the students or teacher).
3. Teachers valued trade books the most, levelled books next, and basals the least.

Hoffman said that it is important for students to be able to "read your room": that is, read resources on the wall, on the shelves, and indeed, everywhere they look. Classrooms should offer varied and extensive literacy collections.

If you would like to read the article, "Levelled Texts for Beginning Readers: A Primer, A Test and a Quest" by James Hoffman, Nancy Roser and Misty Sailors, contact the balanced literacy resource team (phone 555-123-4567). A copy of the article I received at the James Hoffman sessions has been sent to them for sharing with others.

Please e-mail me if you would like any more information regarding these sessions.

Mary Sims, Pine Street School

At the School Level

It is easier to conduct post-conference discussions if the entire staff attends certain sessions. If attendance must be spread over several sessions, teachers could be encouraged to summarize their session for colleagues, distribute a key article, and prepare two or three article-based discussion questions. These discussion questions could serve as "starters" for sharing points in the professional development portion of a staff meeting.

5. Creating a Team of Experts Who "Lead the Way"

In the early stages of raising awareness about balanced literacy, it is necessary to assemble the team that will initiate implementation. It is helpful if the following personnel are included: literacy experts, teacher leaders, and what we like to call "practical people."

Literacy experts are people who can act as balanced literacy consultants, running inservices, demonstrating lessons in the classroom, and coaching teachers. They should possess:

- a rich range of knowledge concerning the literacy development of children in the elementary grades
- comprehensive knowledge about literacy programming options, materials, assessment techniques, and teaching strategies suitable for the selected age group
- experience in providing teacher inservices
- skill at giving demonstration lessons in kindergarten-through-grade-six classrooms
- ability to communicate effectively with teachers, engaging in collaborative coaching and consultation with them.

In the balanced literacy program used by Edmonton Public Schools as well as in the surrounding area, all of the balanced literacy consultants were fully qualified reading specialists with graduate degrees in the literacy development and assessment of students. It is vital to have a strong team of consultants who have the knowledge and skills to assist teachers in implementing balanced literacy programming.

The program also needs teachers who are energized and keen to work on balanced literacy in their classrooms. These teachers would be willing to pilot techniques and would be good role models for other staff members.

Finally, the program needs "practical people" who are skilled in costing out models and options, and who can arrange the day-to-day aspects of co-ordinating materials, booking speakers, and organizing meeting schedules.

At the District Level

Organizing the team of experts to lead the way is best accomplished at the district level. All system staff should be under consideration during the selection of a resource pool of people with strengths in particular areas. When that is the case, the needs-based question "Do we have a literacy expert who can serve as a knowledgeable deliverer of inservices and as a coach?" can be answered readily.

Because literacy learning is such a crucial element in all elementary schools, invariably there will be in-district educators who focus on Language Arts instruction. In large districts there may be a Language Arts supervisor, reading specialists, and curriculum consultants. In small school districts, the role of Language Arts curriculum leader may be included with the supervision of other curriculum areas. These educators could schedule initial speakers and gather together the team of experts who will begin the implementation of balanced literacy programming in the district.

At the School Level

If the plan is to initiate balanced literacy within a single school, full program implementation will likely present an immediate challenge. There is little doubt that the teaching team will include "practical people" who can lead the way. However, the team may not include a literacy expert who can provide inservices, demonstration lessons, and coaching. If an external resource must be contracted, a cluster of schools might be able to join together to implement balanced literacy, thus reducing expenses.

6. Encouraging Staff to Visit Balanced Literacy Classrooms

After initial presentations, videotapes, and print materials have exposed staff to balanced literacy programming, it is helpful for them to visit established balanced literacy classrooms.

At the District Level

Inter-school visits can be co-ordinated at the district level, if there are schools that already have balanced literacy programming in place. However, when this type of literacy programming is new in the district, there is little alternative but to approach other districts that already have such programs. If those districts are far away, representatives such as language arts curriculum supervisors, reading specialists, or experienced teachers could make initial visits to the balanced literacy schools in those areas. In addition, the district staff could arrange opportunities for discussions with established balanced literacy teachers and with program organizers in their school district.

At the School Level

A school may wish to organize its own staff visits to another school more experienced in balanced literacy programming. In Edmonton, for example, visits from new schools considering the implementation of balanced literacy are encouraged. Schools either organize their own visits or consult with a balanced literacy consultant for school recommendations. There is nothing more powerful than actually observing a classroom that is using the techniques and approaches teachers have read about or seen on videotape. Of course, if a school is the first in its district to start balanced literacy, visits may entail travelling to another district. In this case, one or two teachers could be sent. Alternatively, a district level representative who has made an out-of-district observational trip could make a presentation.

Whether visits are arranged at the district or school level, it is important to be sensitive to the needs of the balanced literacy school being visited. Visiting personnel usually hope to observe in several classrooms, and they also need time to discuss and ask question. We recommend that the visitors offer to pay for a substitute teacher in the afternoon. The visitors could then observe regular balanced literacy teaching-learning in the morning, and a lead teacher could be "freed up" to meet with the observing teachers in the afternoon.

Observational Questions to Guide a School Visit

Visual Overview

- Do the classrooms have obvious indicators of balanced literacy programming? (Examples include: a Word Wall for kindergarten to grade three or Tricky Words area for grades four to six; a reading station chart for grades one to three; an area for guided reading; and writing organizers and class writing checklists posted on the walls.)

Organization

- Does the teacher vary organization for learning? (whole class, small group, and individual)
- What support is offered to struggling learners?
- How does the teacher vary learning for advanced learners?

Components

- What is taught in Language Arts?
- For how long is each component taught?

Materials

- How do the children share print materials read by the whole class?
- How does the teacher meet children's needs with multilevel materials?
- How does the school centralize materials?
- What system is in place for sharing resources?

Continuity

- Will the children experience continuity in Language Arts as they move through the grades?
- Are teachers aware of what is happening in Language Arts in other classes and grades?
- Have teachers decided what information to hand on to the next teacher?
- How do teachers use information from children's previous teachers?

Contact with the Balanced Literacy Consultant

- What is the role of the balanced literacy consultant?
- What aspects of inservices, demonstration lessons, and coaching do the teachers find helpful?

In Appendix B, we have included classroom visit checklists. These can be taken on school visits and used to guide observations. Separate checklists are included for visits to kindergarten, primary, and upper elementary classrooms. If more than one class is visited, a separate observational guide can be completed for each room. We have also included a school guide on which teachers can note, and enquire about, school-based aspects of balanced literacy programming.

Bibliography

Professional References

Brailsford, Anne. *Balanced Literacy: Division 1*. Edmonton, AB: Edmonton Public Schools Learning Resources, 2002.

Brailsford, Anne. *Balanced Literacy: Division 2*. Edmonton, AB: Edmonton Public Schools Learning Resources, 2003.

Videotapes

Educational Resource Specialists (San Diego, CA), 1999:
- Successful Classrooms: Effective Teaching Strategies for Raising Achievement in Reading and Writing

Heinemann. *Primary Literacy Video Collection*, 2001:
- Classroom Management: Managing the Day
- Classroom Management: Planning for Effective Teaching

Pearson Education Canada. *The Literacy Backbone: Connecting Teaching-Learning Approaches*, 1996:
- A Balanced Literacy Program.
- Success in Early Literacy Instruction
- Classroom Management
- Matching Children and Books
- Guided Literacy: Emergent - Early

Pearson Education Canada, 1997:
- Phonics in a Balanced Literacy Classroom

Stenhouse. *Strategy Instruction in Action* series, 2002:
- Using Strategies to Enhance Book Club Discussions
- Creating a Culture of Thinking
- Modelling Questioning in a Reading Workshop
- Reading and Understanding Nonfiction

Selecting a Program

When a school district or school is planning a balanced literacy program, the following elements and related questions need to receive attention.

- **Essential Characteristics**
  Question to ask: In what philosophy of literacy learning is this program grounded?

- **Teaching-Learning Components**
  Question to ask: What components are planned for a comprehensive Language Arts program in kindergarten, primary, and upper elementary grades?

- **Time Guidelines**
  Question to ask: How do we structure Language Arts time in our program?

- **Grouping and Teacher Support**
  Question to ask: How are grouping arrangements varied to meet student needs and to offer varying degrees of teacher support?

- **Core Materials**
  Question to ask: Does the program recommend any core materials for the classroom?

- **Assessment**
  Question to ask: What key assessment strategies are recommended to guide and modify classroom instruction?

In this chapter, examples of each of the above elements will be drawn from *Balanced Literacy: Division 1* and *Balanced Literacy: Division 2 Programs* (Brailsford, 2002, 2003).

Essential Characteristics of a Balanced Literacy Program

Essential characteristics form the criteria for evaluating a program during the selection process. In the Balanced Literacy Program used by

Edmonton Public Schools and surrounding districts, the following characteristics listed below are incorporated into programs for kindergarten through grade six.

Essential Characteristics

1. The program is based on the view that literacy learning occurs in social contexts and in "rich print" environments; that is, environments where there are books as well as student- and teacher-made print materials on the walls, and where print materials are integrated into most classroom activities.

2. The program is comprehensive, in that it covers the Language Arts curriculum.

3. The program meets the needs of diverse learners by:
   • varying groupings to permit whole class, small group, and individualized learning
   • promoting teaching that moves from offering support to the learner to offering independent practice on materials at each child's optimal learning level
   • providing multilevel materials
   • offering teacher demonstrations of all strategies
   • emphasizing the daily teaching of strategies and the application of these strategies in new print contexts.

4. The program offers continuity by:
   • teaching all program components every day
   • linking learning across Language Arts components and content areas
   • operating across grade levels, in every classroom in a school
   • providing practical home links to involve parents in their children's literacy learning.

5. The program builds "assessment that guides instruction" into the daily teaching process.

Program Organization

The following charts illustrate the components, time guidelines, grouping arrangements, and teacher support required in a balanced literacy program that integrates the essential characteristics with the teaching-learning components. The program is structured to flow from kindergarten through grade six (Brailsford, 2002, 2003).

The Kindergarten Balanced Literacy Program

In some school districts, kindergarten is a full day program; in others, it runs for half days, or for two or three days each week. Therefore the times suggested in the following chart of components will need to be flexible. In full day kindergartens, for example, the 10-to-15-minute word study period may be repeated, so that the children experience one session on high-frequency words in the morning and another on phonemic awareness in the afternoon. In half day kindergartens, high-frequency words could be presented one day, and phonemic awareness could be emphasized the next day. Kindergarten teachers need to map a program that maximizes literacy learning within the time available. Overall, we recommend building a strong language and literacy environment that immerses children in meaningful listening, talk, and print.

Establishing a Language and Literacy Context

- Encourage listening and talking in whole group, small group, and individualized contexts. Incidental conversations between adults and children serve to extend and clarify communication in supportive ways, for example: Child: "He gots a colour." Adult: "You're right. He got a red crayon from the box."
- Create a Word Wall for children's names and some high-frequency words.
- Provide poems, chants, and big books for shared reading.
- Set up centres that weave in literacy incidentally, such as a playhouse with books, a phone book, take-out menus, writing materials, and a "fridge" noticeboard; or a blocks centre with road signs to use in play.
- Set up literacy centres such as a writing centre, a listening and read-along centre, a library corner, a post office, and a story retelling centre for dramatic re-enactments of tales and for reconstructing stories with flannel board characters or puppets.
- Create a mailbox system for receiving and sending notes. The teacher models by writing notes and sending them to children.
- Display meaningful print labels, such as "Remember! Dixie (rabbit) needs lettuce in the mornings," "Scissors," "Pencils," and "Our Journals."
- Maximize time for literacy by, for example, changing the traditional "show and tell" into literacy events such as the interactive, shared writing of news or a word-building and writing activity such as Getting to Know You (Hall and Cunningham, 1997).
- Display fiction and nonfiction books in a library corner, and also incorporate books into centres and table displays.
- Use adult resources such as aides or parent volunteers. Adults can read to and with children, and can support them in writing.

With these components, time guidelines, grouping arrangements, and teacher support elements in place, the teacher can build a classroom timetable. The following full day kindergarten timetable represents a possible daily plan. If the kindergarten program runs half days, the morning section of the full day timetable can be adopted.

Sample of a Full Day Kindergarten Timetable

Time	Activity	Duration
8:50 – 9:00 a.m.	Transition into beginning of school day: rereading familiar shared reading books and emergent-early levelled reading materials	10 mins.
9:00 – 9:10 a.m.	Teacher writing demonstration with modelling and verbal commentary on writing concepts, e.g. "I'm going to start writing here…"	10 mins.
9:10 – 9:25 a.m.	Interactive writing: children contribute news and ideas, and are invited to add letters and words to co-write with the teacher	15 mins.
9:25 – 9:40 a.m.	Journal writing: children draw and write in their journals, with the teacher offering support	15 mins.
9:40 – 10:00 a.m.	Shared reading with the whole class	15 mins. (plus 5 mins. transition time to recess)
10:00 – 10:15 a.m.	Recess	15 mins.
10:15 – 10:35 a.m.	Read aloud	15 mins. (plus 5 mins. transition time to centres)

10:35 – 11:05 a.m.	Centres: the teacher works with one small group on shared or guided reading	30 mins.
11:05 – 11:45 a.m.	Other curricular areas, e.g. math, phys. ed., music	40 mins.
11:45 – 12:00 noon	Letter, sound, and word study	10 mins. (plus 5 mins. transition to lunchtime)
12:00 – 1:00 p.m.	Lunchtime	60 mins.
1:00 – 1:20 p.m.	Read aloud	15 mins. (plus 5 mins. transition time from lunchtime)
1:20 – 1:35 p.m.	Shared reading	15 mins.
1:35 – 2:05 p.m.	Centres: teacher works with another small group on shared or guided reading	25 mins. (plus 5 mins. transition time to recess)
2:05 – 2:20 p.m.	Recess	15 mins.
2:20 – 2:45 p.m.	Writing and Reading Buddies: engaging in partner writing and reading experiences with older students and community volunteers	20 mins. (plus 5 mins. transition time from recess)
2:45 – 2:55 p.m.	Letter, sound, and word study	10 mins.
2:55 – 3:15 p.m.	Other curricular areas	15 mins. (plus 5 mins. end of day transition)

Components – Kindergarten	Time	Grouping Guidelines	Teacher Support
Letter, Sound, and Word Study			
Teacher selects one activity that features, for example: **Letters** Reading alphabet books and designing a class alphabet book, using an alphabet big book and reading mini-alphabet books (e.g. Alphakids and PM alphabet books) with groups; and doing object sorts in hoops to distinguish things that start with various letters (Kitching, 1993) **Words** • Clapping and saying the letters; building words with letter cards; sorting by first letter; and writing in context on a sentence strip • *Children's Names:* adding to Word Wall • *High-Frequency Words:* Using high-usage words found in chants, poems, and stories for inclusion on the Word Wall • *High-Emotional-Impact Words:* Using words that are very important to the children and have emotional appeal e.g. pizza, Mom, Dad, and Love; placing words on Word Wall **Phonemic Awareness** Hearing the sounds in words: e.g. Turtle Talk (Fitzpatrick,1997), which focuses children on "stretching" words and hearing sound sequences **Letter-Sound Associations** Emphasizing letter-sound relationships: e.g. Be the Sound (Fitzpatrick,1997), where words are blended using sounds and letter cards **Concepts of "Letter" and "Word"** Demonstrating concepts: e.g. by cutting a child's name into letters and rebuilding it with the class; verbalizing concepts: "I'm cutting this word into letters."	10 min. If time permits, more than one session is done each day	Whole class Small group and individual practice activities can also be done during centre time	High Low-Moderate, depending on the adult help available

Components – Kindergarten	Time	Grouping Guidelines	Teacher Support
<u>Language Cues for Word Recognition</u> Covering words in sentences or in stories, and working on predictions by reading back and reading ahead to think of words that would make sense; checking predictions by peeling back the word flaps and attending to letter-sound cues			

Reading

Components – Kindergarten	Time	Grouping Guidelines	Teacher Support
a. Read-Aloud • Reading fiction and nonfiction books	15 mins.	Teacher reads aloud to the whole class and models expressive, fluent reading If adult help is available, read-alouds can also take place with small groups and individuals at centre time	High High
b. Shared Reading • Reading big books, poems and chants • Using fiction and nonfiction materials • Utilizing big books with accompanying little books for shared reading groups • Teaching concepts: e.g. front of a book, print holds a message, top/bottom of a page, first word • Teaching strategies: e.g. print tracking, line movement, how to work out words, how to predict events	15 mins.	Teacher reads aloud to the whole class and the children read in chorus (familiar materials) or echo read (less familiar materials) Teacher conducts small group sessions using big books and accompanying little books	High High
c. Guided Reading • Guided reading sessions may only be appropriate for the few kindergarten children who are confident with book handling and print tracking during shared reading groups • Multilevel books are used, starting with Level A (Fountas and Pinnell, 1996) materials • If there are early readers in the class, they will need to read books at their instructional levels (minimum of 70% comprehension, 90% contextual word recognition)	10–15 mins.	Teacher conducts small group sessions, often during centre time; children are provided with sufficient support to enable them to read the books for themselves.	Moderate

Components – Kindergarten	Time	Grouping Guidelines	Teacher Support
d. Independent Reading • Fiction and nonfiction materials are placed in an inviting library corner • Books can also be placed in some centres, e.g. in the playhouse and in the craft centre (simple "how to make" books)	10–15 mins.	Children read the books individually or with partners	Low

Writing

Components – Kindergarten	Time	Grouping Guidelines	Teacher Support
a. Demonstrations • Write alouds: Teacher demonstrates the craft of writing by writing on a chart and talking aloud about the process • Resources and strategies are demonstrated, e.g. "I think that word is on the Word Wall... I'll check" or "I'll say the word very slowly, like Turtle Talk, and see what sounds I can hear"	10 mins.	Teacher demonstrates writing to the whole class	High
b. Interactive, Shared Writing • The teacher demonstrates writing and invites the class to help; the children provide ideas and participate by writing parts of words, or whole words, on the chart • Topics well within the children's experiences are selected to maximize their ability to join in	15 mins.	Children and teacher share writing in a whole class session Small group shared/interactive writing sessions are recommended too, because they enable instruction to be tailored to meet individual developmental needs	High-Moderate
c. Individual Writing	15 mins.	Students write on their own, usually at centres.	Low-Moderate

The Primary Balanced Literacy Program

In the primary years (grades one through three), the balanced literacy program builds conceptually on the kindergarten year, increases the time allotted for each component, and often follows a structured daily routine. Groupings continue to be varied, to enable the teacher to mesh instruction with the children's learning needs. Teaching styles vary from direct instruction to incidental teaching-learning conversations and teaching through the sharing of ideas.

The following timetable represents a possible daily schedule for a primary balanced literacy program:

Sample of a Primary Language Arts Timetable

8:50 – 8:55 a.m.	Transition at the beginning of the school day	5 mins.
8:55 – 9:30 a.m.	Word block	35 mins.
9:30 – 9:45 a.m.	Read aloud	15 mins.
9:45 – 10:00 a.m.	Shared reading	15 mins.
10:00 – 10:15 a.m.	Recess	15 mins.
10:15 – 10:55 a.m.	*Guided reading and independent reading stations	40 mins.
10:55 – 11:30 a.m.	Writing	35 mins.
11:30 – 12:00 noon	Other curricular areas	30 mins.
12:00 – 1:00 p.m.	Lunchtime	60 mins.
1:00 – 3:30 p.m.	Other curricular areas	

*Note : For grade one children, we suggest modifying the above plan, scheduling one guided reading group before recess and another following recess. This modification allows grade one children to focus attention for two 20-minute periods, rather than the extended 40 minutes that grades two and three children can manage.

Components – Primary	Time	Grouping Guidelines	Teacher Support

Word Study

a. High-Frequency Words (Word recognition and spelling) • Using Word Wall as class dictionary • Introducing 5 core words each week • Adding 3 challenge words for advanced students • Providing fast-paced, hands-on practice activities • Building in review weeks where no new words are introduced; focusing on reviews of words that still present challenges to students, through practice activities	10 mins.	Whole group initial teaching, followed by small group and individual practice in reading stations (independent reading time)	High Low
b. Phonemic Awareness, Phonics, Word Patterns (Word recognition, word analysis, word building, and spelling) • Doing phonemic awareness activities: e.g. Talking Ghost (Fitzpatrick, 1997) where students blend sounds together to make words. • Using Making Words techniques and lessons (Cunningham & Hall, 1994 a.) • Emphasizing letter-sound associations, sound sequences, and visual-sound patterns • Expanding emphasis on transfer of word patterns to reading and spelling	25 mins.	Whole group initial teaching, followed by small group and individual practice in reading stations (independent reading time)	High Low

Reading Workshop

a. Read Aloud • Using fiction and nonfiction books • Books may link to content areas, and often link to writing component	15 mins.	Teacher reads aloud to the whole class, modelling fluent and expressive reading	High
b. Shared Reading • Using big books: fiction and nonfiction • Teaching concepts: e.g. first word, rhyming word, capital letter, dialogue marks	15 mins.	Teacher shares reading with the whole class; joining in and echo reading are encouraged Small shared reading groups can also be formed with children who start school with very limited book handling skills and print concepts; they should be considered as lead-ups to guided reading for early grade 1 children with "low book knowledge"	High Moderate

Components – Primary	Time	Grouping Guidelines	Teacher Support
c. Guided Reading • Children with similar reading needs and Instructional Levels are grouped together • Groups are flexible and change frequently • Each group reads Instructional Level materials and progresses through a gradient of text levels • Lessons are structured to provide support and some challenges, and prompts are used to engage the children in problem solving	40 mins.	Teacher works with two small groups (20 mins. each) and provides small group and individualized support to enable the students to read the books themselves While the teacher is conducting guided reading groups, the other children are reading independently at stations	Moderate
d. Independent Reading • Work board is used to highlight appropriate reading stations for each group • Levelled books are placed in book tubs and the children read Independent Level books (slightly easier than they use in guided reading) • Other stations are provided to help children focus on print and reading: e.g. a word-study practice station, a browsing box of shared reading materials for buddy reading, a listening and reading station, and a poetry station	40 mins.	Children engage in independent reading practice when they are not scheduled for guided reading lessons with the teacher; the primary activity is reading, with some literature response journal writing, and the children read on their own or, occasionally, with a small group or buddy	Low

Writing

a. Demonstrations • Write alouds: teacher writes a brief account and talks aloud, verbalizing thoughts about the writing process • Shared writing: teacher invites children to contribute ideas. • Interactive writing: teacher shares the felt marker and children offer ideas and add letters, words, phrases, and punctuation. • Mini-lesson: direct teaching, usually of a convention: e.g. dialogue or capitalization • Graphic organizers: used for each type of text structure in the planning stages of writing; use of these planners is often featured in the demonstration component • Read alouds: often linked to demonstrations, since they provide links to the text structure being featured in writing	10 mins.	Whole class teaching on aspects of the writing craft; teacher elects to use a write aloud, shared or interactive writing, or a mini-lesson for the demonstration component	High

Components – Primary	Time	Grouping Guidelines	Teacher Support
b. Guided Writing • Children engage in various types of writing: developmentally appropriate instructions ensure that children start with "retelling" and progress to more complex text structures • Text structures covered include: retelling, story analysis, traditional fiction (myths, legends, and fables), sequence, descriptive paragraph, reports, persuasion, comparison, cause and effect, problem-solution, newspaper articles, letters, and poetry • Types of writing are often linked to literature through read alouds and shared reading, and can also be related to content areas • A large portion of the writing is text-structure based, with the teacher setting a topic and the children developing their own versions: e.g. *Text Structure:* Narrative *Topic:* Updated Fairytales *Literature Link:* Teacher reads updated versions of fairytales to the class *Demonstrations:* Shared writing of an updated fairytale by teacher and class *Guided Writing:* children select a fairytale and write their own updated versions • Text structure organizers are used as planners for each type of writing. Children progress from planning to drafting, revising, editing and, sometimes, publishing	25 mins.	Children work on their own Teacher helps individual children or works with a small group when several children need support in the same area	Low Moderate
c. Guided/Independent Writing • Sometimes the children write on self-selected topics during regular writing time, or during reading station time (literature response journals)		Children work on their own writing Teacher supports writers who need assistance	Low Moderate

The Upper Elementary Balanced Literacy Program

Word Study, Reading, and Writing continue to be the three broad Language Arts areas in the upper elementary program. The chart starting on page 152 illustrates the Word Study and Reading segments. Writing content and process remain unchanged, with students in grades four to six demonstrating increased depth and breadth as writers. As in the primary years, grouping arrangements continue to be varied to allow teachers to meet students' needs. The program is more flexible than the primary program. For example, the Reading Hour occurs daily but the mini-components vary, while writing lessons are increasingly scheduled across content areas.

The following timetable illustrates a typical Language Arts schedule in a grades 4-6 classroom. Writing usually occurs in Language Arts on two days a week. It is integrated into content areas on the remaining three days.

Sample of an Upper Elementary Language Arts Timetable

8:50 – 9:00 a.m.	Transition at the beginning of the day, plus self-selected reading	10 mins.
9:00 – 10:00 a.m.	Reading hour: In this sample, there is a read aloud allied with a class strategy lesson and book study groups. On other days, the mini-components of the reading hour will vary.	60 mins. (15 mins. read-aloud; 15 mins. class strategy lesson; 30 mins. book study groups)
10:00 – 10:15 a.m.	Recess	15 mins.
10:15 – 10:40 a.m.	Word study	25 mins.
10:40 – 11:20 a.m.	Writing	40 mins. (10 mins. teacher demonstration; 30 mins. students writing)
11:20 – 12:00 noon	Other curricular areas	40 mins.

12:00 – 1:00 p.m.	Lunchtime		60 mins.
1:00 – 3:30 p.m.	Other curricular areas		

Components – Upper Elementary	Time	Grouping Guidelines	Teacher Support
Word Study			
Word Recognition and Spelling Activities • Study of high-frequency words • Word building and analysis with Making Big Words lessons (Cunningham & Hall, 1994 b.) • Word building and analysis with prefixes and suffixes • Word pattern activities: e.g. What Looks Right?, Brand Names, and Nifty Thrifty Fifty (Cunningham & Hall, 1998) • Cloze activities at the paragraph and discourse levels to review using contextual language cues when reading • Easy and difficult content is included in each lesson to meet the needs of learners: e.g. in the Making Big Words lessons, word lengths vary from three letters to multisyllabic; students are provided with models if the words are challenging for them	25 mins.	Whole class teaching of word recognition and spelling strategies	High
The Reading Hour			
• Teacher selects a balance of components from the following options: read-aloud, shared reading, class strategy lesson, book study groups, and independent reading	60 mins.	Teacher decides on the component used each day and the amount of time needed; for example, on one day the teacher plans for a read aloud (15 mins.), a class strategy lesson (15 mins.) and book study groups (30 mins.)	
a. Read Aloud • Read alouds often support the theme selected for the book study and shared reading materials: e.g. *Star in the Storm* by J.H. Harlow may be selected as a read-aloud if a grade 4 class is reading materials from the "Join In" theme in Literacy Place (Scholastic Canada)		Teacher reads aloud to the whole class	High

Components – Upper Elementary	Time	Grouping Guidelines	Teacher Support
• Read alouds can also be linked to writing: e.g. a book of Canadian aboriginal myths can be read when the students write their own myths • Content area links can also be forged: e.g. reading *Ticket to Curlew* by C.B. Lottridge when the students are studying Canadian settlers • Read-aloud selections include fiction and nonfiction texts			
b. Shared Reading • Student engage in supported reading of materials by using choral reading • Teacher always reads along to provide an expressive reading model • Shared reading materials often support the theme selected for book study groups and read alouds: e.g. the themed magazine articles can be used for shared reading when using Literacy Place (Scholastic Canada). • Materials can also relate to content areas, and to writing topics and text structures: e.g. choral reading of a letter to the editor from the local newspaper when letters are being written.		Variety in groupings is provided: e.g. whole group, small group, and buddy choral reading, plus buddy Paired Reading (Topping, 1989; Northern Alberta Reading Specialists' Council, 1991)	Moderate
c. Class Strategy Lesson • Direct instruction is provided on using a reading strategy: e.g. using context to elicit vocabulary meanings, summarizing information you have read, linking prior knowledge with new information, or self-questioning during reading • Content for the strategy instruction is provided by the class read-aloud book or by the materials used for shared reading • New strategies are practised with Instructional Level materials in book study groups		Whole class instruction	High

Components – Upper Elementary	Time	Grouping Guidelines	Teacher Support
d. Book Study Groups • Multilevel texts are used; students with similar reading needs are grouped together to read a book at their instructional level • Fiction and nonfiction materials are used • Although there may be 4 or 5 book study groups reading different books, all books relate to a theme to facilitate inter-group communication and instruction on strategies to the whole class • Three types of book study groups can be implemented: *Guided Reading:* teacher works with one group, providing appropriate support to facilitate their reading of the text, while the other book study groups read their own books and write journal responses *Literature Circles* (Daniels, 2002): students take roles (e.g. the "Connector," who makes connections between the book and life experiences or other books read) and these roles are used to stimulate book discussions *Book Clubs* (McMahon & Raphael, 1997): students read sections of the book and use prompts to guide oral discussions and written literature responses		Small group and individual instruction Teacher runs guided reading lessons with book study groups, or facilitates discussions and students problem-solving with literature circles and book clubs	Moderate
e. Independent Reading • Students self-select books to read		Teacher has individual contact with students: sometimes students decide to read the same book with a buddy, or to form a small group book club; teacher contact varies, depending on group needs Individual conferences and assessments can occur during this time	Moderate

Writing

See the primary program descriptions. The writing process is continuous through all elementary grades. In the upper elementary program, some of the familiar text structures such as narratives and descriptive paragraphs are reviewed, while new emphasis is placed on more complex text structures such as problem-solution, business letters, newspaper articles, and cause and effect writing.

Classroom Print Materials

Balanced literacy programs require a varied collection of fiction and nonfiction that will not only engage readers but also provide success by meeting each child's instructional learning needs. In the Balanced Literacy Program that operates in Edmonton Public Schools (Brailsford, 2002, 2003), all schools use a list of the core materials needed to meet the needs of children in kindergarten through grade six. Using core materials facilitates communication during professional development sessions. The core materials are stored in a communal book area in each school and are borrowed as needed. Books in this core set are levelled according to the Fountas and Pinnell criteria (1996), with minor adjustments made by teacher committees.

Core Set of Materials		
Grade	**Materials**	**Components**
Kindergarten	High-Frequency Readers (Scholastic) Alphakids (Scholastic)	Shared Reading Shared Reading (small group)
Grades 1–3	PM Starters (Nelson) Beanbags and Bookshop (Scholastic)	Guided Reading Guided Reading (Big Books used for Shared Reading)
Grades 4–6	Literacy Place (Scholastic)	Book Study Groups (Magazines used for Shared Reading and Class Strategy lessons)

Although we have indicated grade levels, we intend that the list be used flexibly. For example, kindergarten children may well be ready to move into guided reading and use the levelled materials from PM Starters, Beanbags, and Bookshop. These core materials will need to be supplemented by other resources.

Kindergarten Resources

- Read-aloud books that the teacher can read to the class
- Selections of big books, poems, and chants
- Picture books for the library corner and some centres
- Big books and accompanying little books for shared reading
- Sets of levelled books for guided reading groups.

Primary Resources

- Read-aloud books that the teacher can read to the class; content may link to content areas or to other areas of Language Arts (for example, books written in the form of letters provide good models for letter writing instruction)
- Selections of big books, poems, and chants for shared reading
- Articles, flyers, poems, cloze sentences and paragraphs, and plays for shared reading on charts or the overhead
- Sets of levelled books for guided reading groups
- Tubs of levelled books for independent and home reading practice
- Other books that may match themes in content areas, and self-selected library books.

˙For specific examples of suitable supplementary resources, consult *Balanced Literacy: Division 1* manual (Brailsford, 2002).

Upper Elementary Resources

- Magazine and newspaper articles, flyers, poems, cloze accounts, and plays for shared reading and the class strategy lesson
- Read-aloud books that link to the theme being used or to content areas
- Themed, levelled sets of books for book study groups such as literature circles, book clubs, and guided reading
- Books for independent, self-selected reading from classroom and school library resources

*For specific examples of suitable supplementary resources, consult *Balanced Literacy: Division 2* manual (Brailsford, 2003).

Assessment

The Balanced Literacy Program (Brailsford, 2002, 2003) maximizes instructional time. Its "assess-on-the-go" philosophy provides samples of student progress and indicators for subsequent teaching steps. For example, in primary grades, a student book record indicates progress through the levelled texts used in guided reading, while reading strategy checklists and writing rubrics highlight each child's successes and needs across all grades.

Decision Time: Do We Adopt an Existing Program, or Adapt?

When the Edmonton program began in 1997, few resources were available. Pat Cunningham was working on her Four Blocks Program (1999), and Pinnell and Fountas (1996) had written a resource book outlining possible components of a balanced literacy program, with emphasis on the teaching of guided reading. Anne Brailsford designed her balanced literacy program for kindergarten through grade six with the intention of building an integrated Language Arts program that incorporated the essential characteristics listed in this chapter. Currently, more options are available for schools that are considering balanced literacy programming. For example, Cunningham, Hall and colleagues (1999) have fleshed out their program for primary grades, while Fountas and Pinnell (2001) have outlined a detailed program for upper elementary grades.

When selecting a schoolwide balanced literacy approach, the decision has to be made either to adopt an existing program or to adapt a program in order to create a new version. Either route is viable, although the latter route obviously takes more intense planning and organization.

There are some inherent dangers in adaptations. We have seen schools that take just one portion of a balanced literacy program and assume that the component actually represents the entire balanced literacy approach. For example, a school may focus on guided reading and other book study groups, but ignore a daily period of direct instruction and practice in word recognition and spelling strategies. Care has to be taken in adaptations to include a full range of teaching-learning components.

The most frequent adaptation, however, tends to be a "balanced-literacy-in-my-classroom-but-not-necessarily-in-your-classroom" approach. In this case, individual teachers create a micro-climate of balanced literacy programming in their classrooms. While the honest attempt to meet the needs of all literacy learners and the spirit of educational adventure are to be admired, the creation of pockets of balanced literacy programming defeats the overall purpose of providing a continuous Language Arts experience for elementary school students. However, if colleagues are not pursuing balanced literacy goals, a teacher might argue that he or she can at least provide a balanced literacy micro-climate for one year in a child's education. In this situation, literacy leadership needs to be offered by district and school administrators to encourage teachers to develop schoolwide, continuous Language Arts programming.

After careful exploration of all the available options, the "adopt or adapt" decision can be made. However, adoption or adaptations can only be fully implemented in schools when programming decisions are accompanied by a long-term professional development program for teachers. As Lyons and Pinnell note in *Guiding Readers and Writers, Grades 3–6* (p. 238):

Educational change, particularly as it pertains to developing students' critical literacy skills, cannot be halfway or halfhearted. We need comprehensive efforts; we need long-term support provided through specific, clear, understandable professional development.

Bibliography

Professional References

Brailsford, Anne. *Balanced Literacy: Division 1*. Edmonton, AB: Edmonton Public Schools Learning Resources, 2002.

Brailsford, Anne. *Balanced Literacy: Division 2*. Edmonton, AB: Edmonton Public Schools Learning Resources, 2003.

Cunningham, Patricia M., Hall, Dorothy P. and Sigmon, Cheryl M. *The Teacher's Guide to the Four Blocks*. Greensboro, NC: Carson-Dellosa, 1999.

Cunningham, Patricia M. and Hall, Dorothy P. *Month-by-Month Phonics for Upper Grades*. Greensboro, NC: Carson Dellosa, 1998.

Cunningham, Patricia M. and Hall, Dorothy P. *Making Words*. Torrance, CA: Good Apple, 1994a.

Cunningham, Patricia M. and Hall, Dorothy P. *Making Big Words*. Torrance, CA: Good Apple, 1994b.

Daniels, H. *Literature Circles: Voice and Choice in Book Clubs and Reading Groups*. Markham, ON: Pembroke, 2002.

Fitzpatrick, Jo. *Phonemic Awareness*. Cypress, CA: Creative Teaching Press, 1997.

Fountas, Irene C. and Pinnell, Gay Su. *Guiding Readers and Writers Grades 3-6*. Portsmouth, NH: Heinemann, 2001.

Fountas, Irene C. and Pinnell, Gay Su. *Guided Reading: Good First Teaching for All Children*. Portsmouth, NH: Heinemann, 1996.

Hall, Dorothy P. and Cunningham, Patricia M. *Month-By-Month Reading and Writing for Kindergarten*. Greensboro, NC: Carson-Dellosa, 1997.

Lyons, Carol, A. & Pinnell, Gay Su. *Systems for Change in Literacy Education*. Portsmouth, NH: Heinemann,1997.

McMahon, Susan I. and Raphael, Taffy E., eds. *The Book Club Connection: Literacy Learning and Classroom Talk*. Newark, DE: International Reading Association and New York: Teachers College Press, 1997.

Northern Alberta Reading Specialists' Council. *Paired Reading: Positive Reading Practice*. (Manual by Anne Brailsford, and accompanying training videotape.) Distributed in Kelowna, BC: Filmwest, 1991.

Topping, Keith. "Peer Tutoring and Paired Reading: Combining two powerful techniques." *The Reading Teacher*. 42 (7), 1989, 488-494.

Children's Books

Harlow, Joan H. *Star in the Storm*. New York: Aladdin, 2001.

Kitching, Katie. *Sounds Like This*. Twickenham, UK: Belair, 1993.

Lottridge, Celia B. *Ticket to Curlew*. Toronto: Groundwood/Douglas & McIntyre, 1992.

Co-ordinating a Professional Development Program for Teachers

The inservices planned in the "raising awareness" phase are only the beginning of the professional development journey. Implementation of school-wide balanced literacy programming will succeed only if long-term professional development is built into the plan. Initial inservices stimulate interest and motivation, but it is the long-term professional development plan that supports teachers as they learn to implement a complex literacy program.

A Long-term Balanced Literacy Professional Development Program

A balanced literacy professional development program should have the following characteristics:

- a minimum of two years' duration with opportunities for continuous contact through consultation or "updater" inservices beyond the two-year program

- inservices that include information on children's literacy development, the essential characteristics of a balanced literacy program, teaching techniques and strategies, classroom organization, and the selection of materials

- regular classroom demonstrations of teaching components, strategies, and techniques by balanced literacy consultants

- provision for coaching, where the balanced literacy consultant can teach alongside the teacher, then gradually move aside and give supportive feedback as the teacher tries the new techniques independently

- flexibility in the plan, so that the consultant can give more support to teachers who need it

- time for the balanced literacy consultant to discuss school-specific needs with the staff, which may include some initiation of topics by the consultant, but should largely be the teachers' forum for discussing topics they wish to raise

- opportunities for classroom visits within or across schools

- time for teachers to share ideas within the school and with teachers in other schools.

Professional Development, Year by Year

In the Balanced Literacy Program in Edmonton area schools (Brailsford, 2002, 2003), a new school joining the balanced literacy project would experience something similar to the professional development process shown in the following chart.

Summary Chart of a Five-Year Professional Development Plan

Introductory Year	Year One	Year Two	Year Three	Year Four
All Staff • raising awareness	**Kindergarten** • 6 inservices • 3 demonstration/ coaching sessions (minimum)	**Kindergarten** • 4 inservices • 3 demonstration/ coaching sessions (minimum)	**Kindergarten** • continuous contact by request • invitations to attend Years One/Two inservices to review techniques • invitations to attend updater inservices to learn about new techniques and materials	
Primary • initial 1 day inservice (end of the year)	**Primary** (Grades 1-3) • 1-1/2 days' initial inservices • 9 inservices • 9 demonstration/ coaching sessions	**Primary** • 7 inservices • 6 demonstration/ coaching sessions	**Primary** • continuous contact by request • invitations to attend any Year One or Year Two inservices to review techniques • invitations to attend updater inservices	
	Upper Elementary • initial 1 day inservice (end of the year)	**Upper Elementary** (Grades 4-6) • initial 1-1/2 days • 9 inservices • 9 demonstration/ coaching sessions	**Upper Elementary** • 7 inservices • 6 demonstration/ coaching sessions	**Upper Elementary** • continuous contact by request • invitations to attend refresher and updater inservices

Introductory Year

- The staff attends an information meeting to raise awareness.

- The staff explores balanced literacy and decides whether to enroll in the project. They may visit other schools where balanced literacy is in operation, read resources, invite a balanced literacy consultant to the school to answer queries and provide further information, and possibly view videotaped highlights of program components.

- If the decision is positive, the staff then asks for support from a balanced literacy consultant and begins making preparations.

- A school professional development library is started, using lists of resources provided by the balanced literacy consultant.

- The school orders the core print materials needed for the classroom, as well as some of the support materials, such as student dictionaries, student and teacher alphabet letters and kits for the Making Words lessons, and wall charts of text structure organizers for writing (Learning Resources, Edmonton Public Schools, 2001).

- In June, teachers of grades one to three are released from the classroom to attend a professional development day about the Balanced Literacy Program. (Substitute teachers will be needed in their classrooms.) This gives them a comprehensive overview of the Balanced Literacy Program. Usually the primary teachers start the program in the first year, and the upper elementary teachers begin their program in the second year; this is a sequence that enables school budget decision-makers to focus on providing materials for grades one to three in the first year, and for the upper elementary grades in the next year.

- Teachers read some professional development resources over the summer.

Year One

- Kindergarten inservices and the demonstration-coaching component start. The kindergarten teachers attend six inservices and participate in a minimum of three demonstration-coaching lessons during the year. The schedule is flexible and additional classroom visits can be arranged if the teacher would like more information or support.

- Primary teachers attend a further one-and-a-half days of inservices, which provide an overview of the three large teaching-learning components: the word study period, the reading workshop, and the writing block.

- Once school begins, balanced literacy consultants commence monthly school visits and start demonstration lessons in the primary classrooms. Extra visits can be scheduled if a teacher requests more demonstrations. Demonstration lessons continue throughout the year, but gradually give way to coaching and feedback sessions as the teachers learn the new techniques.

- When the consultant visits the school to demonstrate techniques in the classrooms, a lunchtime meeting is also held. This meeting provides time for teachers of kindergarten through grade three to discuss their needs.

- Following the initial inservice sessions, primary teachers attend nine other monthly inservices. Each inservice group comprises several school staffs, to provide opportunities for the exchange of ideas. Ideally, inservice locations are rotated around participating schools, to give all teachers the chance to visit new classrooms and talk about materials and classroom organization with other teachers.

- Towards the conclusion of Year One, the upper elementary teachers attend their initial inservice day, and are provided with resource materials to read over the summer.

Year Two

- The kindergarten teachers attend four inservices. The balanced literacy consultant provides a minimum of three demonstration and teaching lessons, and more if requested by a teacher. Kindergarten teachers receive a participation-completion certificate at the end of their second year of professional development.

- The primary teachers' inservices, demonstration lessons, coaching sessions, and meetings with their balanced literacy consultant continue. The number of inservices is reduced from nine to seven, with inservices spread over the year. As teachers develop more confidence with the new program, they move from support to independence in implementation. They receive a participation-completion certificate at the conclusion of the second year of professional development.

- The upper elementary teachers complete their initial inservices (one-and-a-half days) at the beginning of the school year. They then engage in nine monthly inservices over the course of the year. They receive classroom demonstration lessons and coaching, following the same professional development pattern as their colleagues from the primary grades. They join the lunchtime meetings when the balanced literacy coach visits the school.

Year Three

- Kindergarten and primary grade teachers are encouraged to attend any of the inservices for new teachers entering the program, if they feel the need for "refreshers" in any area. They may also request consultant time if they need support or have new enquiries. Quite frequently, these more experienced balanced literacy teachers may be asked to share their experiences with new teachers at inservices, or to welcome them as visitors in their classrooms.

- Because a balanced literacy program is always evolving and new materials, techniques, and strategies may have emerged since the kindergarten and primary teachers completed their two years of

professional development, one or two "updater" inservices are offered by the consultants.

- Upper elementary teachers complete their second year of seven inservices, six demonstration lessons, and coaching sessions. They receive a participation-completion certificate at the conclusion of their second year of professional development.

Year Four

- All of the "initial enrollment" kindergarten, primary, and upper elementary teachers have now completed their respective professional development courses. They are welcome to attend new teachers' inservices for topic-specific "refreshers," and are also invited to "updater" inservices. They continue to serve as mentors for new teachers in their own school and other schools, and may continue to access consultant time if they wish.

- Teachers may continue the lunchtime meetings at their schools. Sometimes they meet in primary and upper elementary groups, and at other times they have whole-staff discussions. These meetings can be used to continue to share ideas, to order new materials, and to problem-solve when new issues emerge. A balanced literacy consultant may occasionally be asked to join a meeting.

Content in the Professional Development Plan

Although the content of inservices will vary, there are five elements that should be part of all sessions.

> ### Common Elements for Inservices
> 1. Links
> 2. Review
> 3. Strategy development
> 4. Teacher sharing
> 5. Goal setting

Links

In the Links section, the consultant introduces brief items that help participants to connect one aspect of their program to another, or one classroom with another. For example, a typical topic in a Links section would be the introduction of one or two new children's books that provide good introductions to various text structures for writing. Another topic might be a short presentation by a teacher who has discovered, for example, a new way of practising Word Wall words, or a way of linking a shared reading lesson with interactive writing.

Review

This section of the inservice provides a review of an approach or strategy used at a previous inservice. For example, once prompts in guided reading groups have been introduced, they will be reviewed frequently, using overheads that display examples of readers' miscues and discussions of prompting options.

Strategy Development

Strategy development focuses on enhancing teaching across all components of the program. It may include a demonstration of a technique, an explanation of the underlying relationship to children's literacy development, and finally, suggestions for possible applications in the classroom. For example, if the strategy development portion of the inservice addresses the use of prompts in guided reading lessons, the consultant may show a videotape that demonstrates the use of prompts with emergent, early, and more fluent readers. The video will be analyzed and discussed, and the consultant will explain the role of prompting in assisting children to problem-solve when reading. Teachers will then practise using the prompts by looking at examples of readers' miscues. Application will start in the whole inservice group, with support from the consultant, and then progress to small group practice with the consultant moving from group to group as a facilitator. A goal will likely be set for the teachers to use prompts in guided reading groups over the next month, with the consultant providing in-class demonstrations.

Teacher Sharing

Although aspects of teacher sharing may be built into the Links section of the inservice, small group interactions are also important, allowing more teachers to share ideas. Sharing time in inservices is usually linked to goals set the previous month. For example, if increasing accountability in independent reading stations is one month's inservice goal for primary teachers, the following month's sharing session will allow teachers to discuss how they have fared. Small groups will report back to the whole group. A final summary of ideas will be provided by the consultant.

Goal Setting

Goal setting is always reviewed before the inservice concludes. Each month teachers are asked to focus on one or two aspects of their Language Arts program, such as using prompts in guided reading, trying a literature link with a text structure organizer for persuasive writing, "sharing the pen" with students during interactive writing, or enriching the transfer of word patterns into reading and spelling in a Making Words lesson.

Congruence Between Inservice and Teaching-Demonstration

The content of the professional development plan needs to be carefully outlined by the inservice provider and there must be congruence between the inservice component and the teaching-demonstration lessons. This type of cohesion can be established in two ways. First, the content of the inservices needs to be related to the content of the practical teaching component. For example, if the word study area is being covered in the inservices, that area should receive prominence in the demonstration and coaching model. Although it is not possible to keep inservice topics and demonstration lessons entirely parallel, it is vital that key topics be covered in inservices before being demonstrated in classrooms. Secondly, congruence will be enhanced if the balanced literacy consultant who provides the inservices is also offering the demonstration and coaching lessons in the classroom. Thus, teachers hear about the strategies and observe them being used by the inservice provider in their own classrooms.

Inservice Topics

Inservice topics for kindergarten, primary, and upper elementary groups are listed in the following section. The topics reflect the strategy development and some review portions of the inservice, keeping in mind that links and teacher-sharing sections need to be added each month. The teacher-sharing and goal-setting segments should be flexible and structured to fit teachers' needs. Suggested teacher goals are provided on the charts, although these should be modified to meet the needs of individual teachers during the classroom coaching sessions.

On the inservice topic charts, we have also suggested demonstration and coaching sessions for each month. During demonstration lessons, the balanced literacy consultant offers a practical illustration of a component or strategy in each teacher's classroom. During most visits, time should also be built in for coaching, as the teacher demonstrates a particular lesson for the consultant.

Kindergarten Inservice Topic Chart: Year One		
Strategy Development (six inservices)	**Teacher Goal**	**Demonstration and Coaching (minimum three sessions)**
September Developmental Continuum for Language, Reading & Writing Learning	Observe a child's oral language; engage in supportive clarifying and extending conversations	
October Kindergarten Balanced Literacy Program • essential characteristics • teaching-learning components	Continue with clarifying and extending conversations; map out a timetable to include teaching-learning components	

Strategy Development (six inservices)	Teacher Goal	Demonstration and Coaching (minimum three sessions)
November Building a Literacy Context in the Kindergarten • maximizing time • changing "show and tell" to a literacy event • weaving literacy into centres	Modify centres to encourage literacy events to occur: e.g. place books, flyers, paper and writing tools in the playhouse Try a "show and tell" session as a literacy event, e.g. bringing objects that start with **b** (3-4 children: vary letters for other children's turns)	Demonstrate a "show and tell" session as a literacy event Optional consultation on weaving literacy events into centres
January Read Aloud and Shared Reading Components • purposes • strategies • roles in developmental literacy learning continuum	Include enhanced strategies in read aloud and shared reading	Demonstrate whole class shared reading with enhanced strategies Coach: "show and tell" as a literacy event Consult: maximizing literacy time in centres; teacher's timetable
February Phonemic Awareness, Letter-Sound Relationships and Words • use of rhymes and chants • work on word/letter and sound concepts: for example, use the first letter in children's names to identify letter-sound relationships • use of Word Wall for high-frequency words	Include daily phonemic awareness activities Start Word Wall Use letter-sound relationships in shared reading, "show and tell" activities, and writing	Demonstrate a phonemic awareness, a Word Wall, and a letter-sound activity Coach shared reading with strategies
March Writing • write aloud • shared/interactive • personal	Try a write-aloud journal entry Try sessions of shared/interactive writing	Demonstrate shared/interactive writing Coach a phonemic, letter-sound, or word activity

Kindergarten Inservice Topic Chart: Year Two		
Strategy Development (four inservices)	**Teacher Goal**	**Demonstration and Coaching (minimum three sessions)**
September Literacy Assessment for Emergent Readers and Writers Review of Phonemic Awareness, Letter-Sound Awareness and Words: e.g. use the Getting to Know You activity (Hall & Cunningham, 1997)	Try assessment tools Try the Getting to Know You activity	Demonstrate an assessment tool, e.g. letter recognition or book handling checklists Coach shared/interactive writing
November Literacy Development in Small Groups • shared reading • guided reading • writing • progression from whole class lesson to small group sessions to meet the needs of students at different stages on the literacy learning continuum	Try movement from large to small group in shared reading: e.g. move from a whole class shared reading lesson to a small group lesson with little books	Demonstrate the movement from large to small group in shared reading Demonstrate the use of an assessment tool in the small group shared reading session: e.g. observing two key print-tracking concepts for each group member
January Guided Reading Groups • book levels • matching books and readers • essential parts of a guided reading lesson • sample plan for a Level A book • video of a lesson	Integrate assessment tools into small group shared reading Try guided reading with children ready to move on from shared reading	Demonstrate a guided reading lesson Coach small group shared reading where an assessment tool is being used
March Guided Reading Groups • small group planning of a guided reading lesson • use of prompts for emergent and early readers Celebrate completion of two years of professional development; discuss continuance of professional journey	Engage in guided reading groups with children ready to move on from shared reading Use prompts to guide readers with problem solving	Demonstrate guided reading with prompts Coach guided reading

A Sample Year One Inservice on Writing for Kindergarten Teachers

The following is a sample plan for a two-hour inservice on writing held at Bonaventure School in March of the first year. It shows how inservice components provide the basic backbone for each session, despite varied content.

Links

1. The balanced literacy consultant begins by making some book recommendations.

   • *While You Were Sleeping* by John Butler (Scholastic, 1996) is a counting book showing creatures from around the world.

   • *Bunny's Noisy Book* by Margaret Wise Brown (Scholastic, 2000) and *From Head to Toe* by Eric Carle (HarperCollins, 1997) are books that encourage interactions such as joining in with the actions or sounds.

   • *Boomer's Big Surprise* by Constance McGeorge (Scholastic, 1999) is a book that can be used to encourage children to make predictions about story content, and to help them link story events to personal experiences.

   • *Phonemic Awareness* by Jo Fitzpatrick (Creative Teaching Press, 1997) is a professional book recommended for the school collection. It is useful for quick phonemic awareness activities. Concentrate on the Rhythm and Rhyme and Parts of a Word (sound sequencing; onsets and rimes) activities first.

2. Margaret from Bonaventure School will explain how she has integrated literacy events into her Blocks centre, and will invite the group to visit her classroom after the inservice.

3. An announcement: Woodlands School is hosting a book fair, featuring materials which support balanced literacy instruction, from 3 to 6 p.m. on April 23.

Review

1. The balanced literacy consultant reviews what the participating teachers have learned so far about children's writing development and teaching writing.

   - Writing develops along a continuum when appropriate experiences are provided.

   - Appropriate experiences for kindergarten children include:
     – meeting the needs of all children; for example, a write aloud by the teacher should include "talk" that covers early directionality concepts such as where to start writing as well as more advanced concepts such as how to use the Word Wall as a resource for words
     – opportunities to move from support to independence.

   - Demonstrations provide mediated experiences to children whose learning occurs within a social context. They need to see experienced writers modelling the process.

2. The consultant then shows a selection of children's writing samples that provide evidence of growth as a consequence of demonstrations.

Strategy Development

1. The balanced literacy consultant provides a handout on writing demonstrations.

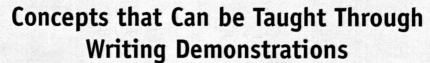

Concepts that Can be Taught Through Writing Demonstrations

Print Directionality: where to start writing; left to right progression; line movement

Print Conventions: letter formations; capital and small letters; periods; commas; "speech marks" for dialogue

Terms and Concepts: letter; word; sound; first letter, last letter; first word, last word; top of the page, first line, bottom of the page, last line

Cues for Spelling: Word Wall words; charts and labels in the room; first letter sound, last letter sound; saying a word aloud (and slowly) and listening to the sounds

Syntax: word order is important; ideas have to make sense; we can reread to see if it makes sense and sounds right; written language is different from speech

Content: can be true or imaginary; has to make sense to a reader; can be a mixture of pictures and print

Tips for Teachers

- Keep the lesson short and well paced.
- Read aloud the journal entry with the children afterwards.
- Use markers with intense colours and ensure that printing is large enough for all to see.

2. The consultant demonstrates a write-aloud journal entry on chart paper. The demonstration should include "talk" that features a variety of developmental concepts. The write-aloud technique provides total support in writing, as the teacher generates ideas, writes, and talks aloud about thought processes.

Shared/Interactive Reading

- Select a shared experience that enables all children to contribute.
- Keep the lesson short and well paced.
- Use unlined chart paper, because children's fine motor control is highly variable.
- Use large-tip, chunky markers. These enable the children to see the print clearly, and help them to handle the fine motor aspects of writing when it's time to share the pen.
- Reread the piece of writing several times on this and subsequent days.
- Hang it on a chart rack so that the children can reread it during centre time.

3. The consultant then demonstrates shared/interactive writing. In this approach, the "talk" about developmental concepts continues, but the children will be invited to share ideas and to contribute by adding letters and words.

Teacher Sharing

Teacher sharing covers a previously inserviced and demonstrated topic.

1. The balanced literacy consultant divides the teachers into small groups and provides a guiding question to focus teacher sharing: *What phonemic awareness, letter-sound relationships, and Word Wall (high-frequency) words activities are now included in your program?* The teachers then write the activities that group members have used on a large wall chart.

Phonemic Awareness	Letter-Sound	Word Wall
• Turtle Talk • clapping syllables	• initial letters-sounds in masked words during shared reading	• children's names

2. After the discussion concludes, each small group shares one activity from each area with the whole group, using their wall charts to point out examples.

Goal Setting

The balanced literacy consultant concludes the inservice by describing the teacher goals appropriate for the upcoming month.

1. Do a write-aloud journal entry demonstration in the classroom.
2. Do shared/interactive writing demonstrations in class.
3. Read sections one and two of *Interactive Writing: How Language and Literacy Come Together, K-2* by Andrea McCarrier, Gay Su Pinnell and Irene Fountas, (Heineman, 2000).

Inservices for Primary Grades

The following pages outline an inservice plan for teachers of grades one to three.

Initial Inservice Topics Grades 1-3

This chart shows what is covered in the two-and-a-half days of initial inservices, comprising active demonstrations by the consultants, videotape footage, hands-on teacher practice, and teacher sharing.

Day One (June, at the end of the "raising awareness" year)
Morning: Overview of the Program • Rationale and theoretical underpinnings for a balanced literacy program • Teaching-learning components that form the program • Overview of materials for professional development and classroom use • Putting the program in the timetable on a daily basis *Afternoon: Word Block* • High-frequency words for word recognition and spelling (purposes and rationale): — use of a Word Wall — core words for each grade — daily practice activities (demonstrations) — use of personal dictionaries — weekly spelling quiz — home practice activities • Phonemic awareness, word analysis, and spelling strategies (purposes and rationale): — demonstration of Making Words lessons (Cunningham and Hall, 1994a) — equipment — spelling and word recognition by analogy (the Sort and Transfer stage of Making Words)

| **Day Two** |
| (In August-September of the first year of enrollment in the project) |

Review of Word Study
Review of Word Wall, Making Words, and Sort and Transfer activities, emphasizing the strategies and concepts that can be taught and providing hands-on practice for the teachers

Reading
- The role of demonstrations and the movement from supported to independent literacy learning in each component
- Review of the components (purposes and rationale)
  — read aloud (integration with content areas; the use of multiple genres; concept teaching and modelling; and the program links between read alouds and writing)
  — shared reading (integration with content areas; use of many genres; and the use of strategic teaching)
  — guided/independent reading (running the two components simultaneously; the use of independent reading stations; selecting stations that emphasize reading practice; the use of levelled materials; options for grouping students; and an overview of a guided reading lesson)

| **Day Three** |
| (Half a day in August-September of the first year of enrollment in the project) |

Writing
- The writing process (stages, purposes, and rationale)
- The role of writing demonstrations in the program
- The movement from support to independence with teacher modelling (write alouds); teacher and children interacting to produce text (shared and interactive writing); and children writing with guidance and independence
- Literature and information text links with writing
- The developmental use of text structure organizers for planning
- Using text structure organizers for Story Analysis and Descriptive Paragraphs to illustrate stages in the writing process

Primary Inservice Topic Chart: Year One

Strategy Development (nine inservices)	Teacher Goal	Demonstration and Coaching (minimum nine sessions)
September Getting Started in Balanced Literacy (panel of experienced teachers describe the "getting started" process) or Substitute a Classroom Organization Videotape (See list of classroom organization videotape titles on pages 125–127.) Making Words Lesson including Sort and Transfer (review from initial training) Writing • descriptive paragraph and story analysis (review from initial training)	Start Word Wall (High-frequency words) Start Making Words: Grade one: one-vowel words (Cunningham & Hall, 1997) or use the Special Child activity first (Cunningham & Hall, 1997) Grades 2 & 3: Making Words lessons (Cunningham & Hall, 1994) Grades 1-3: Start using the descriptive paragraph and story analysis text structure organizers for analysis of books from read alouds Grades 2 & 3 start using the organizers for writing	Demonstrate Word Wall practice activities and a Making Words lesson
October Read Aloud and Shared Reading • strategies to match developmental needs • use of fiction and nonfiction materials • oral retellings Writing • review of write alouds • shared/interactive writing and mini-lessons, using personal experience retellings for examples • demonstration of a journal entry (write aloud), a literature response (interactive writing), and a mini-lesson	Implement a full range of daily practice activities for Word Wall words Grade ones move to Making Words with one-vowel words (Cunningham & Hall, 1997) if they engaged in the Special Child activity in September Use a range of strategies in shared reading Link read aloud to writing text structures and organizers Use journals for retelling	Coach a Word Wall activity and a Making Words lesson Demonstrate Sort and Transfer plus, briefly, interactive writing (journal entry)

Strategy Development (nine inservices)	Teacher Goal	Demonstration and Coaching (minimum nine sessions)
November Independent Reading Stations • emphasis on reading • selection of stations • use of multilevel materials • establishing routines Sequence Writing • using personal experience with a literature link	Start reading stations with careful teacher supervision Use text structure organizer for sequence writing	Demonstrate shared reading using a full range of strategies Coach a Sort and Transfer lesson Consult on independent reading stations
December Guided Reading • use of levelled books • analysis of supports and challenges in texts • lesson planning	Start guided reading (one group a day, initially) Use a selection of text structure organizers in writing: e.g. descriptive paragraph, story analysis, and sequence	Demonstrate a guided reading group Coach a shared reading lesson
January Guided Reading • use of prompts Writing • persuasive writing with a literature link	Move to two guided reading groups each day Add persuasive writing to text structures in writing lessons	Demonstrate guided reading with an emphasis on prompts Coach a guided reading lesson
February Levelling Independent Reading Materials • underlying rationale • explanation of criteria and techniques • hands-on small group work in levelling books brought by the participants	Level books in classroom for the independent reading tubs Continue using a variety of text structures in writing	Demonstrate writing with a literature link to text; use of the text structure organizer; and consult on how to complete the class account Coach a guided reading lesson

Strategy Development (nine inservices)	Teacher Goal	Demonstration and Coaching (minimum nine sessions)
March • review the writing process from demonstrations through to a class story and individual writing • an experienced balanced literacy teacher provides examples from her/his classroom to highlight the process • consultant demonstrates the process, using traditional fiction writing as an example	Teachers now use retelling, descriptive paragraph, story analysis, sequence, persuasive, and traditional fiction writing in the classroom	Demonstrate the revising and editing stages of writing Coach on prompts in the guided reading lesson
April Assessment in Balanced Literacy • theoretical underpinnings • assess-on-the-go during reading time (i.e. use assessment strategies that inform instruction and that can be completed during instructional time) • whole and small group work on analysis of book levels and readers' strategies	Use assess-on-the-go reading techniques	Demonstrate an assessment strategy Coach a writing lesson that uses a text structure planner Consult on levelled books record
May Assessment in Balanced Literacy • writing rubrics • strategies Whole and Small Group Work • analysis of student writing samples Writing • friendly letter	Use a writing rubric to assess an assignment Add friendly letter writing	Optional demonstration: teacher's request Coach the revising and editing stages in writing

Primary Inservice Topic Chart: Year Two

Strategy Development (seven inservices)	Teacher Goal	Demonstration and Coaching (minimum six sessions)
September Comprehension Strategies • weaving them into guided reading groups lessons • using in literature response activities	Use a comprehension strategy in a guided reading group Use the comprehension strategy in a literature response activity following guided or independent reading Create a book recommendation bulletin board where children can write quick reviews for each other	Demonstrate a guided reading lesson using a comprehension strategy: e.g. Retelling, Relating and Reflecting (Schwartz & Bone, 1995) Coach/consult on reading stations (content and student accountability)
October Guided Reading with Longer Texts • fiction and nonfiction chapter books • chunking into readable units • linking across chapters • use of prediction and anticipation guides • use of comprehension strategies • use of literature response activities Poetry Writing • demonstration of structural poems: e.g. diamond, haiku, and repeated pattern poems	Use a longer text with at least one guided reading group and try the strategies demonstrated in the inservice Use a structure to engage class in poetry writing	Demonstrate starting a longer text study with prediction or anticipation guides Coach comprehension strategies in a guided reading group

November
Report Writing
• grade one report types (e.g. a visual report such as a concertina booklet)
• more advanced reports
  - research
  - planning
  - doing a class report with group work (building a report from a series of related descriptive paragraphs)
  - linking ideas across paragraphs
  - introduction and conclusion
  - progressing from class to individual reports
	Work on reports in the classroom	Demonstrate one aspect of the report writing process: planning a class report, taking notes on the descriptive paragraph organizer, or converting notes into a paragraph or into writing links between paragraphs
		
		Coach: work alongside the teacher as the students write: e.g. help run a writing support group for children with similar needs

Strategy Development (seven inservices)	Teacher Goal	Demonstration and Coaching (minimum six sessions)
January Refining Guided Reading by Revisiting • prompts • integration of comprehension strategies Report Writing • teacher presentation on report writing • teachers provide samples of report writing stages	Use emergent, early, and fluent reader prompts and comprehension strategies in guided reading groups	Optional: teacher's choice of a demonstration lesson. Teacher chooses an area where he/she needs more support. Coach: review Word Wall, Making Words lesson, or Sort and Transfer
March Variety in Word Study • use of new practice activities for high-frequency words • transfer of patterns to new words Writing • comparison writing	Use new word activities in the classroom Add comparison writing to the students' repertoire of text structures	Demonstrate 2-3 new word activities Coach the area the teacher selected for additional support last month
April Assessment Revisited • teacher presentation of the tracking and monitoring devices used to assess one child's progress • group work on analysis of a child's literacy progress over a year Assessment-Instruction Link • planning instruction from assessment procedures Writing • cause and effect	Share assessment monitoring devices with other primary teachers at the school. Plan for continuity: What information do we need to share with next year's teacher to ensure continuity of instruction and learning? Introduce cause-and-effect writing to grade three students. Provide examples for grades one and two students, such as using examples in the read-aloud session and analyzing ideas on the cause-and-effect organizer.	Demonstrate a writing mini-lesson for comparison or cause-and-effect writing Coach: 2-3 new word activities

Strategy Development (seven inservices)	Teacher Goal	Demonstration and Coaching (minimum six sessions)

May
Celebration and Sharing
• reflecting on the professional development journey
• sharing strategies, student work samples, and experiences
• planning the next stage:
  - school-based sharing groups
  - across-school visits
  - expanding the professional development library
  - building regular professional development activities into staff meetings
	Plan for continuity in staff professional development	Consult on teacher's continuing professional development plan

A Sample Year One Inservice for Primary Teachers

The following is a sample plan for a two-hour inservice on guided reading held at Arrowhead School in December of the first year. It shows how inservice components provide the basic backbone for each session, despite varied content.

Links

1. The balanced literacy consultant begins by recommending some literature links for writing.

    - Story analysis, using books about journeys:
      — *Penguin Small* by Mick Inkpen (Hodder, 1992)
      — *Harvey Slumfenburger's Christmas Present* by John Burningham
        (Candlewick Press, 1993)
      — *Stickeen* by John Muir retold by Donnell Rubay (Dawn Publications, 1998)
        These books could be used to stimulate story writing about a journey.

    - Story analysis, using a winter story about animals decorating a tree to add colour to the forest:
      — *The Snow Tree* by Caroline Repchuk (Templar, 1996)
        This repeated action story could provide a model for the students' own writing.

- Descriptive paragraph for nonfiction:
  — *Exploring Space*, *A Tree for All Seasons*, and *Insects* (National Geographic Big Books)
  These big books could be used as literature links when creating a whole class descriptive paragraph.

2. Joe, a grade two teacher from Wheatcroft Elementary School, explains his method for increasing on-task reading in independent stations. He adds a sharing time at the end of some independent reading sessions, where a selection of students talk about their reading activities.

3. Anne (a balanced literacy consultant) and Adrienne and Mary Lou (grade one teachers) show writing samples to illustrate how some grade ones spontaneously transferred the sequence writing organizer to their personal journal writing.

4. A reminder: this month's classroom demonstrations are about guided reading. Let your balanced literacy consultant know the title of the book you wish to be used in the demonstration. Coaching will feature a shared reading lesson with the types of strategies you saw demonstrated last month.

5. An announcement: start to gather independent reading books together after Christmas, ready for the February inservice on book levelling. These should be books with titles that are not already levelled in Matching Books to Readers (1999).

Review

The balanced literacy consultant reviews some topics in guided reading.
- Two methods of organizing guided reading:
  — placing all the children in groups that have similar reading needs, and preserving the same groups for the independent reading stations
  — placing children in mixed level groups for the reading stations, and drawing out a group of children with similar needs for guided reading.

- Reasons for grouping children with similar needs for guided reading:
  — need to match readers with instructional level texts to ensure progress
  — can teach strategies more effectively when children have similar reading needs
  — can track reading behaviours (such as print directionality concepts or rereading to self-monitor) more effectively if children's needs are relatively homogeneous.

Strategy Development

1. The balanced literacy consultant demonstrates how teachers can rapidly monitor book level progress for each child over the course of the year, using a levelled book chart (Brailsford, 2002) for all of the core books.

2. The balanced literacy consultant shares a guided reading lesson plan with the group. *Will You Play With Us?* (Bookshop: Level D fiction text) is used to demonstrate an analysis of "supports and challenges" the readers will experience when reading the book. The consultant models analyzing the text for "supports and challenges" and talks aloud while filling in the lesson plan.

Supports	Challenges
• repeated language pattern	• word recognition, e.g. climb
• picture support	• change of pattern on last page
• matches children's experiences	• question mark

3. Teachers analyze books for "supports and challenges." Teachers bring one fiction and one nonfiction text from the core materials (for example, *The Old Woman Who Lived in a Vinegar Bottle*, Level L fiction; *I Eat Leaves*, Level C nonfiction) and analyze these in small groups. They fill in their books' "supports and challenges" on lesson plan overheads and then discuss their findings with the large group.

4. Using *Will You Play With Us?* the consultant demonstrates how to convert the "supports and challenges" into a brief, focused book introduction.

Tips for Teachers

- Group placement is flexible and will change frequently as children move along the literacy continuum.

- Children who are less advanced as readers will need more guided reading sessions than the most advanced group.

5. The consultant completes the lesson plan, talking about each step to model the process for teachers. The following points are emphasized:

- Provide support to the readers, but avoid solving all problems before asking children to read, since reading involves personal problem-solving.
- Provide a purpose question before reading, which focuses children's thinking as they read.
- Maximize children's actual reading time.
- Hear children read and observe reading behaviours (one or two a lesson).
- Observe, specifically, for child's use of an effective reading strategy, which can be discussed during concluding section of the lesson.
- Provide a simple activity for "early finishers," such as rereading the book with a partner or answer the purpose question on a sticky note.
- Emphasize comprehension in the conclusion.

Here is a sample lesson plan to hand out to the teachers.

<table>
<tr><td colspan="2" align="center">GUIDED READING LESSON PLANNER — DIVISION ONE
(FOR NARRATIVE OR EXPOSITORY TEXT)
Date: December 7th   Grade: 1   Group: Chocolate
Text: Will You Play With Us?   Level: D</td></tr>
<tr><td colspan="2">Supports: Repeated language pattern, picture support, good match with children's experiences.
Challenges: Word recognition [e.g. climb/conjunctions on, up to], change of pattern on last page, question mark, story summary at higher level than text.</td></tr>
<tr><td colspan="2" align="center">Teacher Does</td></tr>
<tr>
<td valign="top">Introduction
· Predictions and building background knowledge
· Link to children's experience
· Point out supports and some challenges</td>
<td valign="top">• Show front cover: Read title together/discuss question mark.
• Open out back cover: Read 'blurb' to group
• Predictions: What games will they play? Where will they play?
Orally emphasize to, in by etc. in responses.
• Choral Read pp. 2-3 Purpose: Where will they play?
Point out repeated lanuage pattern, picture support e.g. for climb.
Discuss purpose question.</td>
</tr>
</table>

Children Reading
• Set comprehension purpose
• Set activity for early finishers
• Teacher listens to children read, and checks on strategies used and needs of readers
• Use prompts
	• Children read whole book independently.
	• Purpose:
	  What did they do that was the most fun?
	• Early finishers: Reread story with a buddy.
	• Teacher:
	  - hears two children read
	  - monitors for use of work recognition strategies
	  - uses prompts to help child problem solve.

Conclusion
• Check purpose question
• Check on comprehension
• Discuss successes
• Mention a "Good Reading" strategy
• Discuss challenges
	• Review purpose:
	  What did they do that was the most fun?
	  Share opinions.
	• Comprehension:
	  When did the dog have the most fun?
	  Why did the other kids keep joining them?
	• Discuss a good reader strategy.
	• Discuss challenges.

Follow-up Activities Focus on: What is your opinion? (Comprehension)	**Students Do** Make bookmark: on one side draw a picture of the play activity that they think was most fun for the children. On the other side draw what was most fun for the dog.

6. In grade-level groups, teachers write a lesson plan on one of the two texts they have brought to the inservice.

Teacher Sharing

In groups of five or six, teachers talk about the types of independent reading stations currently underway in their classrooms. They "showcase" activity samples, writing all of the activity ideas on a chart and displaying the chart for other teachers to examine. One idea per group is then shared verbally with all of the teachers, who are encouraged to ask questions and offer comments. The balanced literacy consultant supports the interactions, and responds to questions as needed.

Goal Setting

The balanced literacy consultant ends the inservice by explaining the goals that teachers could accomplish in the upcoming month.

1. Start one guided reading group a day. Write lesson plans to ensure that all key elements are included.
2. Bring two lesson plans, and the accompanying books, to next month's sharing time.
3. Revisit a selection of retelling, descriptive paragraphs, sequence writing, and story analysis in writing.

Inservices for Upper Elementary Grades

The following pages outline an inservice plan for teachers of grades four to six.

Initial Inservice Topics (Grades 4-6)

This chart shows what is covered in the two-and-a-half days of initial inservices, comprising active demonstrations by the consultants, videotape footage, hands-on teacher practice, and teacher sharing.

Day One
(June)

Morning: Overview of the Program
- Rationale and theoretical underpinnings for a balanced literacy program
- Teaching-learning components that form the program
- Overview of materials for professional development and classroom use
- Putting the program in the timetable on a daily basis

Afternoon: Word Study
- High-frequency words for word recognition and spelling (purposes and rationale)
  — use of a Tricky Word Wall
  — sources for core words
  — individual and buddy practice activities (demonstrations)
  — use of personal dictionaries
  — weekly spelling quiz
  — home practice activities

- Word analysis, vocabulary, and spelling strategies (purposes and rationale)
  — demonstration of Making Big Words lessons with the Sort and Transfer component (Cunningham and Hall, 1994 b)
  — demonstration of other approaches, such as teaching prefixes and suffixes using the Nifty Thrifty Fifty list (Cunningham and Hall, 1998); vocabulary using context clues; building words from roots; and spelling by analogy (accessing word patterns and meanings)

Day Two
(August-September)

Review of Word Study
- Review of Word Wall, Making Words, and Sort and Transfer activities, emphasizing the strategies and concepts that can be taught and providing hands-on practice for teachers

Reading Hour
- The role of demonstrations and the movement from supported to independent literacy learning in each component

- Review of the flexible components (purposes and rationale)
  — read aloud (use of an anchor book to tie together the themed, levelled book study work; the content from read-aloud books is often used for class strategy lessons; read alouds can also be used to highlight Social Studies and Science themes)
  — shared reading (use of co-operative reading strategies to enable a class to share content from one level of text; links to

other components, especially the class strategy lesson; use of many genres of materials)
— class strategy lesson (teaching reading strategies using content from read aloud and shared reading; applying strategies learned in the whole group to Instructional Level texts in the book study groups
— book study (use of themed, levelled fiction and nonfiction books for guided reading, literature circles, and book clubs; book study asks students to reflect on their reading through discussions and written literature response
— independent reading (use of self-selected books; individual reading or informal, self-selected book clubs)

- Planning a unit (overview and demonstration of a unit plan to illustrate the links across the components)

Day Three
(Half a day in August-September)

Writing
- The writing process (stages, purposes and rationale)
- The role of writing demonstrations in the program
- The movement from support to independence with teacher modelling (write alouds), teacher and children interacting to produce text (shared and interactive writing), and children writing with guidance and independence
- Literature and information text links with writing
- The developmental use of text structure organizers for planning
- Using text structure organizers for story analysis and descriptive paragraph to illustrate stages in the writing process

Upper Elementary Inservice Topic Chart: Year One

Strategy Development (nine inservices)	Teacher Goal	Demonstration and Coaching (minimum nine sessions)
September Getting Started in Balanced Literacy (panel of experienced, upper elementary balanced literacy teachers giving tips to new teachers in the program) *or* Substitute a panel of grade three teachers if this is the first year of the upper elementary project. (Primary grades will have started the previous year, and grade three teachers will have had a year's experience with the program). Review a Making Big Words Lesson Writing • review descriptive paragraph and story analysis writing (from the initial training sessions)	Start the word study periods with Making Big Words Try descriptive paragraph and story analysis writing Add book series (e.g. Literacy Place from Scholastic) to the school's levelled bookroom	Demonstrate a Making Big Words lesson

October
Word Study
• planning a balanced month
• review of other areas for study and other techniques, e.g.:
  - Sort and Transfer (from Making Big Words lesson)
  - word trees for expanding root words
  - use of prefixes and suffixes for word building, word analysis, and word meanings
  - using a Tricky Word Corner and personal dictionary for high-frequency words
• group work to create a word study monthly plan
 	
Writing
• persuasive writing is demonstrated with a literature link
	Plan a month's word study
	
	Implement a range of word study activities in the word study period each day
	
	Do persuasive writing using a text structure organizer
		Coach a Making Big Words lesson
		
		Demonstrate Sort and Transfer and another word activity

Strategy Development (nine inservices)	Teacher Goal	Demonstration and Coaching (minimum nine sessions)
November The Reading Hour • review of the components: read aloud, shared reading, class strategy lesson, book study (guided reading), and independent reading Core Comprehension Strategies • explanation and demonstration of strategies, e.g. 5Ws and HI (Brailsford and Coles, 2002) and QAR (Raphael, 1984) • use of strategies in the teaching-learning components Writing • sequence writing using personal experience (e.g. directions, recipes, and "how to do it" instructions) • sequence writing using a literature link: e.g. "Off the Wall" (Literacy Place Grade 6 magazine, *In the Spotlight*, which describes the steps in painting wall murals)	Start using the core comprehension strategies in class strategy lessons; use content from read-aloud books or magazines (if using Literacy Place) Do sequence writing in addition to other text structure organizers in writing	Demonstrate an introduction to sequence or persuasive writing using a text structure organizer Coach a Sort and Transfer lesson
December Planning a Unit • integration of teaching-learning components in a unit plan • use of core comprehension strategies in the plan • use of a unit planner • sample units for each grade level Writing • comparison writing with emphasis on making the transition from the class organizer to the first draft through interactive writing	Plan the first unit with a colleague or small group at school Co-ordinate the themed, levelled materials for the unit Do comparison writing in Language Arts or content areas	Coach a writing lesson that features the introduction of a text organizer Demonstrate interactive writing to convert a text structure plan into a first draft; add some revisions with the class

Strategy Development (nine inservices)	Teacher Goal	Demonstration and Coaching (minimum nine sessions)
January Shared Reading and the Class Strategy Lesson • co-operative reading techniques for shared reading (for example, choral reading) to enable all students to share content from a text • integrating the class strategy lesson with shared reading • topics for the class strategy lesson • samples of integrated lessons Writing • friendly letter (e.g. communicating with a younger buddy)	Start co-operative reading techniques when one level of text is used (in content areas in addition to Language Arts) Start shared reading and class strategy lessons Start friendly letter writing	Demonstrate a shared reading and a class strategy lesson using a core comprehension strategy Coach the word study period, e.g. contractions, word trees, prefixes and suffixes, or figurative language
February Book Study Groups: Guided Reading • links to read aloud, shared reading, and the class strategy lesson • use of themed, levelled materials • fiction and nonfiction materials • class organization for book study groups • essential components of a lesson • literature response activities Writing • newspaper articles	Start guided reading groups in the book study period Add newspaper article writing to the students' writing repertoire	Demonstrate an introduction to a book study using the class read-aloud and a KWL chart. Use the back and front covers of the read aloud (on overheads) to ask the class to make predictions and ask questions. Students then analyze the front and back covers of their levelled books in their book study groups Coach/teach alongside, working with the book study groups as they create KWL charts for their books
March Indepth Guided Reading • essential components (analysis of videotaped lessons) • lesson planning • the use of prompts to assist students in problem solving as they read • using checklists and a quick miscue analysis (Brailsford, 2003) to monitor reading strategies Writing • business letters	Add refinements to teaching guided reading, e.g. prompts Add business letter writing	Demonstrate a guided reading lesson with prompts and a core comprehension strategy Coach shared reading with a class strategy lesson on a core comprehension strategy

Strategy Development (nine inservices)	Teacher Goal	Demonstration and Coaching (minimum nine sessions)
April Levelling and Theming Supplementary Novels • use of novels in school storerooms • each school brings one novel from each set • explanation of process and the book level criteria • hands-on small group work on levelling the books - verification discussions - listing the books - moving among tables to cluster for themes (Booklists will be provided later that month, with the book titles, levels, possible theme, and school names. Inter-school loans and book trades are encouraged.)	Add levelled and themed supplementary novels to the school's levelled book collection for book study groups	Demonstrate another guided reading lesson with prompts and a core comprehension strategy Coach a guided reading lesson
May Literacy Assessment • theoretical underpinnings • assess-on-the-go approach • assessments in: - word study - reading - writing Writing • cause and effect	Use literacy assessment techniques in the classroom Try cause and effect writing in addition to other text structure forms	Demonstrate a component requested by the teacher Coach a writing lesson that focuses on interactive writing and the revising process

Upper Elementary Inservice Topic Chart: Year Two

Strategy Development (seven inservices)	Teacher Goal	Demonstration and Coaching (minimum six sessions)
September Literature Response Activities • part of levelled book study groups and independent reading • integrating core comprehension strategies with literature response activities • examples of other literature response activities, such as Plot Profile (Tompkins, 1998), Character Silhouettes (Brailsford, 2003), maps of settings or a journey Panel • experienced balanced literacy teachers provide examples and respond to questions	Integrate new literature response techniques into book study groups and independent reading	Demonstrate a class strategy lesson to introduce a literature response technique Coach a guided reading lesson
October Traditional Fiction Writing • characteristics of fairytales, myths, and fables • literature links to each narrative form • examples of each form • process of writing: progressing from a class version to individual accounts Revisiting prompts in guided reading • practical examples of readers' miscues • group discussion of prompts	Add traditional fiction to the students' writing repertoire (select a fairytale, myth, or fable) Emphasize word recognition and comprehension prompts in guided reading	Demonstrate a writing lesson: run a writing support group, or emphasize the brainstorming stage as students move from the class prototype plan to personal writing (fairytale, myth, or fable) Coach a class strategy lesson to introduce a literature response technique

Strategy Development (seven inservices)	Teacher Goal	Demonstration and Coaching (minimum six sessions)
November Book Study Group Alternatives • literature circles and roles (Daniels, 2002) • book clubs and prompts (Day, Spiegel, McLellan & Brown, 2002; McMahon & Raphael, 1997) • methods and rationale • role of class strategy lessons in introducing and maintaining these book study methods • variety in book groups in order to look at comprehension through "different windows" Writing • problem-solution	Plan a unit with literature circles or book clubs Use problem-solution writing in content areas	Demonstrate an introduction to literature circles or book clubs Coach/teach alongside during literature circles or book clubs, & model how to facilitate discussions
January Report Writing • research • planning a class report • small group work on a section of the class report • linking the paragraph sections to form a report • adding the introduction and conclusion • individual reports following the process learned in the whole class plan	Use report writing techniques in content areas	Demonstrate a mini-craft lesson during the report writing process Coach a portion of the report writing process (e.g. a support group) or a book study group, depending on which area the teacher identifies as needing the most support

Strategy Development (seven inservices)	Teacher Goal	Demonstration and Coaching (minimum six sessions)
February Assessment Revisited • use of student writing to inform instruction (small group work on using the rubrics with student writing samples) • use of the oral reading form (Brailsford, 2003) to inform instruction (use examples of teacher analysis and discuss) • benchmark assessment of a reader new to the class (Brailsford, 2003) to decide on a book level • discussion of the assessment sample in partners and whole group Writing • poetry - structured (e.g. haiku or limerick) - free form - use of figurative language	Use the assessment strategies in the classroom Work with a colleague or small group to evaluate class writing samples using the rubrics Add poetry writing to the writing program	Demonstrate an assessment strategy Coach the word study area, or a mini-lesson in writing (e.g. using conventions for adding dialogue to written accounts)
March Oral Language and the Written Form: Speeches, Interviews, and Plays • characteristics of each oral and text form • examples of each text form • use of text forms such as Literacy Place magazines and overheads of a play in shared reading and class strategy lesson • use of text forms such as Literacy Place's "Dramarama" theme for grade 6 book study groups • moving from oral to text forms or from text forms to oral production	Teach class strategy and shared reading lessons using one or more of these oral and written forms Build wall charts to demonstrate the characteristics of each form Link to writing and develop speeches, interviews, or plays into written form with the students	Demonstrate the introduction of one form (choosing from speeches, interviews, or plays); show how to build a list of characteristics of the form on a wall chart Coach the use of an assessment strategy in book study groups

Strategy Development (seven inservices)	Teacher Goal	Demonstration and Coaching (minimum six sessions)
May Celebration and Sharing • reflecting on the professional development journey • sharing strategies, student work samples, and experiences • planning the next stage: e.g. school-based sharing groups, across-school visits, expanding the professional development library, building regular professional development activities into staff meetings	Plan for continuity in staff professional development	Optional consultation regarding the professional development goal with the balanced literacy consultant

Sample Year One Inservice for Upper Elementary Teachers

The following is a sample plan for a two-hour inservice on writing held at Bonaventure School in January of the first year. It shows how inservice components provide the basic backbone for each session, despite varied content.

Links

1. The balanced literacy consultant begins by recommending some literature links for read-alouds.

   • Mini-craft lessons in writing can be based on the class read-aloud book. Use *Skateway to Freedom* by Ann Alma (Beach Holme Press, 1993) as an example. Link the book to a lesson on crafting interesting lead sentences (many of the chapters have suitable introductory sentences).

- Links to native culture, using two picture books that are suitable for older students:
  — *Sootface: An Ojibwa Cinderella Story* retold by Robert San Souci (Bantam, 1994). Link to alternative fairytales from other cultural perspectives.

  — *Maple Moon* by Connie Brummel Crook (Stoddart Kids, 1997). A young Mississauga boy, who is teased about his physical handicap, saves his tribe from hunger by discovering maple sugar. Link to writing "discovery" stories.

- Link to descriptive writing:
  First on the Moon by Barbara Hehner (Scholastic/Madison, 1999). The book documents the first human landing on the moon in July 1969. Use as a read-aloud for the "Voyagers" theme (Literacy Place: Grade 5 unit), or link to descriptive paragraph or sequence writing. The section on "The Eagle Has Landed" would be excellent for interactive sequence writing with the class.

2. Steve, a grade four teacher at Mountain Heights School, shows his card strips of word patterns that he displays on the wall. They are helpful for students who need more spelling support, and for the weekly spelling test that includes five words transferred from word patterns taught during the Making Big Words lessons (Cunningham and Hall, 1994 b)

3. A reminder: this month there will be demonstrations provided on shared reading and class strategy lessons. The coaching will be on word level activities that you are using in your monthly plan. Select activities that move beyond Making Big Words and the Tricky Word Corner.

Review

The balanced literacy consultant reviews the transfer steps in the Making Big Words lessons. (This had emerged as a need for many people during the coaching sessions in the previous month).

- Remind the group to generate two to three new words based on the word pattern sorts that stem from the lesson. Use a rhyming

dictionary if help is needed in finding new words with the same pattern.

- Provide a context, such as, "I am writing a letter to a friend, and I want to say that our neighbour was complaining that Spooky, our dog, had got through the fence again. I need some help with spelling 'complaining.' Is there a pattern we studied that could help me?"

- Check patterns studied. Ask the students to decide on the appropriate pattern (*ain* in this case) and spell the word together.

- "Word patterns can help you read and spell new words." Make this point explicit for students.

Strategy Development

1. The balanced literacy consultant focuses on shared reading and a class strategy lesson by reviewing the need to use co-operative reading strategies to support students. The consultant emphasizes the following co-operative reading techniques.

    - Do choral reading with pairs, rows, and the whole class. This approach can be used with magazines, content area materials, plays, or texts copied onto overhead transparencies

    - Create paired reading teams, pairing weaker readers with stronger readers. A portion of the Paired Reading videotape (Northern Alberta Reading Specialists' Council, 1991) is shown to illustrate this approach, and a handout describing the technique is provided. It is suggested that this technique be featured at lunchtime meetings in schools, and that schools could add it to their agendas.

    - *3-Ring Circus* (Cunningham, Hall, and Sigmon, 1999) is a way of dividing the class into three reading groups. One group reads the material independently, another group reads chorally with a buddy, while the third group reads chorally with the teacher.

2. Shared reading is often allied with class strategy lessons. The consultant recommends that the teachers consult the Balanced Literacy: Division 2 manual (Brailsford, 2003) for a list of topics for class strategy lessons.

3. The consultant shows the group a class strategy lesson that is combined with the shared reading component. An overhead outlines the key information.

The consultant treats the group of teachers as a temporary "class" and demonstrates how to combine shared reading with reflections.

- Use a hand signal to indicate pauses for reflections. The teachers read chorally and pause when the consultant uses a prearranged hand signal.

- Use "talk alouds" to reflect on textual information. The group choral-reads the first paragraph and the consultant reflects aloud as teachers would in their classrooms: " 'I wonder if the Ojibwa name their children from dreams … what could some of the names be…?' Invite the teachers' reflections. Read the next two paragraphs and reflect aloud, 'This part interests me. There's a big build-up of suspense before we find out her name. I think her name is either going to sound really important or be funny. What are you thinking?' "

> **Materials:**
> - "The Naming Ritual," a story from the Literacy Place *Snapshots* magazine. (The teachers have been asked to bring copies of the magazine to the inservice.)
> - Wall chart of "Reflecting" prompts (Retelling, Relating and Reflecting, Schwartz and Bone, 1995)
>
> **Strategy:**
> Reflecting on what you read (interpreting, evaluating, wondering)
>
> **Shared Reading:**
> Choral reading with the whole class.

- Continue the pattern of choral reading, pausing to model reflections, then continuing to read together. After the consultant has modelled the technique, members of the group are invited to add their reflections. Then the consultant finalizes the demonstration by explaining that these oral reflections are precursors to the stage when students can generate their own reflections as written literature responses.

4. The consultant introduces the text structure organizer for a friendly letter (Brailsford, 2002, 2003) and recommends trying this in the classroom. Tips are provided for using the text structure.

Teacher Sharing

1. Nina, a grade five teacher from Bonaventure School, uses children's writing samples to share her persuasive writing project with the group. She provides an overhead of an organizer that has been used to create a class plan, a persuasive account on chart paper produced by a "class write," rough notes on brainstormed ideas, and overheads of children's writing samples.

2. The whole group of teachers divides into small groups. Teachers share their class writing samples with colleagues.

Goal Setting

The balanced literacy consultant recommends suitable goals to implement in the classroom during the coming month.

- Start co-operative reading techniques in shared reading.
- Do strategy lessons with shared reading.
- Start friendly letter writing. Continue with a selection of other text structures, such as sequence writing, story analysis, and descriptive paragraph.

Bibliography

Professional References

Brailsford, Anne. *Balanced Literacy: Division 1.* Edmonton, AB: Edmonton Public Schools Learning Resources, 2002.

Brailsford, Anne. *Balanced Literacy: Division 2.* Edmonton, AB: Edmonton Public Schools Learning Resources, 2003.

Brailsford, Anne and Coles, Jan. "Literacy Place in the Balanced Literacy Classroom," in *Literacy Place Teacher's Tool Kit: A Guide to Using Literacy Place in Your Classroom.* Markham, ON : Scholastic Canada, 2002.

Cunningham, Patricia M. and Hall, Dorothy P. *Month-by-Month Phonics for Upper Grades.* Greensboro, NC: Carson-Dellosa, 1998.

Cunningham, Patricia M. and Hall, Dorothy P. *Month-By-Month Phonics for First Grade.* Greensboro N.C.: Carson-Dellosa, 1997.

Cunningham, Patricia M. and Hall, Dorothy P. *Making Words.* Torrance, CA: Good Apple, 1994a.

Cunningham, Patricia, and Hall, Dorothy P. *Making Big Words.* Greensboro NC: Carson-Dellosa, 1994b.

Cunningham, Patricia M., Hall, Dorothy P. and Sigmon, Cheryl M. *The Teacher's Guide to the Four Blocks.* Greensboro, NC: Carson-Dellosa, 1999.

Daniels, Harvey. *Literature Circles: Voice and Choice in Book Clubs and Reading Groups.* Markham, ON: Pembroke, 2002.

Day, Jeni P., Spiegel, Dixie L., McLellan, Janet, and Brown, Valerie. *Moving Forward with Literature Circles.* New York: Scholastic, 2002.

Fitzpatrick, Jo. *Phonemic Awareness: Playing with Sounds to Strengthen Beginning Reading Skills.* Cypress, CA: Creative Teaching Press, 1997.

Fountas, Irene C. and Pinnell, Gay Su. *Matching Books to Readers: Using Levelled Books in Guided Reading, K-3.* Portsmouth, NH: Heinemann, 1999.

Hall, Dorothy P. and Cunningham, Patricia M. *Month-By-Month Reading and Writing for Kindergarten.* Greensboro, NC: Carson-Dellosa, 1997.

McCarrier, Andrea, Pinnell, Gay Su, and Fountas, Irene. *Interactive Writing: How Language and Literacy Come Together, K-2.* Portsmouth, NH: Heinemann, 2000.

McMahon, Susan I. and Raphael, Taffy E., eds. *The Book Club Connection: Literacy Learning and Classroom Talk*. Newark, DE: International Reading Association and New York: Teachers College Press, 1997.

Northern Alberta Reading Specialists' Council. *Paired Reading: Positive Reading Practice* (Manual by Anne Brailsford, and accompanying training videotape) Distributed Kelowna, BC: Filmwest, 1991.

Raphael, Taffy E. "Teaching learners about sources of information for answering comprehension questions," *Journal of Reading* 27 (4): 303-311.

Schwartz, Susan and Bone, Maxine. *Retelling, Relating, and Reflecting Beyond the 3Rs*. Toronto: Irwin, 1995.

Tompkins, Gail E. *50 Literacy Strategies*. Columbus, OH: Merrill, 1998.

Children's Books

Alma, Ann. *Skateway to Freedom*. Vancouver: Beach Holme Press, 1993.

Brummel Cook, Connie. *Maple Moon*. Toronto: Stoddart, 1999.

Burningham, John. *Harvey Slumfenburger's Christmas Present*. Cambridge, MA: Candlewick Press, 1993.

Butler, John. *While You Were Sleeping*. New York: Scholastic, 1996.

Carle, Eric. *From Head to Toe*. New York: HarperCollins, 1997.

Hehner, Barbara. *First on the Moon*. Toronto: Scholastic/Madison Press, 1999.

Inkpen, Mick. *Penguin Small*. London: Hodder, 1992.

McGeorge, Constance, W. *Boomer's Big Surprise*. New York: Scholastic, 1999.

Muir, John (as retold by Donnell Rubay). *Stickeen*. Nevada City, CA: Dawn Publications, 1998.

Repchuk, Caroline. *The Snow Tree*. Dorking, UK: Templar, 1996.

San Souci, Robert D. *Sootface: An Ojibwa Cinderella Story*. New York: Bantam, 1994.

Stewart, Sarah. *The Gardener*. New York: Farrar Straus Giroux, 1997.

Wise Brown, Margaret. *Bunny's Noisy Book*. New York: Scholastic, 2000.

Teacher Support Materials

Edmonton Public Schools Learning Resources (2001) Tel. (780) 429-8122

- Student Dictionaries
- Student and Teacher Alphabet Letters and Kits for the Making Words lessons
- Text Structure Organizers for Writing

Classroom Book Series

National Geographic Big Books

- *Exploring Space* (1999)
- *A Tree for all Seasons* (1999)
- *Insects: A Three-Part Story* (1999)

Scholastic: Bookshop

- Phinney, Margaret. *Will You Play With Us?* (1995)
- Douglas, Ann. *The Old Woman Who Lived in a Vinegar Bottle* (1997)
- Vandine, JoAnn. *I Eat Leaves* (1995)

Scholastic: Literacy Place

Implementing Balanced Literacy in the School

Once the type of program has been selected or created, and the professional development plan has been organized, the focus turns to the school community. An enabling environment is vital when the program moves from the planning phase to the practical realities of implementation.

Roles

Administrators, teachers, librarians, and balanced literacy consultants all have parts to play as the program is put into operation.

Administrators

If the program is to be successful, administrators need to be part of the implementation scheme. Here are the ways they can be helpful.

- Administrators can join staff in the inservices as well as lunchtime meetings with the balanced literacy consultants. In addition, it is helpful if they observe the program in operation in the classroom. If they have a thorough understanding of the program being implemented, they can accommodate staff needs and share information with parents.

- Administrators should provide time at staff meetings for a balanced literacy professional development component. This ensures that all staff receive and discuss new information about the program, and demonstrates that balanced literacy is a priority at the school.

- Administrators can assist staff in clearing space for a school bookroom or book area. It is important for administrators to demonstrate in this way that they are part of the literacy team.

- Administrators can be resourceful in obtaining the materials needed to operate the program, since funding may well be limited and priorities have to be created. For example, the core print materials may be purchased and older materials used for independent reading until more funding is available.

- It is crucial for administrators to support the staff as they engage in a two-year commitment to balanced literacy professional development. It would be wise for administrators to help staff focus on balanced literacy professional development by refraining from asking them to enroll in other inservice series during the implementation period. In addition, administrators should ensure that inservice days are free of commitments for teachers. In the Edmonton project, for example, when inservices occurred once a month from 3 to 5 p.m., principals ensured that teachers were able to leave the school promptly so that they could make the transition from the classroom to professional development sessions.

- Administrators can offer practical teaching support in the classroom. For example, as teachers begin to implement independent reading stations and guided reading in the primary grades, it would be helpful if administrators could help out in the classroom.

- Administrators should work on the timetable to permit as much uninterrupted Language Arts time as possible; for example, assemblies, plays, concerts, and similar events should be scheduled when they won't hinder Language Arts. Similarly, in the Edmonton and area project, we always recommended that physical education and music occur outside the morning Language Arts block for primary grade students.

- Administrators can ensure that school events do not conflict with the days when the balanced literacy consultant will be visiting the school. Usually these dates are scheduled and teachers need to clear time to work with the consultant in the classroom and during lunchtime meetings.

- Administrators need to build an open relationship with the balanced literacy consultant. The consultant will not reveal classroom observations; any observations of teaching practices and teaching suggestions will be shared only with the teacher. Although the administrator needs to be aware that the consultant has no role in teacher evaluation, it is still possible to approach the consultant as an administrative facilitator, asking, "Is there anything more I can do to enable this program to be successful in our school?"

- Administrators are in a position to "see the overall picture" when segments of the program are being implemented. Teachers will need to focus on their own classrooms as they start the program, but administrators must not only view what is in place but plan for the next stages. For example, often schools start with the kindergarten and primary programs, adding the upper elementary grades to the program in the next year. Administrators need to plan ahead to fund the new resources that will be needed and to organize the transition into the other grades. They also have to anticipate the time when all the teachers will have completed the professional development component, and plan for continuation of the program with the assistance of the balanced literacy consultant.

Teachers

In the first stages of balanced literacy implementation, teachers need to make a commitment to be fully engaged in the professional development plan. This will involve: attendance at inservices; bringing work samples to share with other teachers; reading professional books and articles; observing demonstration lessons in the classroom; obtaining feedback from a coach as they teach; meeting the coach at lunchtime; and planning with other teachers at the school. As the program gets underway, teachers will have a vital role to play in the program's success.

- Teachers need to establish a relationship with the balanced literacy consultant. The consultant who provides monthly inservices will likely also be the coach who works in the classroom. To maximize learning opportunities, a warm and open relationship with the coach is important. The coach is not in the classroom to evaluate, but to provide enough support to enable the teacher to operate the

new program and strategies effectively. At first, it is entirely normal to feel some discomfort with having a new person in the classroom. Most teachers, however, come to welcome the opportunity to see new strategies demonstrated with the class they usually teach, and to have someone teaching alongside until they feel confident.

- Teachers should connect and share with other teachers who are starting the program, as well as with teachers who are more experienced in balanced literacy. Opportunities for such connections are provided at inservices. Teachers can also form informal support groups within the school, where they can discuss new techniques and materials. If professional development days are staggered in the school district, new teachers may have opportunities to visit the classrooms of more experienced balanced literacy teachers. During those visits, it is often helpful to focus on one area, such as how to run a guided reading group, or how a teacher introduces a writing organizer.

- Teachers will need to organize new and old materials in a centralized book room or book area. This requires teamwork, but it is only a large job in the first year of program implementation. In subsequent years, it is simply a matter of slotting new materials into an established structure.

- Above all, teachers need to focus on implementing the teaching-learning components and new strategies in the classroom. The degree of change they will experience depends on previous Language Arts programs they have taught. For some teachers, change will be relatively small, but for others, the new program may represent significant classroom modifications. Support is the watchword here. Teachers, administrators, and consultants who share the belief that they are entering this new experience as a team, and thus need to support each other, will be assured of a successful year.

Key Teachers

Within a school, one or two teachers emerge as key planners and motivators in moving balanced literacy into the school. These teachers

have likely been instrumental in raising awareness and launching professional development activities. Such teachers may have official designations, but more likely they will identify themselves simply by their enthusiasm for the project. It is helpful if key teachers are identified for both primary and upper elementary grades. As well as their role in the classroom, they enhance program implementation in several ways.

- Key teachers become the contact people for the balanced literacy consultant. The consultant feeds messages to the key teachers, who in turn disseminate information to the teachers in the school. Similarly, teachers can channel questions and ideas to the consultant through the key teacher.

- Key teachers can organize the classroom schedule for visits by the balanced literacy consultant. They discuss the scheduled visit with the consultant and the teachers, and then send the proposed timetable, listing the demonstration lessons and coaching sessions for each classroom, to the consultant. Sometimes a key teacher may forward materials from the teachers to the consultant—such as a book for the preparation of a guided reading demonstration lesson— before the consultant's visit.

- Key teachers will plan the agenda for the lunchtime meetings with the consultant. These monthly meetings should largely follow an agenda that relates to needs within a school, and the teachers need to formulate items for discussion with their consultant.

- Key teachers, one each at the primary and upper elementary levels, can promote sharing sessions among teachers, as well as communicating with each other, and with the consultant and administrators.

Librarians

Librarians are rare human resources in some parts of the country. In areas where budget cuts have been deep, professional teacher-librarians have often been replaced by technicians or volunteers. However, if librarians are still available, they can lend invaluable support to the implementation of the balanced literacy program.

- Librarians provide rich and engaging literacy experiences as they read to children. If they use a wide variety of genres for read alouds, they will certainly complement the classroom program.

- Librarians can use some of the text structure organizers when helping teachers and children plan written research projects. In one school in Edmonton, the librarian took an active role in integrating the text structure organizers into her research-oriented sessions with the students.

- Librarians can supply some levelled materials for independent reading when classroom resources are limited. This is not to suggest that library materials should be levelled on the shelves. Children need to choose their own library materials with limited guidance. However, it sometimes happens that, as schools start the balanced literacy program, they may have few levelled books for classroom reading tubs. The librarian could assist by using *Matching Books to Readers* or the United Library Services' lists to find book titles that could be included temporarily in the classroom's levelled book collection. As soon as funding is available to supplement the classroom tubs, those books should be returned to the open book collection in the library.

The Balanced Literacy Consultant

The balanced literacy consultant plays a pivotal role in the implementation of the program.

- The consultant seeks to develop a warm and trusting relationship with the teachers. A supportive team approach with the teachers works best.

- The consultant visits the school regularly to provide demonstration lessons and coaching sessions.

- The consultant knows how to modify the pace of demonstration and coaching lessons to meet the needs of each teacher. For example, some teachers may need only one demonstration of a

Making Words lesson, while others may need two or three, with the consultant teaching alongside, until they feel confident.

- The consultant can provide written feedback to teachers following coaching. This feedback should contain a column for observations and a column for suggestions. Such feedback is intended to be entirely private and the balanced literacy consultant should not share it with any other staff member. The feedback can be used to stimulate discussion and to help set a goal for the next visit.

- The consultant encourages teachers to develop their own agendas for the regular lunch meeting with the consultant. The content of these meetings will be tailored to match a school's specific needs.

- The consultant maintains contact with the school's administration, and is available to respond to questions and to enhance teamwork.

- The consultant keeps in touch with each school's key teachers to ensure that smooth communication is maintained.

- The consultant, like the administrators, must view "the whole picture." Each school and teacher is focusing, quite rightly, on the details of implementation during the first year. The consultant, however, needs to look to the future as well as supporting present needs. For example, primary grades may start the program in the first year, but the consultant, keeping in mind that upper elementary grades may join the following year, can be influential in ensuring that bookroom space is large enough to accommodate materials for all grades. Similarly, the consultant can spend time during the first year helping teachers from the upper elementary grades to co-ordinate a supply and book ordering list, and introducing them to professional materials and concepts from the program.

- Even in the introductory year of the balanced literacy program, the consultant needs to be working towards the time when the school will be maintaining the program independently. Thus it is important that the consultant encourages the school's development of literacy teams who can continue to enhance the

program even after the official professional development period has expired. Promoting the construction of a teachers' agenda for lunchtime meetings in the first and second years of operation is an important step towards increasing such independence.

Materials

During the first year, the collection and organization of materials is labour intensive. However, once the core materials are organized, schools report that yearly resource adjustments and additions are easily handled.

The Professional Development Library

The professional development book collection may have been started during the final part of the "raising awareness" year. As the inservices progress, new materials will be added. We make the following suggestions.

- Most books and articles should be placed together in an accessible location such as the staff room.

- Teachers should have their own copies of materials when appropriate, for example, the books that focus on the Making Words lessons.

- The loan system (for example, sign-out cards) should be simple and clear to all staff members.

    Note: For a list of suitable professional development resources, consult the *Balanced Literacy: Division 1 and Division 2* manuals (Brailsford, 2002, 2003).

The School Bookroom

Early in the first year of the balanced literacy program, or at the conclusion of the "raising awareness" year, materials should be stored in a centralized location. We have found that the need to have a book area has been the motivational force behind many a school's clear-out of old, dusty textbooks. Some schools elect to use storerooms, while others

choose an area in the library or seldom-used classroom space. When arranging the book area, consider the following recommendations.

- Establish consensus that *all* sets of books need to be located in a central area. The bookroom concept works best when all teachers contribute their book sets.

- Use the space for all grades, including kindergarten.

- Use shelves and a bin system for storage. Each levelled book set needs to be stored and many schools use cheap plastic tubs from the dollar store for this purpose. Since it should be easy for teachers to take the sets of books they need, and return them to a specified space after the books have been used, shelves and tubs will need labelling.

- Arrange the books to demonstrate the flow through the levelled materials. In the first year, start by arranging the core classroom book series, forming a skeleton collection that can be supplemented at a later date. The alphabetic levels established by Fountas and Pinnell (1999 & 1996) are linear and easy to follow for primary grades. In the Edmonton and area project, the kindergarten shared-reading series were placed to precede the primary grades' alphabetic levels. We then arranged the Literacy Place Units and support materials, plus supplementary novel sets, to follow the primary series.

- Include extra resources in each levelled book bin. For example, add the audiotape for the Easy reading selection in Literacy Place to the book tub for that unit. Similarly, for the primary core series, any additional big books, audiotapes, sentence strips, and blackline masters need to be placed in the same book bin or nearby. Many schools leave a card in the bin to inform the teacher that a big book and/or sentence strips can be collected to accompany the book resources. They then set up boxes for big books and hangers for sentence strips in the bookroom, to enable teachers to find them easily.

- Establish a very simple loan system. We have found that when loan systems take too much time, they aren't used, and soon there is confusion about the location of materials. Although computer loan systems seem elegantly up-to-date and efficient, they can be viewed as time-consuming by busy teachers. Instead, we recommend that all teachers be given a half-dozen clothes pins with their names on them. When borrowing materials, a teacher clips a pin on the book bin to identify the borrower. The system takes seconds to use and is favoured by teachers!

- Agree on borrowing and returning materials in an expedient manner. A central bookroom will not meet everyone's needs if some teachers borrow class materials and stockpile them in their classrooms for weeks.

    Note: An exception to the fast return of books can be made for children reading A to D Level texts; these children need to reread familiar books. For this reason, it is vital to have a larger range of Levels A to D books in the central collection.

- Use some bookroom space for consumable materials. For example, teachers will ask students to use the text structure organizers to plan their writing (Brailsford, 2002, 2003). Storing extra student-sized versions of the text structure organizers in a central location makes sense.

Independent Reading Materials

Although core and supplementary levelled book sets are best stored in a central location, we recommend that independent reading materials be located in individual classrooms.

- Offer a rich supply of children's books in the book corner and in centres in kindergarten. Books that can go home, so that parents can read to their children, may be obtained from the classroom or school library. The take-home materials can also be from reproducible resources, to enable the students to build a home library. (For more about this, see the Literacy Context section of this chapter, page 218.) If some children have progressed into guided reading groups, kindergartens should contain levelled tub collections for independent reading and for taking home to read to parents.

- Provide levelled tubs of books for independent reading in each primary classroom. (Where resources are extremely limited, classrooms could share a travelling cart of levelled book tubs.) Book tub selections should cover the entire range of readers in the classroom. However, as students progress beyond Levels O and P, they should be encouraged to choose their own books from the library.

- Encourage upper elementary children to self-select books from classroom and library resources for independent reading. However, levelled tubs will still be needed for readers who need more support, and especially for those who are reading below grade level. Hence, sources for independent reading materials should be flexible in the upper elementary grades.

- Go slowly during the first year of implementation of the balanced literacy program! The first job is to level the core book collection and store it in a way that is conducive to a smooth flow of materials across the elementary grades. Once this is done, attention can turn to the independent reading collection. During the first year, we recommend that at least one professional development inservice focus teachers on how to level books. Each school should allocate some professional development time to levelling books within the school.

The Literacy Context

During the process of implementing and running a balanced literacy program, the overall atmosphere in classrooms, the library, hallways, and the office should reflect the strong message that "this school is wholeheartedly committed to promoting literacy learning." There are many ways in which a school can convey this important message to all students, staff, parents, community volunteers, and the community at large.

- Display children's writing in classrooms, the library, and hallways. In balanced literacy schools, students, staff, and visiting adults can often be seen poring over writing samples arranged on walls and bulletin boards, as well as the children's published books,

arranged on library shelves. Kindergarten and first grade children, especially, love to read and reread their own and whole-class "Special Child — getting to know you" booklets (Cunningham & Hall, 1997; Hall & Cunningham, 1997) during Drop Everything and Read (DEAR) sessions with older buddies, and during their independent reading times.

- Invite children, on occasion, to read their book recommendations and written stories and poems to the whole school, during the principal's intercom announcements. Hearing kindergarten, primary, and upper elementary students share their creations over "the principal's ether" often provides an inspiring model for other students to emulate.

- Devote hallway or library bulletin boards to children's and possibly staff's book recommendations. Reading book reviews, by peers and teachers, often encourages children (and staff!) to dip into materials they might not otherwise encounter.

- Run monthly or bimonthly "Writers' Café" meetings (one each per session for primary and upper elementary grades) where the children can read their creations to others. They may wish to dress up as stereotypical writers, for example, sporting French berets for poetry reading, reporters' hats for news reports, baseball caps for sports stories, deerstalker hats for mystery stories, witch-wizard creations for Halloween offerings, sou'westers for stories about the sea, and so on.

- Organize buddy reading-writing partners for occasions such as Drop Everything and Read or Write time blocks (often the first 15 minutes of the afternoon), or for those days when it's either too wet or too cold for children to be outside during recess and lunch breaks. The buddies could be older students or community volunteers pairing up with younger children for read alouds, partner reading, Paired Reading (Northern Alberta Reading Specialists' Council, 1991), language experience dictations, and writing support.

- Schedule buddy reader-writer "mail exchanges" for seasonal occasions such as Valentine's Day, Easter, Halloween, and Christmas. Older children and community volunteers help the younger children to write, mail, and deliver pertinent messages to their friends and teachers.

- Invite educational publishers to hold in-school book fairs for staff, students, parents, and members of the immediate community, once or twice a year. These can be arranged at the beginning of the school year, just before Christmas when family members often buy books as presents, or to coincide with parent-teacher conference times. In these situations, the publishers often allocate a percentage of their overall earnings as "bonus point" dollars that teachers use for buying classroom books.

- Run monthly educational publishers' book clubs, so that children can purchase their own books, and teachers can use "bonus points" to purchase books for classroom use. Children look forward, with great anticipation, to the monthly routine of being able to choose their very own books.

- Organize treasure hunts (inside if the weather is inclement), in which older students read maps with younger children to track down the location of "buried treasure." The treasure is a selection of "bonus points" books, from which both members of the winning pair choose a book to add to their home book collection.

- Send home "yours to keep" reproducible versions of books that young children have read in class (for example, Scholastic: 25 *Mother Goose Peek-a-Books*, 25 *Emergent Reader Mini-Books*; *Round-the-World Folktale Mini-Books*; 25 *Thematic Mini-Books*; *High-Frequency Readers Take-Home Books*; or the *Keep Books* from Ohio State University's Early Literacy Learning Initiative, kindergarten through grade two.) These take-home materials are especially valued by young children whose families can't afford to buy books.

- Run a "book swap" session once or twice a year. Students bring along a book from home that they no longer wish to keep, and trade it for a book that someone else has brought. Children often

bring more than one book, so extra take-home books are available for those children who don't have any books to bring from home.

- Have staff members occasionally buy books at garage and library discard sales. Books purchased at these venues are often in good enough condition to include in classroom and "book swap" collections.

Parent-School Connections

When a new Language Arts program is being introduced in the school, parents need to be aware of the teaching-learning components and how the program will benefit their children. They should also be comfortable with their role in supporting their children's literacy learning. The school needs to plan for sharing information with parents and for reinforcing, or steering them towards, productive home literacy practices.

Early in the school year, parents can be invited to an information session at the school. If the balanced literacy program is starting in the kindergarten and primary grades, those parents should be invited during the first year of implementation. We recommend running separate kindergarten and primary sessions. In general, the parents of kindergarten children need more supported activities to pursue at home. Meanwhile, the primary inservice can provide demonstrations of literacy practices being pursued at school, and links to supportive home literacy activities. The following year, as the upper elementary grades are added, an information session could be held for those parents.

The following areas need consideration when organizing the meetings.

1. *Who will be the focus group?* Will the meeting be solely for parents and caregivers, or will their families be included? Some schools offer an activities room for children, run by older students and adult community volunteers. The children are read to, or play board games, while the parent meeting is underway. They join their parents for refreshments at the conclusion of the meeting.

2. *How will parents be invited?* A letter could be sent home or the meeting could be advertised in the school's newsletter.

3. *Who will run the meeting?* It is a good idea to ask an administrator to introduce the meeting, which demonstrates that both administration and teachers support the new balanced literacy program. All staff members could participate in the large group meeting, or just one or two key teachers. The balanced literacy consultant could also be asked to attend and help with some sections of the meeting. However, it is better if the staff members take a significant role in the meeting because they need to demonstrate that it is their program.

4. *What content will be included in the meeting?* This is an opportunity to share information about the balanced literacy program, and to provide suggestions that encourage parents to support their child's learning. The content needs to include an overview of the teaching-learning components. Brief demonstrations of each component, no longer than five minutes, are often helpful.

5. *Where will the meeting be held?* Meetings often start in a large space that accommodates the whole group, and then move to the classrooms where teachers can briefly explain specific class routines.

6. *Will refreshments be provided?* Snacks could be offered as the parents arrive, after the general introduction, or as a conclusion. Some schools co-ordinate book sales of reasonably priced materials with parent meetings; at other schools, book trades accompany the meeting, with people bringing old books they can trade for another one.

The following part of the chapter provides outlines of introductory inservices for kindergarten, primary, and upper elementary parents. The balanced literacy program described is the one used in Edmonton and area schools (Brailsford, 2002, 2003). You can use these plans, and modify them, to provide parent information meetings at your school.

Information Meeting for Kindergarten Parents

- For parents of kindergarten children, we recommend that the entire information meeting take place in the informal classroom setting, since there is usually a small group of people in attendance.

- Introduce the meeting by reading aloud *Jeremiah Learns to Read* by Jo Ellen Bogart. Explain the importance of learning to read and write, pointing out that we want to give children every opportunity to be readers and writers much earlier in their lives than Jeremiah.

- Show the group the kindergarten timetable and the scheduling of the literacy components. Explain that these literacy components will occur every day. (Use a timetable plan similar to the one outlined on pages 142 and 143. This can be put on an overhead or chart paper.)

- Describe how children learn from demonstrations. Use the example of how Jeremiah demonstrated whittling with a pocketknife and honking like a goose to help children learn the skills he knew. Explain that you are now going to provide demonstrations of the literacy learning components scheduled for the kindergarten and suggest some reading and writing activities for home.

Kindergarten Presentation

The teacher demonstrates briefly and explains each of the three components (Writing, Reading, and Letter, Sound, and Word Study). At the conclusion of each, the accompanying home supports are discussed.

Demonstrations	Home Support
Writing	
• Use the timetable and show how the writing time moves from a teacher demonstration, through writing with the children (shared and interactive writing), to independent writing and drawing. • Do a teacher demonstration of a write aloud: "We are meeting here to discuss how young children can learn to be readers and writers." Teacher writes on chart paper and talks aloud: "I am going to start writing here, and I want my message to say, 'We are meeting here,' so I write 'We' with a big letter to start the word," etc. The teacher could move into interactive writing, if desired, and draw ideas from the parents. They could contribute by adding letters and some words.	Explain that demonstrations are so important for the young child. Recommend that parents demonstrate writing to their child: e.g. using lists, notes, emails, and greetings cards, and even talk aloud as they write on some occasions. Ask parents to provide writing materials for their child (such as scrap paper, blackboards, whiteboards, scrapbooks, markers, pencils) and to encourage their child's writing attempts. Sending written messages to their child is also recommended.
Reading	
a. Shared Reading • Show timetable. • Explain that shared reading invites children to join in with reading when they cannot yet read independently. It is helpful to list a few of the early reading concepts children can learn from shared reading: book handling and print directionality concepts, differences between letters and words, high-frequency words, letter sounds, and word pattern. • Demonstrate shared reading by reading a section of a big book with the parents.	Children will bring books home. Library books should be read aloud to the child. Backpack books should also be read aloud to the child. Explain that every two weeks each child will bring home a special book backpack. It contains a read-aloud picture book, and often an alphabet book or books about colours and numbers. Sometimes a game is included in the backpack, and there is always a little journal in which the parent and child can write and draw about what they have read.

b. Read Aloud • Show timetable. • Explain that listening to read alouds helps children to engage with written language and teaches many concepts: e.g. written text has meaning, there are many types of fiction and nonfiction books, vocabulary, book handling and print directionality concepts.	
c. Small Group Shared Reading and Guided Reading Groups, Plus Independent Reading • Show timetable. • Explain the purpose of each component: e.g. small group shared reading allows the teacher to tailor instruction to meet the needs of the children. Note that most children will be working on learning concepts from shared reading in kindergarten, but a few may move into more formal guided reading lessons. All children will have the opportunity to read books with partners, with older buddies, and on their own in the library corner.	During the year, the children may bring home small books with captions and simple sentences under the pictures. These can be read with the child chorally, just like the shared reading tonight. It is possible that some children may be able to read these small books to their parents.
Letter, Word and Sound Study	
Demonstrate *Turtle Talk* (Fitzpatrick, 1997), clapping syllables in names, cutting a name into letters (to show how words are made up of letters), or finding words that start with **b** in a familiar big book. (Select a couple of activities.)	Suggest that parents read alphabet books: e.g. *Alphabeasts* by Wallace Edwards or *The Christmas Alphabet Book* by Robert Sabuda, or nursery rhymes, songs, poems and Dr. Seuss-type books to provide their child with a sense of the rhyme and rhythm of the language.

• At the conclusion of the sessions, provide a Home Support Handout for each parent. (See Appendix B.) Invite the parents to look at the display of:
   — picture books
   — alphabet, counting and colours books
   — rhyming-rhythmic books

— simple captioned books

— a sample book backpack

— samples of children's early writing

— a collection of writing tools for young children (such as a small blackboard and whiteboard, an erasable board such as Magnadoodle, crayons, markers, pencils, and paper such as the backs of greeting cards, paper scraps, and a scrapbook with plain pages).

Coffee, tea, and snacks can be provided, together with a social opportunity to talk with other parents and the teacher.

Information Meeting for Parents with Children in the Primary Grades

- Gather the parents in the gymnasium, where they can look over the book displays that have been wheeled in on portable bookshelf carts and at the library display of new books and resources. The meeting starts in the gym and is run by the key teacher, supported by other staff members.

- The principal introduces the session:

    Welcome to you all. It is wonderful to see such a good turnout of parents to our meeting. This year, F. T. Buckley School is starting a new Language Arts program and we want to share parts of that program with you tonight. Our teachers will demonstrate some of the techniques we will be using in the classrooms and will also explain how you can support your child's learning at home.

    Our balanced literacy program is just what it says it is: it offers a balance of all areas of language arts on a daily basis. Let us show you the areas it covers:

- The key teacher shows an overhead of the components:

Balanced Literacy Program Components

- **Word Block**
  Word Wall
  Making Words and other word recognition and spelling activities

- **Reading**
  Read Aloud
  Shared Reading
  Guided Reading
  Independent Reading

- **Writing**
  Writing Demonstration
  Guided/Independent Writing

The key teacher explains that Language Arts takes approximately two-and-a-half hours each day and also points out that home support would be helpful to the child. Teachers then explain the program and provide brief demonstrations, along with suggestions for activities at home that will support the child's learning.

Primary Presentation

The teacher demonstrates briefly and explains each of the three components (Word Block, Reading, and Writing). At the conclusion of each, the accompanying home supports are discussed.

Demonstrations	Home Support
Word Block	
a. Word Wall Words • Explain that: - Each child is expected to learn five new words a week (word recognition and spelling). - Words will be the everyday words most needed for reading and writing. - Three challenge words are provided for children who need more difficult words. - Words are introduced each Monday, practised every day at school, and quizzed on Friday. - Previously learned words are also reviewed and included in quizzes.	We will send home a list of new words each Monday so that you can help your child learn the Word Wall words. Hands-on practice activities are included in each list. Spend 10 minutes on two or more nights reviewing the words with your child. Make it fun as you do the practice activities. Some children may need to practise nightly, whereas others may only need two sessions of practice each week. Only do the challenge words if your child finds the regular words easy. Review previously taught words with the child occasionally.
b. Making Words • Explain that: - This activity teaches phonics, word building, and word recognition plus how to transfer skills to new words. - It is a hands-on activity, with the first day focused on building words and the second on transferring knowledge to analyze and spell new words. • Demonstrate three or four words from a Making Words lesson. Other teachers play the roles of the students and build words on their word racks. The key teacher uses a pocket chart and conducts a portion of the lesson.	Your child will sometimes bring home a Making Words lesson for home practice. Support the child in cutting up the letter strip, in building the words, and in recording them. Reread the words with your child.

Reading

a. Read Aloud

- Explain that:

  - This activity provides a model of fluent reading for the child.

  - It helps the child to connect to written language and to love books.

- Demonstrate by reading a page aloud: pause for predictions, read in "character voices" and ask an open-ended question: e.g. "When have you felt as happy as Harriet?"

b. Shared Reading

- Explain that:

  - Shared reading encourages children to join in.

  - Children learn many concepts from shared reading: e.g. print directionality, line tracking, rhyming patterns, letter-sound connections and how to reflect on events and ideas.

  - Support is offered so that all children can read the same book.

- Demonstrate, using a coloured overhead of a book page, and ask parents to join in.

Continue to read aloud to your child.

Some library books will need to be read to the child in the early days of schooling and when the child is interested in a topic and brings home a challenging book.

We encourage public library membership, both for book loans and for the book sharing programs they often run. The child can be encouraged to select simple books for shared reading, or reading to a parent, and more complex ones for the parent to read to the child.

You can read books from the school's book tubs to your child. If the child is hesitant at first, try shared reading (fading your voice as the child gains confidence).

When reading to and with a child, make it a relaxed, enjoyable time. Talk about characters, events and ideas in an invitational way: e.g. "I wonder what..." "I'm thinking..." "What are you thinking about?" "This reminds me of..." Avoid "skill-testing" questions.

c. Guided and Independent Reading

• Explain that:

 - In guided reading the children will read books that are "just right" for them, with support from the teacher.

 - The teacher will teach strategies to a small group and individuals, and monitor each child's progress carefully.

 - In independent reading the children will select books from tubs of "just right" books; these books will be a little easier than those used for guided reading because the intention is to provide successful practice.

 - Some of these books will be selected for home reading.

 - As children become more proficient readers, they will self-select books to come home.

Writing

• Explain that:

 - Children will learn to use many different kinds of writing during their elementary school years. The program builds from personal journal writing and retellings to story writing, descriptive paragraphs, persuasive writing, comparisons, letters, reports, poetry.

 - Every day they will have a writing demonstration lesson from the teacher. They will be encouraged to use the demonstrated skills in their own writing.

 - The text structure organizers are used in the planning stages.

 - Reading is frequently linked to writing.

• Demonstrate using a story analysis organizer to analyze a story known to all: e.g. "Jack and the Beanstalk" or "Goldilocks and the Three Bears."

You can provide writing models for your child at home by, for example, making lists, sending cards, writing emails, sending notes to your child and writing letters.

You can encourage your child to write by providing writing materials at home (e.g. markers, pens, pencils, paper, scrapbooks), by giving positive feedback on writing attempts, and by sharing the writing activity with the child: e.g. writing some ideas and asking the child to write down other thoughts. This type of co-operative writing is useful in the early stages of writing and encourages a child who is reluctant to take risks.

- At the conclusion of the gymnasium session, parents move to their own child's classroom, where the teacher shares the classroom Language Arts timetable and routines with the smaller group. This is an opportunity for specific routines to be explained. For example:
  — File the weekly Word Wall sheets in a binder at home to keep a cumulative list of the year's words. This provides a resource for reviewing words.
  — Making Words practice activities come home once every two weeks.
  — Each child brings a "just right" book home each night. The child should read these to the parent.
  — Library books come home every Wednesday. These are free choice books and some will need to be read to the child.

Finally, the parents are provided with a Home Support Handout, summarizing ideas to support their child's literacy learning at home. (See Appendix B.)

- Once the 10- to 15-minute classroom meeting has concluded, the parents return to the gymnasium for refreshments.

Information Meeting for Upper Elementary Parents

- The parents meet in the gymnasium for the first part of the meeting. Staff, or a combination of staff and the balanced literacy consultant, run the introductory part of the session together.

- An administrator introduces the meeting:

  Beechwood School is using an exciting new Language Arts program that has been linked to academic success in children's reading and writing. Last year we introduced the program in the kindergarten and the primary grades, and we had excellent feedback from parents. This year we are expanding the balanced literacy program to cover grades four, five, and six. We want children to have continuous experiences in Language Arts as they move through the grades at Beechwood. Some of the upper elementary Language Arts program will be similar to the one we previously used in the school, and some parts will be new. This meeting will provide an overview of the program and demonstrations of a few of the techniques the children will use this year. We will also provide suggestions for parents to support their child's learning at home.

  After the general session is completed, we will ask that you move to your child's classroom for 15 to 20 minutes, where you can meet the teacher, and find out about the specific home support routines that will benefit your child. You'll then come back to the gym, look at the library and book club displays, socialize, and enjoy the coffee and snacks.

- On an overhead, staff members show the components of the program and explain that the three basic components are covered each day.

> - **Word Study**
> - **The Reading Hour, with flexible choice of:**
>
>   Read Aloud
>   Shared Reading
>   Class Strategy Lesson
>   Book Study Groups
>   Independent Reading
>
> - **Writing**

Upper Elementary Presentation

The teachers demonstrate briefly and explain each of the three components (Word Study, Reading, and Writing). At the conclusion of each, the accompanying home supports are discussed.

Demonstrations	Home Support
Word Study	
• This 20- to 25-minute block of time is devoted to word recognition and spelling strategies, and to vocabulary development. Many activities will be used. To give a sample, demonstrate the word introduction for the Tricky Word Corner. Explain that: - 5-8 words are learned each week. - Words are added to the child's dictionary. - Words selected are high usage and often confused in word recognition and spelling. - A quiz on 5-8 new words and 5 familiar words is held each Friday. • Demonstrate teaching the words for Tricky Word Corner and invite parents to join in with the practice chants. For example, present the word **once**: "Give me an **o** Give me an **n**... (and so on) What word have we spelled?"	Help your child to practise words from the Tricky Word Corner. A list of words and practice activities will be sent home when the Tricky Word Wall is featured. A sample of the word practice sheet will be provided when you visit your child's classroom. 

• Demonstrate part of a Making Big Words lesson, with staff taking the parts of the teacher and a few students. (If this inservice is run in separate classrooms, rather than with a whole group of parents, then parents can actually engage in a Making Big Words lesson with their child's teacher. They can make the words from cut-up letter strips.) *or* Demonstrate a hands-on word-building activity, in which a root word is expanded with prefixes and suffixes.	Practice activities for Making Big Words and other word-building techniques will be sent home once a week. Please support your child with these activities.

The Reading Hour

• Demonstrate by showing the materials for a unit. (Put the front covers of each book on coloured overheads for a large group.) Explain that: - Students will be reading fiction and nonfiction materials. - Materials for all components other than independent reading will follow a theme. - Teachers will select two to three mini-components each day. (Show overhead of the mini-components: read aloud, shared reading, class strategy lesson, book study groups, and independent reading. • **Example: Voyagers** (Grade 5 theme from Literacy Place: Scholastic) **Read Aloud:** *Adventures with Vikings* by Linda Bailey (Read a page and model fluent, expressive reading.) **Shared Reading:** *Voyagers* magazine from Literacy Place Put a page on an overhead, such as High Drama, p. 44 and engage the parents in shared reading. Explain that if one level of text is used, supportive reading is necessary so all children can read the content successfully.	You can further your child's reading growth by continuing to read to your child. Read books that are somewhat harder than the child can read independently, and read books that both parent and child can enjoy. Read various types of books to the child. Consider nonfiction and poetry books in addition to fiction. You can read a book at the same time as the child and discuss it together in a parent-child "book club." Each person can read the book silently, or with Paired Reading or shared reading techniques. NOTE: a Paired Reading inservice to teach a low stress method for parents and children to read together is scheduled for next month. Watch for the announcement flyer that will be sent home with your child. Combinations of books and tapes do not offer as strong a support as reading with the child, because it isn't always possible to monitor if the child is reading as well as listening, but they are motivating and helpful at times. You can buy them or borrow them from the library. Continue to take your child to the public library for materials and book programs.

Class Strategy Lesson: Use the magazine article highlighted in shared reading.

• Show an overhead of 2-3 reflection prompts from *Retelling, Relating and Reflecting* (Schwartz and Bone, 1995). Demonstrate how the prompts can be used to self-question and think about content when reading. Explain that students will understand, from demonstrations, how to reflect on their reading.

a. Book Study Groups

• Show book covers for multilevelled book groups:

Ghostliners by Robert D. Ballard (Scholastic, 1998)
(Extra Challenging)

Exploring the Titanic by Robert D. Ballard (Literacy Place)
(Above grade level)

Destination Antarctica by Robert Swan (Literacy Place)
(At grade level)

Discovery Mission by Barbara Bondar (Literacy Place)
(Easier text)

To the Top: Climbing the World's Highest Mountain by S. A. Kramer (Random House, 1993)
(For readers needing more support)

• Explain that each group will read and receive support from the teacher. Groups will meet to discuss the themed content.

b. Independent Reading

• Inform parents that students will select materials from classroom and library resources.

• Inform parents that students will often read on their own, but will have small book sets provided if they choose to read with a partner or in a self-selected book study group.

Writing

- Explain that students will write each day.

  - The writing lesson will always be accompanied by a demonstration of a writing craft by the teacher.

  - Writing will usually occur in Language Arts twice a week and in other areas (e.g. Social Studies and Science) three times a week.

  - Text structure organizers are used for the planning stages of writing.

- Demonstrate, using a text structure organizer for cause and effect writing (Brailsford, 2003), on a topic of local interest, for example, "Drought."

Children learn from writing models: e.g. watching parents write letters, lists, emails, and greeting cards. These social models demonstrate reasons for writing.

Encourage children to write as much as possible. Provide writing opportunities, such as a family message board in the kitchen. Support reluctant writers by sharing writing with your child, both contributing ideas, and swapping the pen back and forth so that both of you write portions.

Students will likely bring home parts of their writing assignments. They may be working on text structure organizers, drafting an account, or revising and editing. Offer support. Remind the child to reread the account often to ensure that sense is preserved.

DROUGHT

CAUSE
Little snowfall or rainfall over the last year

EFFECT 1	EFFECT 2	EFFECT 3	EFFECT 4
water shortages: wells dried up & reservoirs low	crops fail to grow	bush fires increase; high fire hazard	no pasture for cattle; have to be moved or sold

The effects can be collected from the audience and mapped on an overhead.

- At the conclusion of the session, parents go to their child's classroom, where the teacher provides information about the Language Arts timetable and shows it to the group. Specific details are covered; for example:
  — use of a binder to file Tricky Word Corner words to be learned by the child
  — tips on helping the child learn the new words
  — use of plastic, zipper-topped storage bags for the take-home word activities (the bags are on the supply list)
  — reading to the child, and with the child, considered as an important part of nightly homework; book records, and book recommendations for other students, explained
  — tip sheet about how to support their child's learning at home. (See Appendix B.)

- The parent group then returns to the gym to look at displays and to socialize.

Bibliography

Professional References

Cunningham, Patricia M. and Hall, Dorothy P. *Month-by-Month Phonics for First Grade*. Greensboro, NC : Carson-Dellosa, 1997.

Fitzpatrick, Jo. *Phonemic Awareness: Playing with Sounds to Strengthen Beginning Reading Skills*. Cypress, CA: Creative Teaching Press, 1997.

Hall, Dorothy P. and Cunningham, Patricia M. *Month-by-Month Reading and Writing for Kindergarten*. Greensboro, NC: Carson-Dellosa, 1997.

Northern Alberta Reading Specialists' Council. *Paired Reading: Positive Reading Practice*. (Manual by Anne Brailsford, with accompanying training videotape). Distributed in Kelowna, BC: Filmwest, 1991.

Children's Books

Edwards, Wallace. *Alphabeasts*. Toronto: Kids Can Press, 2002.

Sabuda, Robert. *The Christmas Alphabet Book*. New York: Orchard Books, 1996.

Reproducible Books

Fleming, Maria. *Round-the-World Folktale Mini-Books.* New York: Scholastic, 1995.

Fleming, Maria. 25 *Emergent Reader Mini-Books.* New York: Scholastic, 1997.

Kovacs, Debra. 25 *Thematic Mini-Books.* New York: Scholastic, 1992.

Moore, Helen H. 25 *Mother Goose Peek-a-Books.* New York: Scholastic, 1993.

Scholastic High-Frequency Readers Resource Book
(Blackline masters of all 18 high-frequency readers in the series)

Keep Books (kindergarten through grade two)
Ohio State University's Early Literacy Learning Initiative
(1-800-678-6484, or www.keepbooks.org)

Implementing Balanced Literacy in the Classroom

The first year of the program is the busiest one for teachers — but starting a new program can be energizing, too. In the first year, the teacher focuses on learning the new techniques and applying them in the classroom. This chapter "walks alongside" the teacher as the program comes to life.

Setting Up the Classroom Space

Sorting out classroom space is a good first step in program implementation because it builds teacher confidence and because, if the space works, the organization of the classroom day runs more smoothly.

Tips for Teachers

- Before translating ideas into action, we recommend that teachers sketch several possibilities on paper. Minor adjustments through the year are to be anticipated, but it could be stressful to drag a Word Wall into three different locations, until just the right spot is found.

- Before finalizing the spatial organization, go around the classroom and sit in each child's seat. Will each child be able to see the key instructional areas and wall

displays? We have found that in most classrooms we visited, adjustments in spatial organization were necessary, because some children did not have clear sightlines for such essentials as the Word Wall or the pocket charts.

- Few classrooms have ideal space available and compromises have to be made. Don't worry if your spatial organization doesn't look like another teacher's. The spatial plan need only work for your classroom.

Using Wall Space

Word Walls and Tricky Word Corners

Kindergarten and primary classes need room on the walls for Word Wall words. Word Walls take up a good deal of room, although less space will be needed for the kindergarten words than for the 125-or-so words usually featured in each primary grade. Since the kindergarten and primary Word Walls are alphabetized, space needs to be allocated for the alphabet letters in addition to the words. Some upper elementary teachers use a corner wall space for the Tricky Word Corner in their classrooms. In upper elementary grades, words are often clustered into groups: contractions, prefixes and suffixes, compounds, words from other cultures, words for writing, and so on. Such groupings can be delineated with headings.

Tips for Teachers

- If you have combined grades, consider two different colours of card, one for each grade level.

- If you have a bilingual program, separate the Word Walls for each language to lessen confusion.

- Challenge words for stronger spellers are often used in primary and upper elementary grades. Because the Word Wall and Tricky Word Corner need to be uncluttered, focusing on a basic dictionary list that everyone is expected to learn, the challenge words should be placed in a different area of the classroom. Some teachers use a distinctive colour card for challenge words and stick them on a closet door or another part of the wall.

- Place Word Walls only as high on the wall as you can easily reach, because the week's words must be filed on the wall every Friday.

Organizers

Samples of each of the text structure organizers, used to plan writing, should be on clear display on the classroom walls in primary and upper elementary grades.

Tips for Teachers

- The samples should be accompanied by the "strong" words used in a particular type of writing. For example, **first**, **second**, **third**, **next**, **then**, and **finally** are considered strong support words for sequence writing and thus need to be pinned up next to the text structure organizer for sequence writing.

- Each year, you will need to add text structure organizers to the walls as they are used in the classroom. They should be placed low enough on the walls for children to be able to consult them.

Pocket Charts

In kindergarten and primary grades, pocket charts are used for Making Words lessons and for reconstructing texts with sentence and word cards. In upper elementary grades, pocket charts are mainly used for the Making Big Words (word-building) lessons. All pocket charts are used for focused instruction and should be highly visible.

Tips for Teachers

- Word cards used in the pocket charts should have print large enough to be visible at the back of the classroom.

- As pocket charts age, the plastic can turn yellow, obscuring visibility. At that stage,

invest in a new pocket chart! Even new pocket charts can have reduced visibility when the sun reflects off the plastic strips. Consider this when you place the pocket chart on the wall.

Independent Reading Station Charts

Independent reading station charts illustrate the group flow during independent reading time in primary grades. Usually picture cards denote the intent of the station.

Tips for Teachers

- These charts need to be visible when you are explaining the daily station assignments just before the students move into independent reading.

- Put the visual representations of each station—for example, outline drawings of a cougar, a polar bear, and a beaver—on a movable card.

- Many teachers use small pocket charts for the reading station picture cards, to make changes easier. Other teachers use Velcro on the back of each picture card.

- Because group members will change, you will also want to keep individual names as portable as possible. For example, a laminated outline of a cougar may contain name cards, attached with tape or Velcro, listing the five children currently assigned to that reading group. When a child moves to a different group, that child's name can be peeled off the cougar and added to the other group's animal outline.

- In kindergarten, the "independent reading stations" will become a medley of centres that cover all areas of developmental play, literacy, and numeracy. Each area can be charted to illustrate group membership and movement.

Charts for Chants, Poems, and Songs

Charts may be featured on walls and, in primary and kindergarten grades, on hanging chart frames.

Tips for Teachers

- Children need to use these charts as resources in shared reading. They may also be used for a Read Around the Room station during independent reading time for grade one. In this activity, children use pointers and read the print on classroom walls.

- Any chant, poem, or song featured on a chart hanger needs to have well-reinforced "hanging holes" to ensure that the charts don't tear off as children use them.

Children's Work

Of course, classrooms need space to display an ever-changing array of children's work.

Tips for Teachers

- Use the space on the hallway walls near the classroom door to display children's work. This invites parents, community members, and other children to read and enjoy it.

Using Floor Space

Kindergarten and primary classrooms need floor space, preferably carpeted, for gathering the children together to listen to a story or engage in shared reading. In upper elementary grades, students can listen at their desks and tables, and join in with shared reading using an overhead projector or copies of magazine articles.

Tips for Teachers

- During read alouds, it is important that children can view the pictures, but less important that they see every textual detail. However, in shared reading, it is vital that children can see the text clearly.

Small Reading Groups

In a kindergarten class, the teacher will convene small groups for shared reading and possibly guided reading sessions. In the primary and upper elementary grades, small groups will be organized for guided reading and other book study groups. For all grade levels, a space should be arranged for the teacher's small group lessons with children. This space should

contain a table and chairs, and a small board for jotting down teaching points.

Tips for Teachers

- A round table will allow you to see all students, and will make discussion easier. (Some teachers are now acquiring specially designed guided reading tables that have a semicircle cut out to enable the teacher to sit closer to the students and observe their reading behaviours more clearly.)

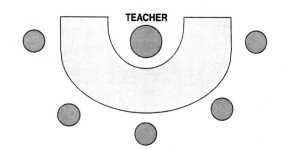

Centres and Stations

Kindergarten teachers will organize floor space for their centres, and primary teachers will organize it for their independent reading stations.

Tips for Teachers

- Position the computer area, the listening station, and any station using an overhead projector (such as a poetry station where poems are selected from overhead transparencies) before you assign other space, because these technology areas must be near electrical outlets.

- Keep supplies portable—for example, by placing book response journals and writing tools in tubs—so that any area can quickly become a literature response area.

- Place a book station or kindergarten library corner near the shelves containing the books. This cuts down traffic across the room.

Using Shelf Space

Books for Independent Reading

Kindergarten teachers will keep most of their books in an open collection in a library corner, and may also include books in other centres such as the playhouse and a "doctor's office" play area. If some kindergarten children move into guided reading groups, levelled book tubs will also be needed to provide resources for home-supported reading practice. Primary grade children will need access to levelled books, placed in tubs and shelved, both for independent reading stations in school and for home reading. The tubs should be clearly labelled and portable. In the upper elementary grades, students may select books from a classroom library collection, from the school library, or from levelled book tubs. The latter will be especially important for students who still need a great deal of support in reading. Levelled books are really separate collections that are used temporarily by readers as they move through the earlier stages of learning to read, when they need lots of successful practice to reinforce their growing range of strategies.

Tips for Teachers

- Levelled tubs are most accessible when stored in the classroom. However, we recommend trading tubs and book titles among several classrooms to increase the variety available to the students.

- Store levelled book tubs on low shelves to make them accessible to children.

- If supplies are desperately low, you might use a mobile trolley of levelled book tubs, but this should be a temporary measure. Similarly, using school library books for the tubs should be only a short-term endeavour, because library resources could be depleted. If library resources must be dispersed among the classrooms, they should be on open shelves so that children have opportunities to select books on their own.

- Familiar books, such as those used for shared reading lessons, can be used for centres in kindergarten and for independent reading stations in primary classes. Store these on shelves or in a big browsing box, together with pointers for partner and small-group reading.

- Add big books featuring collections of class writing, artwork, and group projects to the shelved collection.

- In upper elementary grades, resources for independent reading can be obtained from both school library and classroom collections. It is also a good idea to have small sets of books available for partner reading or self-selected, small-group book studies.

Multilevel Book Sets

Book sets for shared and guided reading, and for literature circles or book clubs will be stored in the school's book room and borrowed for short-term classroom use with small groups.

Tips for Teachers

- In the classroom, it is a good idea to place the materials close to the area used for small group work. These materials are not part of the collection for independent reading, but are used for instructional purposes.

- Some teachers use plastic bins for storing each group's books, and the teacher can also use these lightweight bins to transfer supplies to and from the school's central book location.

Text Structure Organizers

Although samples of text structure organizers are on the classroom walls, students need constant access to these organizers for their own writing. Teachers find it convenient to put piles of 8 x 11-inch organizers on the shelves, as each text structure (Brailsford, 2002, 2003) is introduced. For first graders, who often need more space, we advise enlarging the 8 x 11-inch organizers to 11 x 17 inches.

   Experience has taught us to leave these blank organizers on the shelves! Teachers who left them out accidentally found that children were borrowing them to help with personal writing. This has occurred even in a grade one setting, when a group of children borrowed text structure organizers and used them in their journals.

Tips for Teachers

- Some teachers keep text structure organizers tidy by placing each type (such as Friendly Letter or Persuasive Writing) in a separate plastic basket.

- If space is available, you can place the baskets of organizers on shelves located beneath the wall displays of the organizers and "strong" words.

Making Words Materials

In the kindergarten classroom, large letters mounted on card and strung to form placards can be used to build children's names and to make simple words (Hall and Cunningham, 1997b). These should be accessible for word activities. In the primary grades, student letters and word-building racks need to be placed on shelves, ready to be distributed for the Making Words lessons.

Tips for Teachers

- For the primary Making Words lessons, most teachers store class sets of letters in the type of plastic container that has drawers for nails and screws, purchased from a hardware store. (In the upper elementary grades, paper letter strips are used, for which no shelf storage is required.)

- Teachers in the Edmonton area balanced literacy project use wooden letter racks for each child. Each rack is a simple strip of wood with a central groove. The child builds a word by placing letters, printed on card, in the groove. A lower case letter is printed on one side of each card, and its upper case equivalent on the other side. The teacher (who becomes skilled at reading backwards) can glance around the class and view the words. A local woodworker builds these letter racks. It will save time and mailing costs if you can find entrepreneurs in your community who are willing to make similar racks.

Starting the Teaching-Learning Components

Early in the first year of implementation, the teacher has to take the plunge into starting the balanced literacy program. Although the long-term intent is to create a cohesive Language Arts program, it is best to start with aspects of the program, and gradually expand until the whole program is encompassed.

We recommend starting with an area that is concrete and ensures some "instant success." We usually select the word area as a good starting place, because the activities are outlined (Brailsford, 2002, 2003) and definite. The fast gains from the word study part of the program provide early positive feedback for both children and teacher.

Enhancing areas that are already familiar to the teacher is another low-stress strategy for moving into the program. For example, shared reading may be somewhat alien to upper elementary teachers, but it is highly familiar to primary teachers. Hence, kindergarten and grades-one-to-three teachers could integrate new strategies into their existing skill repertoire. For example, using "talk" that covers all developmental stages when sharing a big book, or discussing "how to read nonfiction texts" would be appropriate enhancements. Upper elementary teachers may feel more comfortable integrating some of the new writing strategies into their program and, for example, using a text structure organizer for a class project on myth writing.

Teachers frequently ask us, "What do we do in the other areas, until we include them in the new program?" For example, if teachers start with the word area, what happens in the reading area until they start the guided reading lessons and book study groups?

Even though this is only an issue in the first year, as the program is slowly phased into the classroom, it is still a common concern. We usually respond to this question by saying, "Do what you've always done in those areas." For most teachers, this is the best advice. Teachers who have read widely may feel confident about introducing a range of new areas simultaneously. The danger here is that teachers who try to incorporate numerous new areas at once may feel crushed if all their ventures don't work out. That is why we suggest focusing on one area at a time, and using familiar routines elsewhere until the first area is running smoothly.

Moving into the Word Area

Movement into the word area can start in the first month of school. At that stage, the teacher will have experienced initial inservices and a demonstration lesson in the classroom.

Kindergarten Letter, Word, and Sound Study

In the kindergarten classroom, the Letter, Word, and Sound block is a brief 10 minutes in a half-day program and 20 minutes in a full-day program. Kindergarten teachers may wish to start with the children's names and the Getting to Know You! activity outlined by Dorothy Hall and Patricia Cunningham (1997). In this activity, a child's name is selected and the class follows a routine of saying and chanting the letters, writing the name, cutting the word into letters, and reconstructing the name. The children then draw a picture of the child. Talk is focused on those important concepts of "letter" and "word," and demonstrations such as cutting the word into letters reinforce the talk.

Tips for Teachers

- You will need to do this type of introductory activity for each child in the classroom. It is worth spending time on because so many important concepts are covered and reinforced when the routine is repeated for each name.

- In an envelope, place the cut-up letters for each child's name, along with a printed model of the name. Place the envelopes in a centre. Write the names in as many different colours as possible — for example, "Eve" in purple letters and "Max" in orange ones — to limit confusion when the children refile the letters into the envelopes.

- Balance this activity with some work on phonemic awareness, such as reading rhyming books and chants, "stretching" words (explained in Step 2), and listening to sounds at the beginning of the children's names.

Primary Word Study

In primary classes, teachers usually start with the Word Wall activities to teach high-frequency words. They print the week's five words on card or paper and focus on the daily practice activities that reinforce learning the new words. They establish routines of introducing the words on Monday, entering the words in personal student dictionaries, sending home the word list and practice suggestions, and using hands-on review activities each day. After the teacher has assessed the range of needs in the classroom, challenge words may be introduced later in September. Once the Word Wall is running, Making Words lessons can be started. The first day is devoted to word building, while the second day is focused on

sorting the words into patterns and transferring the patterns into reading and spelling new words.

Tips for Teachers

- With grade one students, you may wish to start with the Special Child activities suggested by Cunningham and Hall (1997b). In this activity, the class interviews each child and a story about the child is written on chart paper using interactive writing techniques. Then the name is written on a card and chanted, cut up, reconstructed, and compared with other names. As the names list grows, work on word patterns and rhyming is done with the name cards. We usually suggest that classes work on reconstructing the names with letter necklace cards. If the name is "Tracy," then five children are selected. Each child wears a letter card (representing one of the letters from Tracy's name) strung as a placard around the neck. The children, with directions from the class, arrange themselves to form Tracy's name.

- Other than reading attractive alphabet books to the children, we do not recommend any extensive work on letter recognition at the beginning of grade one. When children are immersed in activities such as Special Child, the Word Wall words, and Making Words activities, we find that they learn the alphabet quite quickly, even when they arrive at school with limited alphabet knowledge.

- You should start the Making Words lessons in September. There is sufficient modelling built into the activity to ensure success. Grade one students may start a little later if the Special Child activities are completed first. We recommend starting grade ones with one-vowel words (Cunningham and Hall, 1997b).

- You will need to practise the routines for Making Words lessons before introducing them to your classroom. Practising with a colleague helps to ensure that you have included all of the steps.

- Establish an equipment distribution and collection routine for Making Words lessons at the beginning of the school year. Ask two children to hand a letter rack to every class member, and other children to distribute the letters required to build the word. For example, if the word is "flower," six children will be asked to hand out the letters. Alan gives everyone an **e**; Madison gives everyone an **l**, and so on. At the conclusion of the lesson, the eight children who distributed the materials collect and store them so they are ready for the next lesson.

Jobs	Name
Give out letter sticks	Rahim and Amy
Give out letters	
e	Alan
l	Madison
w	Teague
r	Donovan
f	Jason
o	Riva

Tips for Teachers cont'd.

For grade one, we have found it helpful for the teacher to demonstrate how to give out and collect letter and word racks. A lot of incidental learning can occur during this process. For example, we always say, "This is an **s**," as we put it on a grade one child's desk. Each child who is selected for distributing a letter follows the teacher and states the name of the letter being given out. By the time a child has distributed a letter to about 24 children, there is a strong chance that the letter will be known!

- Make use of transitional time when children are moving from Word Wall activities to the Making Words lesson. Many teachers do a quick shared reading of familiar chants and poems while a chosen group of students distributes the equipment.

- The Making Words lessons are divided by grade in the *Balanced Literacy: Division 1* manual (Brailsford, 2002). When working with a combined grade class, select from either grade's list. The words the children build, and the patterns for transfer they learn, are more important than the complexity of the final word — that is, the "mystery word" at the conclusion of the word-building portion of the lesson.

- Some schools make up packages of the Making Words lessons and store them in boxes or a filing cabinet in the school's bookroom.

- The power of the Making Words lessons lies in the teaching of Sort and Transfer activities on the second day of each lesson. There the patterns are defined, words are compared, and new words are analyzed and spelled. It is vital that teachers provide the second day of instruction for each word lesson. (Note that, as the words become more complex, students in later grade two and in grade three may need two days to complete the word building, and a third day for the Sort and Transfer work.)

- Work on other word analysis and spelling activities only when the teacher and students feel confident with the basic Word Wall and Making Words lessons.

- Build in assessment to guide instruction. For example, the weekly spelling quiz can tell you how well the children have internalized high-frequency words and whether they are using the Word Wall as a resource. If there are unmet needs in these areas, the teacher can institute review weeks for difficult words and talk about the use of the Word Wall more frequently in writing demonstration lessons.

Upper Elementary Word Study

In the upper elementary grades, the Word Study area contains a variety of activities to reinforce word recognition, and spelling and vocabulary skills. We recommend that the teacher plot an initial one-week plan for word study. This plan can be created with colleagues in the initial inservices so that it is prepared for the start of school in September. In the first year, the plan should be simple and contain only two or three activities for the week. You can repeat the first week's plan for each week in September, until you feel confident about the introductory techniques. Over time, you will need to extend the initial plan to ensure that a range of activities is included to develop students' word knowledge.

Sample of a One-Week Introductory Plan				
Monday	**Tuesday**	**Wednesday**	**Thursday**	**Friday**
Tricky Word Corner	Making Big Words lesson	Sort and Transfer lesson for Making Big Words	Buddy review of Tricky Words	Quiz: Tricky Words and transfer words from the Making Big Words lesson

Reference for Making Big Words lessons (Cunningham and Hall, 1994b)
Reference for a Buddy Check method (Pinnell & Fountas, 1998)

Tips for Teachers

- As noted for the Making Words activities for the primary grades, practising the routines with a colleague is recommended before starting them in the classroom.

- The lessons from *Making Big Words* (Cunningham & Hall, 1994b) and *Making More Big Words* (Cunningham & Hall, 1997a) are divided by grade level in the *Balanced Literacy: Division 2* manual (Brailsford, 2003). As noted in the primary tips, if you are teaching a combined grade, you may select words from either grade's list.

- Distribution of materials does not need additional planning in the upper elementary grades, because letter strips for student use are provided with the lessons.

- Lessons can be prepared and packaged in envelopes. Many schools file this lesson collection in the school's bookroom.

- When September's routine is moving with ease, expand Word Study activities in this area so that October's plan is more varied. For suggestions to include in the word area, consult the *Balanced Literacy: Division 2* manual (Brailsford, 2003) and *Month-By-Month Phonics for Upper Grades* (Cunningham and Hall, 1998).

- Build assessment into instruction. Use the weekly spelling quizzes to assess students' retention of tricky words, and their ability to transfer word patterns and construct new words. You may need review weeks for some tricky words, as well as greater emphasis on the Sort and Transfer stage of the Making Big Words lessons if transfer is a problem for some students.

Starting the Writing Program

If schools are already using a process writing approach that includes planning, drafting, revising, and editing, then changes to programming will be moderate in this area. However, there are differences.

First, there is more of an emphasis on balance, in that writing occurs daily as part of a balanced and predictable program. Furthermore, a wide range of text structures is used, so that all children, over the course of their elementary schooling, are exposed to retelling, narratives, descriptive paragraphs, traditional fiction (fables, myths, and legends), poetry,

sequence, persuasive, comparison, cause-and-effect, problem-solution, report, and letter-writing structures. Text structure organizers are introduced and regularly revisited, and both teacher-selected and self-selected writing are featured. Second, daily demonstration lessons preface every writing lesson. The teacher demonstrates a writing craft, helps the students to apply new strategies during interactive writing, or models an aspect of writing through "talk alouds." Third, text structure organizers are used for the planning stages of writing. Over time, and with repeated exposures to their use, these organizer scaffolds can gradually be de-emphasized for students who internalize the nature of the text structure. Finally, there is a strong emphasis on the reading-writing connection. Writing projects and demonstrations are frequently linked to literature.

Kindergarten Writing

In the kindergarten, the teacher can weave writing demonstrations, and shared and interactive writing into the program early in the school year. Links may be made to the Getting to Know You! activity, with the teacher collecting ideas from the children to chart a sentence or two about each child. In kindergarten, the teacher has to seize all opportunities to weave modelling into the program. At first this will be a challenge, and we recommend that teachers specifically plan writing demonstrations, and shared and interactive writing times.

In the centres, a writing area can be organized early in the year. A variety of writing tools should be available, and the children should be encouraged both to draw and to write. Writing tools can be appropriately placed in other centres, for example in the playhouse, in the block construction area (for drawing and writing about creations), and in a café centre (for writing orders, menus, and signs.)

You will be emphasizing early developmental writing in kindergarten, without any intention of introducing the students to text structure organizers and structured writing projects. Instead, the emphasis in the kindergarten program should be on demonstrations, on shared and interactive writing, and on providing opportunities for children to choose their own topics.

Tips for Teachers

- When modelling writing, buy chart paper that is wider horizontally than vertically. Young children need to see whole sentences along a line without having to track downwards to complete an idea. Use markers with strong colours, because children need to see the print clearly. Leave a wide space between each line of print when possible. This allows room for a pointer below each word when the children reread the charts. Slightly exaggerate the word spacing to help children to develop a sense of word boundaries.

- Consider conducting small group, interactive writing lessons. Working in a small group means that instruction can match the children's needs, and that each child can be offered more opportunity to be an active participant than in the large group. (This will be easier to schedule in full day, rather than half day, kindergartens.)

Primary and Upper Elementary Grades

In primary and upper elementary grades, we suggest that teachers start with retelling, story writing, and descriptive paragraph writing. *Retelling* is a key factor in reading comprehension and in descriptive writing. It is flexible enough to be an aspect of, for example, literature response activities, science reports (when added to sequence writing), and autobiographical writing. *Story writing* is a basic structure that can encompass genres such as historical fiction, mysteries, and science fiction. Again, it is a flexible form with many applications. *Descriptive paragraph* writing provides the third foundation for a writing program, as we gradually teach children to build paragraphs into reports and more weighty accounts.

These text structures are the building blocks for both fiction and nonfiction writing. Select one and link the writing project to literature through the read-aloud portion of the program. For example, in a grade two class, a teacher may read Phoebe Gilman's book, *Something from Nothing*, do a demonstration lesson to generate a personal story, and model a journal entry. The children then engage in selecting their own personal stories for their journal entries. A grade five teacher may read *As Long as the River Flows*, Larry Loyie's autobiographical account of his

final summer with his family before being sent to a residential school. Next, the teacher demonstrates how to use the text structure organizer* for a descriptive paragraph to collect ideas on the traditional native life described in the book. The organizer can be filled in, interactively, with the class. In Social Studies, students continue to read about traditional native life and, with a partner, use an organizer to plan a descriptive paragraph on one aspect of this life, such as hunting, food collection, or making clothing. (Later demonstrations will show the students how to translate the planner into a draft, and how to revise and edit. The teacher will use the class paragraph to demonstrate the next stages, and then the children will apply the concepts as they develop their own paragraphs.)

Once the word area is established, start a writing project. Working through the stages may be "rough and ready" at first, but keep in mind a main concept: you can only expect students to progress through the stages of writing when they have been exposed to many demonstrations. (Demonstrations are the teaching sessions you provide on a daily basis, which also emerge from the models of good writing embedded in the texts you read with the children.) Some teachers find writing demonstrations tricky at first. They may not write much themselves, so writing for students, and talking aloud to students about the process, may seem nerve-wracking. Furthermore, demonstrations are unfamiliar to many teachers. Although they may have taught formal lessons about including dialogue in speech, it is more challenging when they have to write the text in front of the students and think aloud about the dialogue needs of that piece of writing. "Making the teacher a writer" is not a primary goal of a balanced literacy program. However, you may find that reflective journal writing during the professional development sessions helps to condition your "writing muscles." In addition, you can practise demonstration writing with a partner or in small groups.

In grade one, the introduction to writing has to follow a slower pace. Retelling in journals provides an appropriate starting place, as you model writing in demonstrations and encourage the children to draw and write. It is best if you start to use the text structure organizers for descriptive paragraphs and stories, as an analysis activity after you read to the children. For example, after you read a story, the children can recall the characters, setting, problem, key events and resolution, and these can be filled in on the text structure organizer for a story. In this way, the students are exposed to the form of the organizers before they ever use them for their own writing. As the students progress into writing, the organizers themselves can form completed written accounts. For example,

* For information regarding the text structure organizers consult the *Balanced Literacy: Division 1 and Division 2* manuals (Brailsford, 2002, 2003)

the students may listen to the teacher read *The Snow Riders*, by Constance McGeorge (1995). They can then, in an interactive writing session, create a class descriptive paragraph on the making of the snow sculpted horses. Next, the teacher and students can brainstorm about other snow sculptures they could make, such as snow bears, dogs, kittens, snakes, and birds, and finally the children can write their own accounts on 11 x 17-inch descriptive paragraph organizers. These accounts can form the final written version of their snow sculpture paragraphs.

In the first year of the program, all the text structure organizers will be unfamiliar to the children, and teachers will need to introduce the forms. In subsequent years, however, the forms will be familiar to all, except for new children entering the school. For these newcomers, text structure planners will need to be used, and some other children may continue to need the support of such planners. However, many others may be able to plot accounts without the tangible planners. Furthermore, use of the planners is going to vary, depending on the text structure organizer utilized. For example, text structure organizers for descriptive paragraphs and story writing are used from grade one onwards, whereas a text structure such as problem-solution is introduced only to upper elementary students. Thus organizers may be used for less familiar structures and dropped for the most familiar.

Tips for Teachers

- Be flexible in using the text structures for writing projects. If your school decides to do one text structure a month, for example, this will reduce flexible application in the classroom, where persuasive writing may be appropriate for one class in December, while being most useful for another in February. Revisit text structures during the year to help the children to benefit from previous experience.

- Build in assessment to guide instruction. For example, rubrics may be used occasionally to explore students' planning, content development, organization of ideas, and use of conventions (Brailsford, 2002, 2003). Findings from these assessments can help to shape future writing demonstration lessons and individualized assistance for students.

- Use writing support groups as vehicles for student assistance. For example, a group struggling with planning could be formed, or a group needing help with editing.

- If you are teaching a combined grade, the writing program will be sufficiently multilevel to meet all students' needs. Demonstration lessons can vary and include content that spans both grades. The writing support group structures will serve to assist teachers in helping writers from both grades. Avoid calling together, for example, a group of grade four writers and then another for grade five writers. Instead, include students from both grades in a writing support group, clustering the students according to their needs.

Building the Reading Program

The balanced literacy reading program has several components. These components may vary slightly as the students progress through the grades, but they all have the same foundations, and all are intended to move children from supported to independent learning.

Maximum Support			→ Minimum Support	
Kindergarten – Grade 3:				
Read Aloud	Shared Reading		Guided Reading	Independent Reading
Grades 4–6:				
Read Aloud	Shared Reading	Class Strategy Lesson	Book Study Groups (Guided Reading, Literature Circles, and Book Clubs)	Independent Reading

When starting the program in the classroom, the teacher needs to keep the whole plan in mind, but institute the components at a comfortable pace.

There is little doubt that read alouds can occur early in the year and continue throughout the year, at all grade levels. This is a familiar practice for all teachers. However, what may take time to incorporate is the balanced literacy program's strong emphasis on reading-writing connections. The program should often link the read alouds to other program components, and especially to the writing sessions. Literature links are used frequently to start writing projects.

Kindergarten Reading

In the kindergarten class, whole group read alouds and shared reading lessons can start at the beginning of the school year, because these practices are familiar to the early childhood teacher.

The next step is to move to small group reading sessions during centre time. Small group lessons ensure that the teacher can tailor instruction to meet the children's varying needs. The teacher should aim for one small group reading lesson a day. All children should experience small group, shared reading lessons with the teacher, progressing from interacting with big books to using little books. Some children may be developmentally ready to move to guided reading groups. We suggest that all children start with small group, shared reading sessions while the teacher gains familiarity with the procedures and notes the children's successes and challenges. The teacher can gradually move to offering guided reading groups if it becomes clear that some children are more advanced emergent readers.

Teachers can offer independent reading opportunities in centres right from the beginning of the school year.

Emergent Reader Characteristics

- Understands that print holds a message
- Demonstrates good book-handling concepts
- Displays some control over directionality concepts, such as knowing where to start reading and sweeping left to right (may be uncertain about line movement and will be inconsistent in word-by-word matching)
- Locates some words around the classroom, such as names, special signs, and words on chants and poems
- Notices some print details, such as "That starts with **M** like my name."
- Uses picture cues to aid in word predictions and to support story meaning
- Has developed memory for text on predictable books and can check some graphic features
- Uses language cues to make predictions
- Uses some letter sounds to assist word recognition

Tips for Teachers

- During shared reading sessions, ensure that "talk" meets the range of children's needs. For example, include book handling concepts (print the right way up, going from front to back, and turning pages) as well as more advanced concepts (print tracking, word predictions, and first letter sounds in words) in each session.

- Choose high-quality children's fiction and nonfiction books for shared reading and read alouds. Avoid "theme dominance," in which weaker texts may be selected just because they fit with a class theme.

- When moving into shared and guided reading lessons with small groups, ensure that the children are very familiar with centre routines. The rule should be that the teacher and the small group are not to be interrupted unless there is an emergency. Now there is a difference between what an adult would call an emergency and how a five-year-old perceives a situation! That is why it is helpful to keep small group reading sessions short (approximately 10 to 15 minutes), and to have a roving adult to support centre activities.

- Observe the children's progress during the large and small book shared reading times. Monitor for students who are ready to move into guided reading lessons. They will demonstrate emergent reader characteristics.

- If you have enough staff or community volunteers, you may be able to build in support during the independent reading centre time. For example, children can have stories read to them or do more shared reading of books already introduced in the class.

Primary Reading

In the primary grades, teachers can progress into read alouds and shared reading early in the year. It will be necessary to train the children in all of the routines for the independent reading stations before starting guided reading groups. Many teachers start guided reading groups sometime in December in the first year of a balanced literacy program. Certainly, guided reading is the most complex area in the reading component and will need the most support from professional development.

Use the shared reading sessions as vehicles for strategy teaching. Reading strategies for contextual word recognition and comprehension can be woven into all shared reading activities. For example, the strategy teaching will focus initially on print tracking, word recognition, and the comprehension of events and ideas. As the children progress through the primary grades, the range of strategies will expand. They will learn how to make reflective responses to literature, and how to utilize the organizational formats of nonfiction texts, such as tables of contents, glossaries, labelled diagrams, and chapter organization.

Establish the independent reading stations gradually and demonstrate the routines and the work expectations at each one. As the children try each station, be available to work on reinforcing expectations. Keep the stations simple and focused on meaningful reading. All activities should have the aim of moving students towards extended daily periods of reading. Depending on the needs of the class, stations should be running for a week or so before a guided reading lesson is started, so that children will know how to focus on their stations and avoid interrupting a guided reading group in progress. Books for independent reading stations may be roughly levelled at first but should be more finely levelled over time. We use the Fountas and Pinnell levelling system and criteria (1996). Working with colleagues to level books is strongly recommended. Although some titles may be listed in *Matching Books to Readers* (Fountas and Pinnell, 1999), professional opinions and consultations about the books and the criteria are needed for others. The first levelling is unlikely to be the last. One word of caution: if there are doubts about the level of a book, always place it in the higher level tub to ensure student reading success. For example, if there are questions about whether a book should be in the F or G tub, place it in the G tub.

Tips for Teachers

- With grade ones, and with older classes in which children have short attention spans, we recommend that you run one guided reading group before recess and one after the break.

- In the first year of program implementation, the group selection process may be a challenge. We take a pragmatic view of the process. For guided reading, you need to match instruction, book levels, and children's reading needs appropriately. In grade one, we recommend starting all the children on level A materials and then moving some of them into other materials as you identify the more advanced readers. In grades two and three, the previous teacher's recommendations can be used as starting points. Make opportunities to hear children read before starting guided reading. You could ask children to read benchmark books at various levels so that you can establish an instructional level. (See the *Balanced Literacy: Division 1* manual, Brailsford, 2002 for explanations of benchmark book assessments.) When you form the first groups, be aware that changes will occur frequently.

- In subsequent years, teachers find group placement to be straightforward. Many of the children will have been in balanced literacy the previous year, and the previous teacher will provide lists of book levels and strategy needs. Only new children coming into the program will need benchmark book assessments, to establish an appropriate guided reading group.

- If there are more than six primary children reading the same level book, consider splitting that large group into two smaller groups.

- Plan the guided reading lesson to ensure that it stays focused, provides the support the children will need to read the text, and allows enough time for them to read. The intent is to provide a "just right" book (at instructional level, with appropriate supports and a few challenges) for a group of readers who share similar reading needs. Teacher talk should focus on providing an introduction that introduces some supports and challenges; setting a purpose for the readers; providing prompts to help readers problem-solve; and drawing ideas together in a conclusion, perhaps by reviewing the purpose for reading, discussing challenges (including comprehension), and pointing out an observed "good reader" strategy.

- The children in your class should receive just enough guidance to enable them to read the levelled text independently. They should be left with some problems to solve as they read.

- As books become longer and more complex, you will need to divide content over several guided reading lessons. Allow enough time for discussion of content and linkages across chapters.

- A basic form of tracking and assessment can occur as soon as the guided reading groups start. A book record should be kept, indicating the child's journey through the levelled materials. We recommend that teachers keep strategy checklists to guide observations of students. We suggest focusing on one or two strategies for each guided reading lesson and observing each reader's use of the strategies. Assessment procedures should be practical and linked strongly to instruction.

- In combined grades, none of the reading areas presents any organizational difficulty. In fact, the guided reading group structures are extremely helpful in providing instruction for a wide range of learners. You can cluster the children according to their needs for guided reading, irrespective of grade placement. In the Edmonton area project, we had a small school where the teacher combined grades one to three in the classroom and the reading components worked smoothly in those circumstances.

Just as readers need "just right" books, teachers need "just right" assessment techniques that provide focused information for instruction, without detracting from instructional time.

Upper Elementary Reading

In upper elementary grades, read alouds can begin immediately. Teachers select books to read aloud to the class that match the theme of the shared reading and book study groups. Read alouds can also be chosen to link to the text structure being used in writing.

Independent reading can also start at the beginning of the school year. The teacher should use this time to help students with book selections and to work diagnostically with them. This will assist the teacher in clustering readers into book study groups with levelled materials.

The teacher may then venture into the class strategy lesson, using content from the read aloud or from shared reading. This may be done as a preface to book study groups. For example, the teacher may select the Time Detectives theme from Literacy Place, a grade six nonfiction theme that addresses bringing the past to life. As the class strategy for the lesson, the teacher elects to focus on interpreting photographs, knowing that students will need this skill in their book study groups and as they read content area materials. The class uses an article from the *Time Detective* magazine (pages 6 to 8), called "Can Pictures Talk?" The article discusses how historical pictures can be analyzed for information about the past. Two class photographs from 1889 and 1912 are shown. The students and teacher choral read the introduction to the article. Then, on a prepared chart, the teacher jots down the children's remarks about the time, place, and people depicted in the first class photograph, and asks them to provide clues, or evidence, to support their ideas.

	Information	Clues
Time (When?)	- 1889 - old-fashioned dresses (Victorian) - boys in knee breeches	- page 6 (first paragraph) - black and white photo showing outfits
Place (Where?)	- Revelstoke, British Columbia - old wooden schoolhouse with few windows	- page 6 (first paragraph) picture shows a building behind the students — it's probably a school
People (Who?)	- a male teacher - 28 students ranging from age 5-6 to mid-teens	- picture shows one teacher - little children in the front row and older students standing behind

The children then read the pictorial labels with a buddy. Following the partner reading, the teacher asks for further information. The class discusses the clues they used to make their decisions and these are added to the chart by the teacher. The teacher summarizes and reinforces the idea that the children can use pictorial clues to give information about the historical time, the place, and the lives of the people. The children may then form groups to chart their ideas about historical pictures and photographs provided by the teacher. Alternatively, this strategy can be

used to start book study groups. The students can move to their book groups and apply the strategy to analyzing the front cover of their book.

Once the teacher has ventured into read alouds, class strategy lessons, shared reading, and independent reading, book study groups can begin. A teacher new to the program cannot launch into literature circles, bookclubs, and guided reading all at once. Instead, we recommend starting with guided reading groups, and adding the other book study formats later in the first year.

If you are using the Scholastic Literacy Place units, the *Teacher's Tool Kit* (2002) offers valuable help in planning for the Reading Hour. Each *Tool Kit* has book study grouping suggestions, a core comprehension strategy, and literature response activities. It also includes list of books that can be used as read alouds, or as materials to extend the Literacy Place selections to better meet the needs of very advanced readers as well as those needing a great deal of support.

Tips for Teachers

- You can enhance independent reading by providing a variety of book resources. Although many children may choose to read independently, offer small sets of books for readers who want to read with a partner or a small group. Vary the levels of the books and change the sets over the school year. Consider adding plays and books of poems to the sets. For independent reading, let the students choose both their book and their reading colleagues.

- While we recommend that upper elementary readers choose their own books, you may find that a few children may still need the support offered by levelled resources. If so, offer a few levelled tub books.

- Class strategy lessons should teach the students how to apply core comprehension strategies and how to write literature responses for the materials they read. Keep literature responses simple and link them to a core comprehension strategy whenever possible. For example, if a core comprehension strategy is Retelling, Relating, and Reflecting (Schwartz and Bone, 1995), then a literature response journal should feature reader responses that use these strategies and prompts.

- You will need to cluster students into appropriate book study groups, using levelled materials which ensure that all students can engage with the text. If balanced literacy was introduced in primary grades at your school the year

Tips for Teachers cont'd.

before being extended to upper elementary grades, then the grade four teacher can use information from the grade three teacher to help form initial book study groups. Grades five and six teachers may also use information from previous teachers, but they will likely need to use other sources as well. Again, we recommend grouping pragmatically, by using the selected book study books as benchmark texts. Teachers can use the texts for quick assessments (Brailsford, 2003) to decide on appropriate reader-text matches.

- With classes which include some children with short attention spans, we recommend that you run one guided reading group before recess and one after the break.

- Keeping track of each child's book study books will provide indications about their relative progress. It will only be a rough assessment guide, and more details can be provided by using strategy checklists, benchmark assessments, and reading observations, such as the Oral Reading Observations anecdotal records (Brailsford, 2003). As in primary grades, assessment in grades four to six should be integrated with instruction as often as possible, since otherwise assessment can erode valuable instructional time.

- With combined grades, the reading components work well as they are designed to function in classes with a wide range of learners' needs. Only in the combined grades three-four class will some modifications be necessary in the transition

The Time Detectives Theme

(grade six)

These were the book choices one teacher made for his book study groups

Extra Challenging
(2-3 Grade Levels Above)
Castle Diary: The Journal of Tobias Burgess, Page
by Richard Platt

Challenging
(1-2 Grade Levels Above)
The Secrets of Vesuvius
by Sara C. Bissel
(Literacy Place)

Average
(At Grade Level)
Mysteries of Time
by Larry Verstraete
(Literacy Place)

Easy
(1-2 Grade Levels Below)
Knights in Rusty Armour
by Pat Hancock
(Literacy Place)

Easy Plus
(2-3 Grade Levels Below)
Ice Mummy
by Mark Dubowski and Cathy East Dubowski

The teacher was wondering whether to place Tony in the group reading *Knights in Rusty Armour* or in the one reading *Ice Mummy*, and used *Knights in Rusty Armour* for a benchmark assessment of word recognition and comprehension (Brailsford, 2003). Tony had only 85% contextual word recognition and 60% comprehension on the piece of text selected for analysis; the teacher decided the text was too challenging for Tony. He achieved far more success on *Ice Mummy* (94% contextual word recognition and 90% comprehension) and was fascinated by the photographs in the book. Therefore the teacher placed Tony in the *Ice Mummy* group. As the example shows, we believe that quick assessments on the books themselves are far more reliable than a formal reading test.

from the primary to the upper elementary program. We suggest that the Language Arts program be run on the primary model for at least part of the year, and perhaps the whole year, but with modifications in

Tips for Teachers cont'd.

materials. In guided reading, many of the grade threes will continue to need the range of materials from the primary program. Many of the grade fours, meanwhile, can move on to the materials from Literacy Place, but the program will run as a small group book study, rather than as a themed unit for the whole class. Of course, advanced grade three readers will be able to use the Literacy Place

materials and grade four readers needing more support can read either the Bookshop or Literacy Place extender materials (See *Teacher's Tool Kit*: Scholastic 2002, for the "Easy Plus" books for Literacy Place). This pattern may continue all year, or a transition to Literacy Place or supplementary materials could be made during the year.

Concluding Thoughts

In the wonderful children's book, *The Pumpkin Blanket*, by Deborah Turney Zagwyn, five-year-old Clee owns a colourful, cosy patchwork quilt. Across many cold autumn days, she and her father pick apart the threads holding the patchwork squares together and then use each square to protect a pumpkin from the frosty nights. On Halloween, Clee and her

father go into the garden to collect the pumpkins. The wind whirls the quilt pieces up into the sky, where they fuse into the ebb and flow of glorious Northern Lights.

Like Clee and her father separating the pieces of a quilt, we have "picked apart" a balanced literacy program to illustrate the steps teachers, schools, and districts move through when implementing this literacy approach. However, we don't want to leave you with the impression that the program remains simply an array of steps or pieces! Like Clee's quilt, the balanced literacy program we describe has a whole that is greater than the sum of its parts. It can, when combined with skillful teachers, become an integrated, fluid network of literacy experiences that meets the learning needs of children throughout their elementary schooling.

Bibliography

Professional References

Brailsford, Anne. *Balanced Literacy: Division 1*. Edmonton, AB: Edmonton Public Schools Learning Resources, 2002.

Brailsford, Anne. *Balanced Literacy: Division 2*. Edmonton, AB: Edmonton Public Schools Learning Resources, 2003.

Cunningham, Patricia M. and Hall, Dorothy P. *Month-by-Month Phonics for Upper Grades*. Greensboro, NC: Carson-Dellosa, 1998.

Cunningham, Patricia M. and Hall, Dorothy P. *Making More Big Words*. Torrance CA: Good Apple, 1997a.

Cunningham, Patricia M. and Hall, Dorothy P. *Month-By-Month Phonics for First Grade*. Greensboro NC: Carson-Dellosa, 1997b.

Cunningham, Patricia M. and Hall, Dorothy P. *Making Words*. Torrance, CA: Good Apple, 1994a.

Cunningham, Patricia, M. and Hall, Dorothy P. *Making Big Words*. Greensboro NC: Carson-Dellosa, 1994b.

Fountas, Irene C. and Pinnell, Gay Su. *Matching Books to Readers: Using Leveled Books in Guided Reading, K-3*. Portsmouth, NH : Heinemann, 1999.

Fountas, Irene C. and Pinnell, Gay Su. *Guided Reading: Good First Teaching for all Children*. Portsmouth, NH: Heinemann, 1996.

Hall, Dorothy P. and Cunningham, Patricia M. *Month-by-Month Reading & Writing for Kindergarten*. Greensboro NC: Carson-Dellosa, 1997.

Pinnell, Gay Su and Fountas, Irene C. *Word Matters: Teaching Phonics & Spelling in the Reading/Writing Classroom*. Portsmouth, NH: Heinemann, 1998.

Schwartz, Susan and Bone, Maxine. *Retelling, Relating, Reflecting: Beyond the 3 R's*. Toronto: Irwin, 1995.

Children's Books

Dubowski, Mark and Dubowski, Cathy East. *Ice Mummy*. New York: Random House, 2001.

Gilman, Phoebe. *Something From Nothing*. Markham, ON: Scholastic Canada, 1992.

Loyie, Larry. *As Long as the Rivers Flow*. Toronto: Groundwood Books / Douglas & McIntyre, 2002.

McGeorge, Constance W. *Snow Riders*. San Francisco: Chronicle Books, 1995.

Platt, Richard. *Castle Diary: The Journal of Tobias Burgess*, Page. Cambridge, MA: Candlewick Press, 1999.

Zagwyn, Deborah Turney. *The Pumpkin Blanket*. Markham, ON: Fitzhenry & Whiteside, 1990.

Literacy Place Materials

Bissel, Sara C. *The Secrets of Vesuvius*. Markham, ON: Scholastic/Madison Press, 1990.

Hancock, Pat. *Knights in Rusty Armour.* Markham, ON: Scholastic Canada, 1999.

Verstraete, Larry. *Mysteries of Time*. Richmond Hill, ON: Scholastic Canada, 1992.

Teacher's Tool Kit: A Guide to Using Literacy Place in Your Classroom. Markham, ON: Scholastic Canada, 2002.

Time Detective Magazine. Markham, ON: Scholastic Canada, 1999.

Observation Guides for School and Classroom Visits

The following guides are provided to focus your observations during visits to a balanced literacy school and classrooms.

The School Observation Guide covers important aspects of the balanced literacy program that relate to the entire school, focusing the observer on key areas to view and to ask about.

Separate Classroom Observation Guides are provided for kindergarten, primary, and upper elementary grades. Although the central questions that guide observations remain the same, the examples of balanced literacy programming you will see in action will vary at different grade levels. Use a separate guide for every classroom you visit.

In each classroom guide, the left column describes examples of what you may observe. The central column highlights a key question. Brief observations can also be recorded in this column. In the right column, space is provided for your questions. These may include questions for the teachers being observed, which can be asked after classes have finished. They could also be questions to be discussed with colleagues after you return to your own school.

SCHOOL OBSERVATION GUIDE

Examples	Guiding Question/ Your Notes	Your Questions
Continuity • School has balanced literacy program in all primary grades • Kindergarten is included in the programming • Upper elementary grades are also engaged in balanced literacy • At the end of a school year, teachers send book levels, comments on readers' strategies and an end-of-the-year writing sample to the next teacher • Children know the Language Arts agendas at the beginning of each school year (expectations are familiar to them)	How many grades are involved in balanced literacy? What are the indicators that the program offers continuity for students?	

Materials
• Professional development materials
  - Definite location?
  - Easy loan system?
• Materials for guided reading, book clubs, and literature circles
  - Central book room?
  - Labelling of level?
  - Easy loan system?
	How are materials shared by the staff?	

Examples	Guiding Question/ Your Notes	Your Questions
Professional Development The school • Uses reading specialists/consultants • Has long-term inservices Each teacher • Has access to demonstration lessons from consultants • Has access to coaching from consultants • Has opportunities to share and reflect with other teachers in school • Has opportunities to share and reflect with teachers in other schools • Receives in-school mentoring support (for new teachers)	How does the staff access support in implementing balanced literacy programming?	
Focus on Literacy • Schedules daily blocks for all components of balanced literacy • Integrates some components with other curriculum areas • Avoids interruptions during literacy learning time (e.g. schedules school assemblies and events to avoid key literacy blocks) • Starts school day promptly, and with few announcements, so teaching and learning can begin • Schedules meetings and mini-inservices with parents to encourage appropriate home literacy activities • Has part of the staff meeting allocated to professional development and staff sharing of articles and ideas	How does the school make literacy learning a priority?	

CLASSROOM OBSERVATION GUIDE: KINDERGARTEN		
Classroom: _____	Grade: _____	
Examples	**Guiding Question/ Your Notes**	**Your Questions**
Appearance of the Classroom ***Bulletin Boards:*** For example, Word Wall with children's names and a few high-frequency words; samples of shared class writing; meaningful labels such as "Get pencils here" ***Spatial Organization:*** For example, Word Wall in clear view of all students; space for whole group read alouds and shared reading; and tables for small literacy groups ***Materials:*** For example, big books, poem and chant charts; library corner; literacy woven into the centres by including books, telephone directory, paper, pencils, and take-out menus in the playhouse	As you look around the room, what are the indicators of balanced literacy programming?	
Components of the Program ***Reading:*** • Read aloud • Shared reading • Literacy groups for shared and guided reading • Independent reading ***Word/Letter/Phonemic Awareness Work*** ***Writing:*** • Writing demonstration (write alouds, shared writing) • Guided writing • Independent writing	What components of the balanced literacy program did you observe?	

Examples	Guiding Question/ Your Notes	Your Questions
Instructional Approaches ***Examples:*** • Changing from whole class to small group and individualized teaching • Using multilevel methods during whole class teaching, such as providing prompts and comments that meet a range of needs in shared reading and writing • Using multilevel materials	How does the teacher vary classroom approaches and materials in order to meet the children's literacy learning needs?	

CLASSROOM OBSERVATION GUIDE: PRIMARY GRADES

Classroom: _____ **Grade:** _____

Examples	Guiding Question/ Your Notes	Your Questions
Appearance of the Classroom ***Bulletin Boards:*** For example, Word Wall; reading stations chart; writing organizers; letters and racks for Making Words lessons. ***Spatial Organization:*** For example, Word Wall in clear view of all children; guided reading table; space for shared reading and reading aloud to class. ***Materials:*** For example, guided reading book sets; tubs of levelled books; big books; and student-sized writing organizers	As you look around the room, what are the indicators of balanced literacy programming?	
Components of the Program ***Reading:*** • Read aloud • Shared reading • Guided reading • Independent reading ***Working with Words:*** (words, letters, phonemic awareness, word patterns) ***Writing:*** • Writing demonstration (write alouds and shared writing) • Guided writing • Independent writing	What components of the balanced literacy program did you observe?	

Examples	Guiding Question/ Your Notes	Your Questions
Instructional Approaches ***Examples:*** • Changing from whole class to small group and individualized teaching • Using multilevel methods during whole class teaching: for example, varying word difficulty levels in Making Words; using supported, whole class reading approaches; and varying the content emphasized in writing demonstrations • Using multilevel materials	How does the teacher vary classroom approaches and materials in order to meet the children's literacy learning needs?	

CLASSROOM OBSERVATION GUIDE: UPPER ELEMENTARY GRADES		
Classroom: _____ **Grade:** _____		
Examples	**Guiding Question/ Your Notes**	**Your Questions**
Appearance of the Classroom **Bulletin Boards:** For example, area for tricky words and word patterns (words frequently misspelled, contractions, prefixes and suffixes etc.); writing organizers; and writing checklists **Spatial Organization:** For example, word area in clear view of all students; guided reading table **Materials:** For example, guided reading book sets; independent reading books and magazines; literature response journals; student-sized copies of writing organizers	As you look around the room, what are the indicators of balanced literacy programming?	
Components of the Program **Reading:** • Read aloud • Shared reading • Class strategy lesson • Guided reading or Literature Circles/Book Clubs • Independent reading **Word Work:** (word analysis, word patterns, high usage spellings) **Writing:** • Writing demonstration (write alouds, shared writing and mini-lessons) • Guided writing • Independent writing	What components of the balanced literacy program did you observe?	

Examples	Guiding Question/ Your Notes	Your Questions
Instructional Approaches *Examples:* • Changing from whole class to small group and individualized teaching • Using multilevel methods during whole class teaching: for example, varying word difficulty levels in Making Words; using supported, whole class reading approaches; and varying content emphasized in writing demonstrations • Using multilevel materials	How does the teacher vary classroom approaches and materials in order to meet the students' literacy learning needs?	

For Parents of Kindergarten Children:

How to Help Your Kindergarten Child to be a Reader and a Writer

- **Read to your child every day.**

  — Reread favourite books.

  — Read in a relaxed way so that your child enjoys the experience.

  — Read with expression, for example, using different voices for characters.

  — Talk about the book with your child. Ask open-ended questions, such as "What do you think might happen?" or "He is so funny. Does he remind you of someone?"

  Library books will come home every _____, and the book backpack will be sent home every two weeks. Read these books to your child. Join the public library, too! It will increase your book supply and offer some good story-reading programs.

- **If your child starts guided reading this year, encourage your child to read the books to you.** If your young reader gets stuck on a word, encourage the child by reading part of the book out loud together.

- **Demonstrate that you like reading and writing.** Parents are powerful models and a child learns by observing them. Write notes, letters, e-mails, and cards, and let your child see you writing. Invite your child to join in and help write (and draw) a letter to Grandma and Grandpa. Encourage family to write back to the child, which will help the youngster connect writing and reading. Let your child see you reading, and share some of the things you read with your child.

- **Provide writing materials at home and encourage your child to communicate through drawing and writing.** Markers, pencils, paper, a scrapbook, or a blackboard or whiteboard encourage a child to write.

- **Help your child to write special words that are important to him/her**, such as the child's own name, family members' names, a pet, a special toy, food, and interests.

- **Help your child with the sounds of the language.** Read nursery rhymes, poems, rhyming books, and alphabet books with your child.

For Parents of Children in Primary Grades:

How to Help Your Child Develop as a Reader and a Writer

- **Read to your child.** Reading to a child expands vocabulary, builds a strong knowledge of different types of books, helps children to compare books and to relate events in books to their own lives, enhances comprehension, and can be a warm and relaxed time for parent and child.

  — Let your child choose many of the books.

  — Occasionally introduce new books that will stretch your child's experiences.

  — Read in a relaxed, unhurried way and engage the child's interest with your expressive reading.

  Library books will come home every _____. In addition, your child may borrow books from the classroom supply. Join the public library, too! Your child may read some of the books independently, but more challenging books can be read aloud by a parent.

- **Help your child to practise reading.**

  — Your child will bring home books that are "just right" for independent reading. In the early stages of reading, encourage the child to read these books to you and give the child positive feedback. If the child is stuck on a word or seems hesitant, read out loud together to provide support and encouragement.

  — As your child becomes a more fluent reader, he or she may prefer to read independently. Try to share some of your child's book choices and read some together chorally, or read the same chapter silently with your child and talk about events and ideas. Keep your comments and questions open-ended, for example: "I wondered whether…" "What were you thinking when…?" "Do you think he'll…?"

- **Assist your child with the weekly Word Wall words and other word-building activities.**
  - The weekly Word Wall words come home every Monday. File your child's word sheet in a binder so that you can keep a record of the year's new words. We practise these words every day in the classroom, and we'd appreciate your support in using fun and hands-on practice activities at home. Some of these activities are listed on the weekly word sheet. Remember that the challenge words are optional.

  - Every couple of weeks, a word-building activity will be sent home. Cut up the letter strip and form as many words as possible from the letters. Give your child support and reread the words together. If you have time, help your child to sort the words into patterns; for example, all the words that start with **sh** or all the words that have **-ate** as the pattern at the end.

  - Play word games with your child to build interest and skills in this area, such as *Junior Scrabble*, *Spill and Spell*, and children's crosswords.

- **Help your child to develop as a writer.** Provide writing equipment at home, such as paper, scrapbooks, markers, pencils, blackboard and chalk or whiteboard and erasable markers. If you happen to have access to a computer, this can become a tool for writing, too. Encourage your child to communicate in writing. Do some co-operative writing with your child: for example, writing a letter or story together.

For Parents of Children in Upper Elementary Grades:

How to Help your Child Develop as a Reader and a Writer

- **Continue to read aloud to your child.** Many parents stop reading to their child as the child becomes a more competent reader. However, we recommend that you continue to read books to your child that are a little more difficult than he or she can read independently. Reading aloud continues to expand vocabulary and knowledge, and helps your child to comprehend a wide range of information. Let your child choose many of the books you read, but also add "a parent's choice" on occasion, choosing a book that you believe will delight your child, and be an enjoyable shared experience for both of you.

  Library books will come home every _____. In addition, your child may select books from the class library. Take your child to the public library frequently so that there are ever-changing book collections in your home. Some of these books will be helpful for your child's research projects this year.

- **Encourage your child to read as much as possible.**
  — Let your child see you enjoying reading at home.

  — Provide an interesting supply of items to read, including library books and borrowed or bought magazines on topics of interest. Comics can also be motivating and engage the child in reading!

  — Share in reading with your child. If a child struggles to read independently, then read pages together, out loud or silently, and talk about the book. Use open-ended comments and questions that don't "test" the child but welcome discussion, for example: "It makes me think of… What does it make you think of?" "That was scary. I was wondering… What about you?"

  — Be supportive if the child reads aloud to you; children are sensitive about corrections and skill-testing questions, so support your child by reading out loud together when there are tricky parts of the text.

- **Help your child with tricky words and word-building activities.**
  When tricky words in reading and spelling are being studied at school, your child will bring home a word practice sheet. Although we will be practising these words at school, we would appreciate your support in reviewing these important words with your child at home. File the word sheets in a binder at home so that you have a list of all the year's words, and can review some on occasion. Use the hands-on practice activities listed on the weekly word sheet. Remember that the challenge words are optional.

  Every two weeks or so, your child will bring home a word-building activity. Support your child in rereading the words you have built together.

- Play word games with your child, such as children's crosswords and word puzzles, or *Scrabble* and *Spill and Spell*.

- **Support your child as a writer.**
  — Provide writing opportunities with easily found materials in your home. Integrate writing into family life, for example, by having a family message board and by engaging in co-operative writing (sharing a writing activity with both parent and child adding ideas and words).

  — If you have access to a computer, this can be used as a tool to give your child writing practice.

  — If you are helping your child with a school writing project, it is likely to be at the revising ideas and editing stage. (Your child will have done thorough planning and initial writing at school.) Help your child by suggesting reading the account aloud and checking for inconsistencies. Recommend that your child underline doubtful spellings and then you can look them up together. Support, but avoid doing the writing!

Balanced Literacy Achievement Results

The pilot year of the balanced literacy program in Edmonton Public Schools (1997-1998) comprised the grades one and two classes of four schools. At the end of the year, all the children in the school district were tested in reading, using the Highest Level of Achievement Test (HLAT), a locally normed version of the Canadian Test of Basic Skills (CTBS). District scores were calculated, and the results from the classrooms in the balanced literacy schools were compared with the district's scores. In each of the balanced literacy classrooms, all children who had received balanced literacy instruction (word study and reading) for at least seven months were included in the results. The numbers, although small in the pilot year, included funded special-needs students. There were four developmentally delayed youngsters, three children with learning disabilities, four students with behavioural disorders, and several ESL children.

Pilot Year: Achievement in Reading Results (4 schools), June 1998

	Balanced Literacy	District
	Percentage of students at or above grade level	Percentage of students at or above grade level
Reading		
Grade one	94% (N=82)	84% (N=5903)
Grade two	93% (N=55)	83% (N=5842)

Note: At two of the four pilot schools, balanced literacy was combined with Reading Recovery©. One hundred percent of the children at those two schools (grades one and two) were at or above grade level.

In the second year of implementing balanced literacy (1998-1999), 18 schools decided to join the project. The program was enhanced to provide a strong writing component, in addition to the word study and reading areas. The Highest Level of Achievement Test (HLAT) was given in reading. As writing had been included in the balanced literacy programming that year, the writing HLAT (a test normed by Edmonton Public Schools) was also included in the results. Again, comparisons between district scores and balanced literacy results indicated progress for balanced literacy schools that was above the district's overall scores. The grade one results were of particular interest, because these were children who had not previously been exposed to any other formal literacy instruction. In grade one reading, only 8 percent of the balanced literacy group were below grade level. By contrast, in the district group, almost twice as many students — 15 percent — were reading below grade level. Similarly, in grade one writing, the district score of 16 percent below grade level was reduced to 7 percent in the balanced literacy classes. Again, special-needs students were included in both the district and balanced literacy results.

Second Year Achievement in Reading and Writing (18 schools) June 1999*

| | Balanced Literacy | District |
	Percentage of students at or above grade level	Percentage of students at or above grade level
Reading		
Grade one	92% (Below= 8%)(N=533)	85% (Below= 15%)(N=5560)
Grade two	88% (Below=12%)(N=383)	84% (Below= 16%)(N=5866)
Grade three	90% (Below=10%)(N=177)	85% (Below= 15%)(N=5854)
Writing		
Grade one	93% (Below= 7%)(N=533)	84% (Below= 16%)(N=5554)
Grade two	93% (Below= 7%)(N=382)	90% (Below= 10%)(N=5857)

*Since grade three students wrote the provincial writing test, they were not required to complete the district's HLAT writing test.

The number of schools in the project has continued to grow and literacy achievement results have been encouraging.

In 2002 the Edmonton Public School Board decided to explore the literacy achievement of students in schools where the balanced literacy program is being used, and to compare it with achievement in schools without balanced literacy programs. Anne Mulgrew, Supervisor of Student Assessment, conducted a six-year comparison study and presented the report to trustees and principals in September 2002.

Her report stated that 86 elementary schools were engaged in the balanced literacy project in Edmonton Public Schools. However, since some schools were still in the process of implementation, they decided to use the data from 48 schools that had fully implemented the program in primary grades. (Note: Research information was only collected for grades one to three. Due to monetary constraints, it was necessary to focus research on the core program rather than on kindergarten and grades four through six.)

There was a note of caution in the report, indicating that direct comparisons must be tentative because the balanced literacy schools could not be considered a representative sample. In what way were they not representative? The balanced literacy schools in fact included "the 10 highest-need schools in the district, as well as several other schools in very low-income areas."

Thus the balanced literacy schools had a disproportionate number of disadvantaged children when compared to the non-balanced literacy schools.

Comparison of HLAT Reading Results for Balanced Literacy Schools and Non-Balanced Literacy Schools 1997 and 2002

| Population | Grade | Percentage of Students Reading at or above Grade Level | | Difference |
		1997	2002	
Balanced Literacy Schools	1	80.9 (N=1690)	86.5 (N=1538)	+5.6
Other District Schools	1	84.0 (N=4262)	83.9 (N=3898)	-0.1
Balanced Literacy Schools	2	77.4 (N=1604)	82.7 (N=1524)	+5.3
Other District Schools	2	84.4 (N=4064)	86.3 (N=4023)	+1.9
Balanced Literacy Schools	3	78.6 (N=1553)	79.8 (N+1487)	+1.2
Other District Schools	3	86.0 (N=4151)	86.3 (N=4093)	+0.3

Referring to the "Difference" column, the report indicates, "there is a substantial difference in the change in the percentage of grades one and two students reading at or above grade level favouring the Balanced

Literacy cohort" (Mulgrew 2002, p. 3) and a "slightly higher increase," in favour of the balanced literacy schools at the grade three level.

Comparison of HLAT Writing Results for Balanced Literacy Schools and Non-Balanced Literacy Schools 1997 and 2002*

Population	Grade	Percentage of Students Writing at or above Grade Level		Difference
		1997	2002	
Balanced Literacy Schools	1	73.9 (N=1701)	86.7 (N=1546)	+12.8
Other District Schools	1	81.2 (N=4252)	82.9 (N=3881)	+1.7
Balanced Literacy Schools	2	82.3 (N=1605)	87.4 (N=1507)	+5.1
Other District Schools	2	87.0 (N=4048)	90.6 (N=4045)	+3.6

*Since grade three students wrote the provincial writing test, they were not required to complete the district's HLAT writing test.

The report states, "The percentage of grade one students writing at or above grade level changed dramatically over the six-year period for the Balanced Literacy schools, but showed little change in the Non-Balanced Literacy cohort. The change in the percentage of grade two students at or above grade level also favoured the Balanced Literacy cohort." (Mulgrew, 2002, p. 4.)